n

Disorganized Children

of related interest

Tics and Tourette Syndrome
A Handbook for Parents and Professionals
Uttom Chowdhury
Foreword by Isobel Heyman
ISBN 1 84310 203 X

Kids in the Syndrome Mix of ADHD, LD, Asperger's, Tourette's, Bipolar, and More!
The one stop guide for parents, teachers, and other professionals
Martin L. Kutscher MD
With contributions from Tony Attwood PhD and Robert R. Wolff MD
ISBN 1 84310 810 0 hb
ISBN 1 84310 811 9 pb

Asperger's Syndrome
A Guide for Parents and Professionals
Second Edition
Tony Attwood
ISBN 1 84310 307 9

The ADHD Handbook
A Guide for Parents and Professionals on Attention Deficit/ Hyperactivity Disorder
Alison Munden and Jon Arcelus
ISBN 1 85302 756 1

Freaks, Geeks and Asperger Syndrome
A User Guide to Adolescence
Luke Jackson
Foreword by Tony Attwood
ISBN 1 84310 098 3 pb
Winner of the NASEN & TES Special Educational Needs Children's Book Award 2003

Caged in Chaos
A Dyspraxic Guide to Breaking Free
Victoria Biggs
ISBN 1 84310 347 8

Disorganized Children

A Guide for Parents and Professionals

Edited by Samuel M. Stein and Uttom Chowdhury

Jessica Kingsley Publishers
London and Philadelphia

First published in 2006
by Jessica Kingsley Publishers
116 Pentonville Road
London N1 9JB, UK
and
400 Market Street, Suite 400
Philadelphia, PA 19106, USA

www.jkp.com

Library of Congress Cataloging in Publication Data
A CIP catalog record for this book is available from the Library of Congress

British Library Cataloguing in Publication Data
A CIP catalogue record for this book is available from the British Library

ISBN-13: 978 1 84310 148 2
ISBN-10: 1 84310 148 3

Printed and bound in Great Britain by
Athenaeum Press, Gateshead, Tyne and Wear

This book is dedicated to

Miriam & Archie Stein

and

Mina Nath & Mira Chowdhury

He is quick, thinking in clear images;
I am slow, thinking in broken images.
He becomes dull, trusting to his clear images;
I become sharp, mistrusting in my broken images.

Robert Graves, In Broken Images

Contents

List of Tables and Boxes

Tables

Boxes

Introduction

Uttom Chowdhury and Samuel M. Stein

This book on disorganized children has been written at the request of innumerable patients, parents, teachers and other child care professionals. It has arisen directly from clinical work with children and adolescents over a period of several years, and the enjoyable experience of being able to help these young people and their families to live happier and more fulfilling lives. All too often, parents and colleagues who had been part of the clinical assessments asked for access to a detailed text about these children. They equally often expressed marked disappointment at the absence of any theoretically coherent and practically helpful publications. We hope that this book will prove useful in helping both parents and professionals to manage children with mild neuro-developmental problems more appropriately and effectively.

The overall content of *Disorganized Children* is not something novel or creative – physicians have been dealing with, and trying to conceptualize, children with mild neuro-developmental problems for decades. Unfortunately, much of this work is fragmented and widespread across the available literature. As a result, parents and professionals often only gain access to small fractions of the wider field. This text is only unique in that it brings together normal child development with child and adolescent mental health disorders, and then tries to highlight the 'invisible children' who fall somewhere in between. Also, rather than concentrating on any one profession or very specific treatment options, the focus is instead on holistic and comprehensive care provided through coordinated multi-disciplinary and multi-agency collaboration.

HISTORICAL PERSPECTIVE

For nearly 200 years, physicians have been trying to link overt behavioural and emotional difficulties with underlying neurological deficits. As early as 1825, the first patient with Tourette syndrome appeared in the medical literature and, by

1902, a clinical description of Attention Deficit Hyperactivity Disorder (ADHD) had been published. Unfortunately, because of the subtleness of clinical presentation, and the lack of frank neurological symptoms, these difficulties were instead psychologically conceptualized in terms of moral dyscontrol or psychogenic causes rather than as physical conditions. In 1943, infantile autism was defined by Kanner and, in 1944, Hans Asperger identified a group of children with broadly similar difficulties although his description included milder forms of the disorder. He also identified these problems across a wide range of individuals, from those with overt neurological conditions to those with near normal development.

The concept of a characteristic psychiatric syndrome attributable to 'minimal' brain damage was first advanced in 1947. It described a constellation of clinical features including overactivity, inattention and conduct disorder, along with perceptual and learning problems which could not be explained by an intellectual deficit. The concept gained widespread support, and the term 'minimal brain damage or dysfunction' was almost universally employed in child psychiatry and developmental paediatrics from the 1950s. Similar behavioural observations were made in 1955 among children with temporal lobe epilepsy, in 1956 in a group of children with cerebral palsy and in 1957 among children with a variety of neurological problems.

The perception of Tourette syndrome and other neuro-developmental problems as rare, psychological disorders began to change in the 1960s with recognition of the beneficial effects of neuroleptic medication. In the 1970s, the concept of DAMP (Deficits in Attention, Motor Control and Perception) was developed in Scandinavia, and concepts such as Clumsy Child Syndrome or Developmental Coordination Disorder were also used to describe motor dysfunction in children with an average intellectual capacity. Based on research evidence, conditions such as Obsessive Compulsive Disorder, ADHD and dyslexia are now placing increasing emphasis on possible genetic influences, anatomical anomalies, biochemical impairments, difference in brain structure and variations in brain function.

The identification, classification and treatment of this group of children has therefore been attempted several times during the past century. Over time, the confusing combination of neuro-developmental signs and symptoms has been referred to by a wide variety of different names and definitions. Unfortunately, inconsistencies in the use of these terms have created a great deal of confusion, impeding accurate diagnosis and preventing the application of appropriate intervention programmes. During the last three decades, significant attempts have therefore been made to differentiate the various forms of dysfunction, and to establish a more formalized classification. This has focused on dividing general and overarching concepts into more accurately defined but separate units, each comprising a discrete group of symptoms. However, even today, in spite of the strong empirical support for these different medical diagnoses, controversy often pervades media stories and scientific debate.

What is most likely is that we are dealing with a spectrum of symptoms related to emotional, behavioural, social and educational impairments, with textbook cases of mental illness falling at one end of a wide continuum and normality falling at the other.

CHILDREN WITH MILD NEURO-DEVELOPMENTAL DIFFICULTIES

Children and adolescents with mild neuro-developmental difficulties, or 'disorganized children' as they have been described in this book, are increasingly coming to the attention of Child and Adolescent Mental Health Services (CAMHS). They tend to present with escalating emotional, behavioural, social and educational problems. They have often already been assessed by a wide range of other professionals before, without a satisfactory outcome having been achieved. Unfortunately, as a definitive diagnosis is seldom reached, and given the minimal impact of traditional treatment approaches, the disorganized child's presentation is then all too frequently attributed to defiance, disobedience, oppositional attitudes, difficulties with authority or deliberate attempts to be anti-social and naughty.

However, careful assessment of these children and adolescents may quickly identify features of well-established neurological presentations such as attention deficit hyperactivity disorder, Asperger syndrome, obsessive compulsive disorder, dyslexia or Tourette syndrome. Disorganized children may even present with mixed signs and symptoms attributable to more than one of these neuro-developmental conditions, while not definitively meeting the diagnostic specification for any one illness. Difficulties in defining the problem are further heightened by the vagueness of the symptoms, their fluctuating pattern and the invariable presence of good intellectual function. However, as can be seen in Figure 1, children and adolescents may present with a variable range of sub-clinical neuro-developmental problems which are actively present but which do not exceed diagnostic requirements. These difficulties, even if they do not warrant a definitive medical diagnosis, will nonetheless seriously hamper and impair their daily function both at home and at school.

The fundamental difficulties experienced by disorganized children, which may help to explain their presenting symptoms, relate predominantly to the way in which they process complex sequences of information. As a result, they can perform to a very high level on some tasks (which match closely with their strengths) and yet be well below average on other tasks (which fall within an area of weakness). Parents and teachers often struggle to understand this 'patchy' cognitive function, or how an obviously intelligent child can attain high levels of function one minute and significantly reduced levels of function a moment later. This confusion is further increased as the disorganized child, except for isolated and particularly stressful occasions, may not exhibit any symptoms at all. However, as social and academic pressures escalate with age, these inherent neuro-developmental processing limitations increasingly come to the fore. They may subsequently present as either emotional or behavioural difficulties, often within both the classroom and the family setting. Figure 2 highlights the neuro-developmental immaturity with which disorganized children invariably present, and their tendency to operate emotionally and socially at a level expected of younger children. Similarly Figure 3, following the Yerkes–Dodson principle, further highlights how disorganized children, in spite of this immaturity, can function without difficulty until their inherently low anxiety and stress threshold is exceeded by internal and external pressures, after which their performance, coping and behaviour deteriorate markedly.

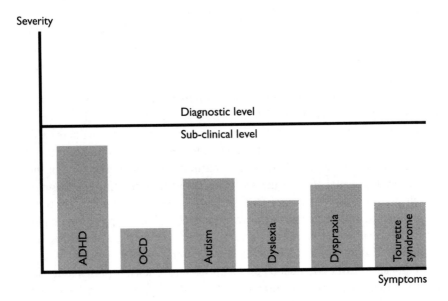

Figure 1

The fundamental processing difficulties experienced by disorganized children also relate to the understanding of complex, abstract and symbolic concepts. These children therefore become easily lost when lessons increase in complexity

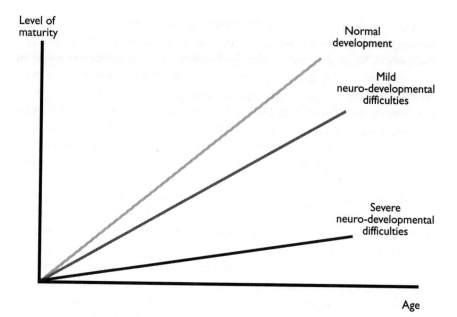

Figure 2

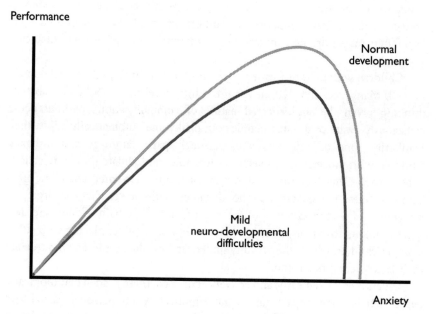

Figure 3

or when instructions are vague. The resulting frustration may lead to a child refusing to undertake the task in question, or even refusal to attempt any other tasks which he or she predicts may lead to failure. These difficulties are often enhanced by a reduced attention span and reduced short-term memory. As a result, their thinking tends to be very linear and concrete with a tendency to work concepts through from first principles. This means that most academic and organizational tasks will take longer, and learning will be enhanced in situations with fewer external stimuli. Children with processing difficulties tend to prefer more structured subjects such as maths, physics and IT and tend to experience greater difficulty with unstructured subjects such as English, drama or art.

Children with mild processing problems struggle to generalize learning from one concept or topic to another. They instead require all new concepts to be built up from basic principles, with clear guidance each step of the way. They will not spontaneously apply something learned in one subject or topic to similar and related subjects and topics unless the links are made overt and clear. All new tasks and learning therefore require significant preparation and gradual introduction as they otherwise leave the disorganized child feeling overwhelmed and left behind. A reduced ability to face academic challenges results as the children come to see all tasks which are not immediately achievable as beyond their reach. These children then tend to 'shut down' when faced with novel challenges rather than rising to the occasion. As a result, they are poorly equipped to respond to pressure, competition, comparison or authority. Instead, they respond far more favourably to gentle, non-threatening, individualized and esteem-enhancing approaches.

Children with mild processing problems often struggle in the social domain as well. Many peer interactions require a high level of symbolic and abstract thinking given the sophisticated nature of communication. Without being consciously aware of it, most people continually and automatically adjust their familiarity, tone of voice, volume, personal space, language and intimacy. Children with processing problems are less able to modulate these interactions appropriately. They therefore tend to miss jokes, and fail to comprehend the often complex rules that govern childhood games. This makes them a target for bullying and victimization as they are often less verbally fluent and less quick-thinking than many peers. As a result, they often prefer playing with either younger children whom they readily understand or older children who tolerate their lack of comprehension.

Unless recognized early, and actively addressed, these hidden neurologically based deficits may impact subtly but significantly on personal, social and educational development, leading to the subsequent emotional and behavioural problems with which these disorganized children ultimately present.

MENTAL HEALTH CLASSIFICATION AND CO-MORBIDITY

As these two important topics are raised repeatedly in various chapters, it seems appropriate to include them in the introduction. This will not only provide an early explanation of these key issues, but will also serve to reduce later repetition and extended reference lists. Mental health classification and co-morbidity, which are essential concepts throughout the book, are therefore discussed briefly below.

Classification is the grouping of disorders according to their signs and symptoms. This serves as a shared language which allows communication between professionals. It also helps in selecting appropriate treatment options, and in determining prognostic and outcome factors. There are two main classification systems currently in use: the *Diagnostic and Statistical Manual of Mental Disorders* (DSM-IV) and the *International Statistical Classification of Diseases and Related Health Problems* (ICD-10). The DSM-IV (1994) is published by the American Psychiatric Association, and is used mainly in North America. The IDC-10 (1992) is published by the World Health Organization and is used world-wide. Both ICD-10 and DSM-IV use categorical systems, requiring the clinician to select from a list of diagnoses, each consisting of identifiable behavioural symptoms. These categories have been based on clinically derived syndromes through professional consensus. At present, there are many similarities between the two classification systems, both of which are continuously evolving and being updated, and either option will prove equally effective clinically if the relevant guidelines are followed.

Co-morbidity, or a co-morbid problem, can be defined as having two or more formally diagnosable conditions at the same time. Many children and adolescents who present to CAMHS clinics have more than one psychiatric diagnosis, and can therefore be said to suffer from co-morbidity. For example, it is not uncommon for children diagnosed to be on the autistic spectrum to also present with clearly defined symptoms of attention deficit hyperactivity disorder. Similarly many children with Tourette syndrome may have associated symptoms of obsessive compulsive disorder. For some children and adolescents, it is the presence and impact of the co-morbid condition, rather than the features of the primary diagnosis, that causes the greatest difficulties. As highlighted in Figure 1, both sub-clinical and diagnosable conditions may readily co-exist within a single child.

HOW TO USE THIS BOOK

Child and adolescent mental health is a rapidly expanding field, with new diagnoses and terminologies entering the lexicon each year. It is therefore not the aim of this book to add yet another new concept to the already growing list. Instead, the emphasis is on avoiding an unnecessary medicalization of children and adolescents with mild neuro-developmental problems. These disorganized children do not need, and are unlikely to benefit from, formal diagnoses or medical treatment. If anything, they are likely to gain most from a move away from tertiary Child and Adolescent Mental Health Services towards community-based provision orchestrated through both home and school.

The aim of this book is therefore to provide user-friendly and practical guidance for parents and professionals on how to identify and manage children and adolescents with mild neuro-developmental difficulties. This can be achieved by first reading the chapters in Part 1 on normal child development. Having gained a basic insight into anticipated chronological achievement, it will then become easier to identify any children or adolescents who are lagging behind developmentally. Part 2 identifies the opposite end of the spectrum, those children and adolescents who will fulfil the formal diagnostic criteria for mental health problems. However, the chapters in this section have not been designed as a definitive guide to the diagnosis or treatment of these conditions. Instead, they are intended to provide an overview for parents and professionals in primary care in order to highlight both those sub-clinical children who do not meet diagnostic thresholds and those children who may need onward referral due to any serious concerns which are raised.

Part 3 relates specifically to the disorganized children whose overt neuro-developmental deficits have been identified in Part 1 but whose mental health does not meet the specific diagnostic specifications highlighted in Part 2. Chapter 19 focuses on how to identify this otherwise invisible group of children and adolescents across a wide range of settings and situations. While clinical examples have been included wherever possible, please note that these are fictitious vignettes which, while based on clinical experience, are not reflective of any one child or adolescent. Finally, Part 4 deals with the specific treatment approaches for disorganized children, which can be combined within the community to provide comprehensive and holistic multi-disciplinary and multi-agency care.

ACKNOWLEDGEMENTS

We would like to thank the various authors for their high quality contributions, and to thank Jessica Kingsley Publishers for their support and commitment. However, most importantly, we want to thank the many children, adolescents and families who taught us everything we now know about disorganized children. We have tried to be worthy conduits for this information, and hope that this book will prove of use to the patients, parents and professionals who may read it.

REFERENCES

American Psychiatric Association (2000) *Diagnostic and Statistical Manual of Mental Disorders*, 4th edn (DSM-IV Text Revision). Washington, DC: American Psychiatric Association.

World Health Organization (1992) *International Statistical Classification of Diseases and Related Health Problems*, 10th revision (ICD-10). Geneva: World Health Organization.

Part 1
Child Development

Chapter 1

From 0 to 5 years

Uttom Chowdhury and Samuel M. Stein

From earliest infancy through to young adulthood, children and adolescents grow and develop according to their age and ability. This developmental pathway is influenced by a wide range of factors, and even 'normal' child development varies enormously. Some parents may report that their child is walking at 10 months, whereas others may report their child as walking from 17 months. While most children will crawl before walking, some will crawl 'commando-style' and others will 'bottom-shuffle'. On the whole, girls tend to develop earlier, particularly with regard to social and communication skills. Yet, all of these changes fall well within anticipated growth and development. However, although the rate of change may differ, it is important to recognize that there is an overall consistency to the pattern of developmental progress over time.

The two main factors which may actively affect development, either positively or negatively, are genetic influences and environmental influences. Genetic factors represent the inherent biological potential of the child, while environmental factors will influence the extent to which the child may achieve this potential. Genetic factors include intelligence, temperament and sex while environmental factors include nutrition, warmth, affection, role models and the opportunity to play. For optimal development to take place, the environment must meet the child's inbuilt physical and psychological needs.

As children can only be fully understood within this fluid context of genetic predisposition and environmental influences, it is essential to understand something about normal development before considering the potential physical and psychological problems which may present during childhood and adolescence. This chapter therefore aims to provide a basic overview of growth and change between birth and 5 years of age. A simple outline of normal development is described for each specific age group including motor function, vision, hearing, speech and social function. Any gross deviation from these milestones may require more detailed reading, discussion with appropriate professionals or further investigation.

THE NEWBORN BABY

- *Motor.* At birth, both arms and legs are usually stiff while the trunk and neck are floppy. The head therefore needs to be supported when the infant is picked up. A number of primitive reflexes are still present, such as the Moro reflex, which involves a sudden outward movement of the arms and an opening of the hands in response to an unexpected loud noise or a rapid lowering of the head or body. Within moments, the baby's arms come together again, simulating an embrace. This reflex, as with other 'survival reflexes', will fade after a few months.

- *Vision.* Infants are able to turn their head towards diffuse light, and close their eyes in response to sudden bright light. However, they cannot focus effectively until 3 months of age. The parent's face must therefore be brought to within 30 centimetres of the baby's face to gain his or her attention.

- *Hearing.* A startle reaction to loud noises is present from birth.

- *Social/play.* Within a few days, babies will make eye contact with their parents and interact with facial gestures.

AT 1 MONTH

- *Motor.* Both arms and legs are now active. Infants are able to open their hands, but these are generally closed. However, fingers and toes will fan out when limbs are extended. If their cheek is touched, babies will move towards the stimulus in an attempt to suckle (rooting reflex). When held standing up, babies will attempt to make 'walking' movements and touching the sole of their foot against a solid surface will produce a 'stepping' reflex. Pressure placed on their palm will initiate a 'grasping' reflex in which the fingers curl and grip.

- *Vision.* Babies' pupils will constrict if stimulated by light and their eyes will shut tightly if any direct light shines into them. They will gaze at toys moved towards and away from their face, and will start to watch familiar faces more closely. From about 3 weeks of age, infants are increasingly alert visually.

- *Hearing.* Infants will be startled by sudden noises, and may appear to 'freeze' momentarily when a small bell is rung. If crying, they may stop suddenly when gentle noises are made.

- *Speech*: At this age, babies may utter some sounds when content. They will 'coo' in response to their parent's voice from about 5 to 6 weeks, and will cry when hungry or uncomfortable.

- *Social/play*: A social smile develops from about 6 weeks onwards, and the baby will stop crying when picked up.

AT 3 MONTHS

- *Motor*: Infants' legs now kick out and, when lying on their front, they will try to lift their head using their forearms for support. When pulled to sit up, there is no longer any head lag and they may hold a rattle for a few seconds.

- *Vision*: There is greater preoccupation with the parent's face. Babies will move their head to gaze at objects, and will follow the movement of a dangling toy. They will also watch their own hand movements.

- *Hearing*: Loud noises continue to produce blinking, crying and distress. They will turn their head towards a nearby voice.

- *Speech*: Babies will make some sounds when spoken to, and 'gurgle' and 'coo' with pleasure.

- *Social/play*: Infants will fix their eyes on the parent's face. They will start to smile, and respond to being tickled or played with. Excited arm and leg movements may occur when they see food or preparation for bathtime. While friendly with adults, they know who their main carer is.

AT 6 MONTHS

- *Motor*: While lying on their back, babies will grab their own feet. If held sitting, they will keep their back straight. When held standing, they will take their own weight on their legs. If lying on their front, they will tend to extend their arms, and they begin to use their hand to hold toys (palmar grasp).

- *Vision*: They will move their head and eyes when distracted, and visually follow an adult around the room. Their eyes should move together, without any evidence of a squint. By now, they will also show interest in 'peek-a-boo' games.

- *Hearing*: Infants will turn towards familiar voices.

- *Speech*: They may laugh and chuckle to themselves, but scream when annoyed. They can vocalize using sounds such as 'goo', 'der' and 'a-a'. They will also try to attract attention vocally.

- *Social/play:* At this age, they tend to put everything into their mouths. They will also put their hand on their mother's breast or a bottle when feeding. They will show delight when engaged in active play. Although they are generally friendly, they start to show some degree of anxiety about strangers from around 7 months onwards. They are excited by familiar toys, and will smile at their own image in a mirror.

AT 9 MONTHS

- *Motor:* Babies may sit unsupported on the floor, and pull themselves up to stand. They can crawl, roll and wriggle on their front. They also begin to point at objects, and use 'scissors' grip (between index finger and thumb) to hold string. Finger feeding and early chewing may be apparent.

- *Vision:* They are very attentive and will stretch out their hands to take a toy.

- *Hearing:* They are attentive to everyday sounds.

- *Speech:* Infants now vocalize as part of communication, and may shout to attract attention. They babble and use syllables such as 'da-da', 'ma-ma' and 'aba'.

- *Social/play:* They can grasp a bell by the handle and ring in imitation of the parent. They can watch while toys are partly hidden and then promptly find them, as well as looking for objects that disappear. They are able to distinguish strangers from familiar adults. They will also throw their body back and stiffen in annoyance, but will stop activities to the command of 'no'.

AT 12 MONTHS

- *Motor:* Children can now rise into a sitting position from lying down. They can also crawl on hands and knees, may shuffle on their bottom or 'bear' walk on the floor. They are able to walk around furniture and step sideways, especially if one hand is held. They can pick up objects with a pincer grip (between thumb and tip of index finger), as well as pointing with their index finger. They can drop toys deliberately and watch as they fall. They can also hold toy bricks in each hand, and bang them together to make a noise.

- *Vision:* Children recognize familiar faces from a distance, and may watch people for a prolonged period of time.

- *Hearing:* They will immediately respond to their own name, as well as recognizing familiar tunes with which they try to join in.

- *Speech*: This takes the form of babbling loudly. There is some imitation of adult vocalization and attempts to converse.

- *Social/play*: Children are able to drink from a cup and hold a spoon. They can stretch their arms out for dressing, and may give toys to adults on request. They will place objects into and out of cups, watching while objects are hidden under a cup before reaching to find the toy. They may clap as part of imitation and wave goodbye on request. They can also imitate actions such as using a play telephone or using a cup and spoon. They will shake their head to communicate 'no'.

AT 15 MONTHS

- *Motor*: Toddlers may try to start walking on their own for a few paces. They are able to crawl upstairs and slide downstairs backwards, as well as kneeling unaided. They can build a tower of cubes and grasp a crayon with their whole hand to scribble.

- *Vision*: They will watch activities outside a window for several minutes, and look with interest at picture books.

- *Hearing*: Children can demonstrate a basic understanding of a small number of words. They can also understand simple instructions such as 'come here' or 'give me the ball'.

- *Speech*: They make a wide range of speech-like sounds, and can ask for objects by pointing.

- *Social/play*: Toddlers will attempt to bring a spoon to their mouth, and chew well. They can push large wheeled objects, open cupboards and close doors. They may also throw objects on to the floor as part of play or rejection. They should be very curious, with a desire to explore their environment. They are able to play 'to and fro' games with trucks, cars or balls.

AT 18 MONTHS

- *Motor*: Toddlers can now walk well, and may even start to run. They can climb into adult chairs, and squat to pick up fallen toys. Hand preference begins to show, and they are able to build a tower of three cubes.

- *Vision*: They can recognize pictures in books, point and turn several pages.

- *Hearing*: An ability to listen to commands which are addressed to them emerges.

- *Speech:* They can use 6 to 15 words or more, and make noises to themselves which have emotional inflections. Attempts to sing are evident, and they begin to repeat words overheard in conversation.

- *Social/play:* Children can obey simple instructions such as 'shut the door'. They are able to point to their own shoes, nose or head on request. They can hold a cup with both hands, and drink without spilling. They begin to let adults know of toilet needs by restlessness and vocalization. They explore their environment with little sense of danger but still like to be near familiar adults. They also imitate everyday activities such as 'sweeping'.

AT 2 YEARS

- *Motor:* By now, children can walk up and down stairs. They may sit and steer a tricycle but cannot yet use the pedals. They will walk into a ball when trying to kick it, but are able to run, both starting and stopping safely. The are able to squat with complete steadiness in order to rest or to play with an object on the ground. Spontaneous circular scribbles should start to emerge and they can build a tower of six or seven cubes.

- *Vision:* They are able to recognize details within a picture book, and also recognize familiar adults in photographs.

- *Hearing:* Increasing attention is paid to communications addressed to them.

- *Speech:* Children should be capable of using about 50 words, while understanding more. They can put words together in phrases, and talk to themselves continuously in long monologues. Echoes of adult speech are evident, with constant asking for the names of objects and people. They enjoy joining in with nursery rhymes and songs. They can also name familiar objects and pictures, and point to their hair on request.

- *Social/play:* They can put on their hat and shoes, and drink well without spilling. They may also attempt to verbalize toilet needs. They can turn door handles and start to engage in make-believe play. They may play near others but will not yet play with them, and may play for lengthy periods of time. They become increasingly resentful of attention shown to other children by familiar adults.

AT 2½ YEARS

- *Motor:* Children can now walk and run well. They can also jump with two feet together and kick large balls. They are able to throw a ball while holding their hand at body level, and can hold a pencil in their preferred hand with an improved grip.

- *Vision:* They will recognize themselves in photographs.

- *Hearing:* They are also more able to start listening to stories.

- *Speech:* Children will use about 200 words or more, and know their full name. They may talk to themselves when playing, and recite a few nursery rhymes.

- *Social/play:* Play with dolls and teddy bears becomes increasingly meaningful. Role plays, such as putting teddy to bed or driving a motor car, may be evident. While they may join in with other children's play, this does not necessarily involve sharing. They can also eat skilfully with a spoon or fork. They tend to be more active and restless, more resistive to restraint and prone to throwing tantrums.

AT 3 YEARS

- *Motor:* Children can walk upstairs with alternating feet, and can manoeuvre around obstacles when running. They are able to ride a tricycle using the pedals and sit with their feet crossed at the ankles. Balls can be kicked forcibly and be caught with extended arms. They can build several bridges from cubes, cut with a pair of safety scissors and draw a person with a head. They may also know the names of some of the main colours, with an ability to match them. Circles and some letters (V, H and T) can be copied too.

- *Vision:* They now enjoy watching television and joining in with songs.

- *Hearing:* An increasing eagerness to listen to stories is evident.

- *Speech:* The child may use personal pronouns, and be able to count up to 10. They also ask a range of questions using 'what', 'where' and 'why'.

- *Social/play:* They are able to wash their hands, and join in with active make-believe play with other children. They may already be dry during the night but this is still variable.

AT 4 YEARS

- *Motor:* They can walk up and down stairs similar to adults, as well as standing and running on tip-toe. They can also stand on one foot, hop and ride a tricycle with ease. Pencils are held with good control and they can pick up objects from the floor by bending at the waist.

- *Vision:* Children are able to match colours without difficulty.

- *Hearing:* They can listen to, and tell, long stories.

- *Speech*: Intelligible speech is evident, which is grammatically correct. There is a continuous asking of questions and they know several nursery rhymes.

- *Social/play*: Children can now brush their own teeth, as well as dressing and undressing except for laces and ties. They are more independent and strong-willed but increasingly able to show empathy for peers in distress. They can also enjoy jokes, with dressing up and imaginative play. Enjoyment of others' company increases and they are better able to understand turn taking. An appreciation of past and future time starts to emerge.

AT 5 YEARS

- *Motor*: Children can stand on one foot with their arms folded. They can move rhythmically to music and play a variety of ball games. They are also able to pick up very small objects, with good writing and drawing control. Competent use of knife and fork is evident. They can copy the main letters of the alphabet, draw a man with limbs, include windows and doors when drawing houses and colour pictures in neatly.

- *Vision*: They are able to read words from standard first school books.

- *Hearing*: They enjoy familiar tunes and stories.

- *Speech*: Fluent speech is evident, with enjoyment of singing and rhymes. They can give their full name, address and birthday.

- *Social/play*: Children are able to choose their own friends, and to comfort playmates if distressed. They are more willing to play with others, and enjoy jokes and riddles. They can also wash and dry their own face and hands.

FURTHER READING

Baird, G. (2002) 'Developmental paediatric assessment.' *Psychiatry 1*, 13–18.

Nicoll, A. (1997) 'Development, language, hearing and vision.' In T. Lissauer and G. Clayden (eds) *Illustrated Textbook of Paediatrics*. London: Mosby International Limited.

Sheridan, M. (1997) *From Birth to Five Years*. London: Routledge.

Chapter 2

Cognitive function in children

Deborah Christie

INTRODUCTION

Cognition (thinking) requires the ability to manage information in order to solve problems. This information must be selected, represented, stored, retrieved and transformed. Cognitive functions therefore describe the different ways in which our brain obtains and uses information about our environment, about ourselves and about other people. Young children learn how these different components of thinking are connected and related through categories, rules, skills and procedures. These theories include a range of processes that allow us to understand our environment, as well as understanding how we can influence it. The processes include learning, memory, perception, attention, language, reasoning and problem-solving. This ability to learn and remember is available from even before birth, and provides the building blocks upon which more complex skills can develop.

Cognitive development (as described with regard to all early development in Chapter 1) is a complex interplay of biological, social and environmental interactions. The ability to develop theories about how the world works is both helped and constrained by biological endowment, current cognitive competence, knowledge and the opportunities provided by the environment. The development of these cognitive skills therefore requires an ability to take in, to make sense of and to use experiences to produce appropriate responses.

As the brain receives and transmits all of the information that a child receives within their environment, early childhood is an important time as the brain is rapidly developing and needs stimulation in order to achieve its maximum potential. This period of development is essential as the brain is growing and constantly making connections in response to different experiences. The brain is therefore heavily influenced by the social and psychological environment, and there is evidence that long-term development can be negatively influenced by a lack of stimulation or damage due to neglect or injury.

EARLY COGNITION

The word infant comes from the Latin meaning 'without speech'. The infant instead communicates through pre-symbolic sounds (as described in Chapter 3), like crying, in order to communicate primary needs such as hunger or physical discomfort. After birth, there is a very rapid period of development during which time the baby starts to smile, achieves head control and discovers the ability to reach and grasp.

Piaget was one of the first psychologists to carefully observe and record the sequence of developmental changes that occur in childhood (Piaget 1970). He described the first two years of life as the sensorimotor period in which children begin to understand the relationship between their actions and the subsequent consequences, as well as starting to differentiate themselves (or 'self') from other objects. Infants come to learn that they can control their world non-verbally, with an action invariably being followed by an event. For example, infants realize that if a toy is thrown onto the floor, it will suddenly reappear, or that crying will bring a familiar face who will pick them up and cuddle them. This ability to learn about, and understand, these interactions allows infants to begin to control and influence their environment.

As a result, they start to develop mental representation of objects, and become aware that these objects are permanent and exist even when they cannot be seen (object permanence). They also start to develop basic short-term memory skills. By the age of 12 months, a baby can recognize faces and can distinguish between familiar and non-familiar faces. Even at this early age, an infant's 'temperament' will influence how easily he or she can be comforted when distressed and how secure he or she is in strange situations. During this time, infant communication is largely through gaze, gesture and babbling.

LANGUAGE

The human brain is organized to allow the development of a symbolic communication system (speech). The part of the brain that is specialized both to produce language, and also to understand it, is on the left side. The right side is less good at language skills, although it can take over if the left side is damaged during early childhood. Normal development of the brain is therefore essential for the acquisition of language. However, social interaction with other children and adults is also essential for the brain to be able to develop this ability. A lack of exposure to the spoken word in early childhood will result in impaired language development in adulthood.

Language involves learning that objects and actions have labels and that, by using these labels, the young child is able to influence his or her environment. From 12 to 15 months, children will use words in order to achieve a particular outcome. For example, saying a particular word will produce food or drink. The use of these labels may also encourage the appearance of certain people, and children find that they can communicate 'yes' or 'no' to indicate a preference.

During the next 12 to 24 months, there is a rapid development of language with less reliance on gesture and an increasing ability to put words together to form short phrases. The child can label actions, and even begin to express future intent (for example, 'me go') and abstract thought (described in Chapter 3). As language develops children can explain how words are similar in meaning to each other, and give reasons for real (or hypothetical) actions or events. This higher-order language is dependent upon understanding behaviour within a social context, and being able to talk about issues which reflect ideas or the development of moral reasoning. The majority of children will have begun to use language to communicate by the age of 3 years. By the age of 5 or 6, children will have acquired a completely intelligible language system.

In the beginning, speech therefore serves a basic communication function that helps children to regulate their interactions with others in the world. Later, it transforms the way in which children learn, think and understand. It becomes an instrument or tool of thought, not only providing a 'code' or system for representing the world but also the means by which self-regulation comes about.

MEMORY

The ability of an infant to recognize its parent is evidence of a basic memory system, and the enhancement of these memory skills is essential for normal development. However, memory is a complex cognitive function with several interdependent components.

The first component is short-term memory. This is the ability to hold on to a certain amount of information for a short period of time, which is sometimes called working memory. We might want to remember a brief instruction (go upstairs and bring down your hairbrush), a series of numbers (like a phone number) or non-verbal information (a clapping sequence in a song). A child's working memory gradually increases with the ability to hold more and more 'bits' of information in his or her head. By about the age of 12, most children will be able to remember between five and nine bits of information which is the same as the adult short-term memory capacity.

The next stage of memory is being able to store and recall the information over a longer period of time. This means that the information (either verbal or non-verbal) needs to be encoded and transferred to a short-term memory store. Thereafter, it is transferred to a long-term memory store for extended recollection. Unfortunately, memory can be disrupted at any of these stages. Difficulty with memory can therefore be due to a failure to efficiently code information being transferred between the short-term memory store and the long-term memory store. In children, more often than not, this is because they did not attend to the task and allowed the information to slip away. A second problem may be in the ability to recall information that has been stored due to difficulty in organizing information. This difficulty in accessing information can be improved by learning efficient recall strategies.

During the pre-school years, memory grows with language development. During the school-age years, improving memory is related to the child's more sophisticated strategies for processing information (as described in Chapter 4). School-age children remember more than pre-schoolers because they intuitively apply rules for recalling information. They have learned to sort information by time, place, category and other cues, all of which serve to organize memories and thus facilitate recall. As the ability to think in categories improves, so does memory as these categories allow for more effective storage of information (Kagan 1984). School tasks, for example, encourage children to remember information intentionally. The capacity for retrieval of information stored in memory improves in middle childhood, but this ability is also reinforced by the need to retrieve information to answer questions in class. Motivated by school tasks, older school-age children create strategies for remembering such as repeating information to themselves, creating mental cues, designing new categories or finding images that help them to remember.

ATTENTION

Attention is the process of focusing on relevant information in the environment, and the inhibition of responses to irrelevant intruding material. Attention can be sustained over time or be selective for specific information. It is a critical process for all other cognitive functions as attention controls the amount and quality of information available for higher-order cognitive processes. The process of focusing our senses on what is happening in our environment allows us to make sense of information (and to remember things) more efficiently.

Development of attention requires the biological growth of structures found at the front of the brain which are involved in this ability to focus as well as being involved in the interactions with the environment from which the child learns to attend. Like memory, attention is a complex process involving several components.

Self-monitoring and regulation develop quickly as the child begins to develop an ability to focus on external events (such as reading a book or playing with a toy). By the age of 4 or 5, the child will be developing dual attention capabilities in which there is a need to concentrate on two events and then pick out the relevant information before choosing an appropriate response. For example, while in a busy classroom, the child will need to listen to the teacher but not be distracted by other activities.

Finally, around the age of 6 or 7, children start to develop a capacity to inhibit or prevent responses and to produce alternative responses, for example, waiting to speak or not making inappropriate comments out loud. Developmentally this is helped by a shift in the ability to attend for longer periods of time and for attention to come under increasing internal control. For this reason, attention difficulties are a common impairment in many neuro-developmental conditions (as described in Part 2).

The ultimate mature expression of attention is sometimes called executive function. This process is involved in organizing information and directing attention. It is also involved in complex memory and the inhibition of impulsive and inappropriate adult behaviour. Normal levels of executive function can usually be measured in children by early adolescence (Gilmour 2003).

VISUO-SPATIAL FUNCTION

The right side of the infant's brain is preset to make sense of and manipulate visual and non-verbal information. The young child first develops an ability to represent two-dimensional figures, which slowly take on perspective and depth to become three-dimensional objects. The child also develops an ability to fill in gaps in partial images, and to make sense of complex patterns. For example, by 30 to 33 months, a child can recognize shapes and orient pieces in a nine-piece jigsaw puzzle. From 15 to 24 months, a child can increase the height of a tower of blocks from two to eight or even more. From 33 months through to 4 or 5 years, the child is increasingly able to copy and construct matching models. Initially, these copies are based on three-dimensional models but children quickly develop an ability to copy models from a two-dimensional plan or picture. In parallel with the development of fine motor control, children develop an ability to copy straight lines in appropriate orientation (50% by 36 months) and draw basic figures like circles and squares (50% by 60 months).

Under 6 years of age, a child tends to see only one dimension of a problem (Siegler 1991). For example, pre-school children asked to compare complex figures, such as two houses which are alike except for the number of windows, will say that the two figures are the same. This is based on finding only one similarity, without further exploration of possible differences. In contrast, children of 7 or 8 will explore both houses systematically before deciding whether the two figures are alike or different. This ability to move back and forth between parts and wholes, between details and larger organizing ideas, is the basis of categorization and classification. As they move through middle childhood, children's ability to view reality in categories which have multiple variables or perspectives gradually increases.

AWARENESS OF TIME AND SPACE

By the age of 6, children will know their right from left. However, they will have difficulty in saying which is the right or left side of a person sitting opposite them. This will only fall into place by the age of 7 or 8. Time orientation also begins to develop by 7, and a clearer sense of how time is organized allows school-age children to think ahead and to plan their actions more efficiently than a pre-schooler. At this age children become less bound by the organization (or lack of organization) of visual materials and are able to reorganize materials into patterns that are more interesting or satisfying.

The school child can look beyond surface perceptions to imagine new patterns. For example, if asked to clean up his or her room, a 5-year-old is likely to feel overwhelmed by the number of toys strewn across the floor because he or she is not yet able to construct an image of the room with everything in its place. While many children do not like to clean up their rooms, an 8-year-old is capable of doing this without assistance because he or she can mentally bring some order to the external chaos, actively thinking about where things should go.

THINKING AND PROBLEM-SOLVING

Pre-operational thinking (2 to 6 years) is the period during which the majority of the basic cognitive functions are developed. Piaget described the subsequent period, from 6 to 11 years, as the period of concrete operations. This is when thinking and problem-solving come to be based on the symbolic understanding of concrete objects (Chapter 3) and the relations between them (Chapter 4). It is the beginning of sophisticated mental operations.

Children arrive at middle childhood with a great deal of knowledge about the categories in their world. Much of this understanding is coded and labelled in their everyday language. During the pre-school period, the child slowly developed the ability to represent experiences mentally, a process that goes hand in hand with the development of language. Mastery of language, which proceeds rapidly across the pre-school period, similarly provides the school-age child with a vehicle for organizing experience mentally. By the end of infancy, children can classify a collection of objects into two classes (such as blue objects and red objects) even when other attributes differ (if some of the blue objects are toy boats and others are wooden dolls).

During early childhood children's vocabularies grow and differentiate to include a vast array of category distinctions organized around basic terms and hierarchies. As a consequence, by the time they are 7 or 8 years old, they have a large fund of organized conceptual knowledge to draw upon in their thinking about the world. Knowledge of categories to which objects belong is crucial to the development of thought. It permits children to reason about an individual category, even ones they have never seen.

As these cognitive skills improve, children develop the ability to think about the world in a particular way. Piaget called this the period of concrete operations (6 to 11 years). This way of thinking relates to real objects, and thoughts about these objects, such as mentally comparing the sizes of several items. Children are increasingly able to use verbal cues to understand problems based on a sophisticated grasp of language and their improving capacity for strictly mental representation. The physical world becomes more predictable as children come to understand that certain real aspects of objects (such as size, density, length and number) remain the same even when other aspects of their superficial appearances have changed. This is known as conservation. For example, if the same amount of liquid is poured into a small wide container and a taller thin container, the volume of liquid remains the same even though the tall thin container may look more full. In pre-operational thought, 3- and 4-year-old children will say that the taller container has more liquid in it, focusing on a single attribute of an object. Around the age of 5 or 6 years, children's understanding of conservation goes through a transitional stage. At this point, children seem to realize that it is necessary to consider both the height and the width of the containers. Unfortunately, they still have difficulty keeping both containers in mind simultaneously, and coordinating the changes, so that they can properly compare them.

By about 8 years, children begin to master the principle of conservation. They understand that one container is both taller and thinner, but that a change in one dimension of the container (e.g. height) is affected by a change in another dimension (e.g. width). Children who have acquired the concept of conservation of volume recognize that it is logically necessary for the amount of liquid to remain the same, despite the change in appearance.

Thus, as children develop, they can increasingly think about different alternatives when they try to solve problems. They are also able to retrace their steps if they want to. Kagan pointed out that school-age children make more use of 'executive processes' than pre-school children, by which he means the skills used in approaching and thinking about problems. While a pre-school child is likely to persist in solving certain problems in the same way, even if he or she is not succeeding, a 9- or 10-year-old is more likely 'to discard inefficient solutions that are not working and to search systematically for better alternatives' (Kagan 1984).

CONCLUSION

Over time, children show an increase in both knowledge and expertise. This greater expertise is paralleled by better cognitive performance in all domains. The improvement follows ongoing maturation of the brain's information-processing capacity, and neurological-based increases in the speed of processing, both of which are determined by age.

The fundamental processes of cognitive development are therefore *learning, memory, perception* and *attention*. Without some form of *memory*, children would live only in the 'here and now'. In order to remember, children must *learn* what is familiar. A cognitive system therefore cannot develop memory without simultaneously developing learning. At the same time, both learning and memory would be impossible if children are not able to *perceive* the world around them with sufficient levels of *attention* and concentration.

While it is helpful to think of childhood development as accurately following the theoretical stages described above, we must not forget about cultural and historical influences or the more immediate and direct social influences, particularly parents and other significant adults, which contribute to cognitive change. Adults serve to guide, support, inspire and correct children's problem-solving. By engaging them in such guided participation, society helps children to reach their maximal level of cognitive functioning. In this way children actively learn much as an apprentice does, by observing more competent others and trying out new skills under the direction of adults.

REFERENCES

Gilmour, J. (2003) 'Specialist neuropsychological assessment procedures for children and adolescents.' In D. Skuse (ed) *Child Psychology and Psychiatry: An Introduction*. Oxfordshire: The Medicine Publishing Company.

Kagan, J. (1984) *The Nature of the Child*. New York: Basic Books.

Piaget, J. (1970) *Science of Education and the Psychology of the Child*. New York: Viking.

Siegler, R.S. (1991) *Children's Thinking*, 2nd edn. Englewood Cliffs, NJ: Prentice-Hall.

Chapter 3

Abstraction and symbolization

Rebecca Chilvers and Samuel M. Stein

INTRODUCTION

Throughout history, some of the world's greatest thinkers have sought to explore the origins and development of human thought. In particular, there has been much unresolved debate concerning the so-called 'higher order' cognitions or thought processes such as deduction, analogical reasoning and abstraction. Are they uniquely human capabilities? At what age do children acquire them? Do they have essential roles in aiding survival and facilitating social success? This chapter attempts to provide a brief overview of two critical aspects of thought and communication – *symbolization* and *abstract thinking*. It also gives examples of how these aspects play a role in communicating with and understanding others, and the world we live in.

ABSTRACT THINKING

Children learning mathematics may first be taught to add or subtract with wooden blocks or sweets. This forms a concrete example, or representation, of the mental operation which they are performing on those objects in their own mind. But, as they get older, children will be able to perform these mental operations in their own mind without either the blocks or the sweets being necessary. This is known as abstract thinking, in which new notions or ideas can be developed from a series of past experiences or past examples (exemplars) without any of these exemplars needing to be actually present. As children develop, this kind of abstract thinking becomes more sophisticated and it may later prove very difficult to establish exactly which concrete exemplars initially contributed to subsequent abstract concepts such as 'justice' or 'freedom'.

Development of abstract thinking

Theorists of child development have long debated the age at which abstract thinking becomes evident in children. Piaget's theories regarding the developmental stages of childhood remain the most well-known. He proposed that young children begin development as 'cognitively egocentric'. They perceive and interpret the world around them in terms of themselves. While children's reasoning gradually becomes less self-centred, Piaget claimed that it is not until the fourth and final stage of development (when children are around 12 years of age) that they have the ability to think and reason in an abstract manner. For example, during early development children tend to conceptualize death as a reversible phenomenon. It is not until much later in their development that they begin to conceptualize death in a more abstract manner, and work hard at making some sense of it.

Piaget divided children's cognitive development into four stages. During the 'sensorimotor' period (0 to 2 years), infants understand the world through overt and direct actions (concrete exemplars). They are unable to recognize that an object exists even if it is out of view (object permanence). For example, until 18 months of age, a child would lose interest if presented with a toy which was then covered over as he or she would not realize that the toy was still there.

Within the second, 'pre-operational', stage (2 to 6 years), the child develops an ability to use mental examples and representations to solve problems. The child is able to 'try out' solutions to a problem mentally within his or her own mind rather than physically needing the concrete experiences or exemplars. As a result, when the child acts, the solution is more efficient and adaptive. The child is also able to think about the past and imagine the future in a way that vastly expands his or her cognitive capabilities.

The third, 'concrete operational', period (6 to 11/12 years) refers to the development of more organized systems of internal mental actions. This would include the principle of conservation and invariance discussed in Chapter 2. Most children at the concrete operation stage are able to see that the quantity remained the same (invariant) despite the changes in perceptual appearance. However they still have difficulties with abstract thought.

Piaget claimed that it is not until the final stage, the 'formal operation' period (aged 12+), that previous cognitive limitations can be overcome by the ability to use hypothetical arguments, deductive reasoning and abstract thought. In this stage, reasoning moves away from immediate reality and into the realms of what *might* be true. An example would be the ability to reason contrary to fact. If a child at this stage was asked the question 'what would happen if we were all to live forever?', he or she would be able to use that question to form the basis of an argument.

Since these stages of development were first described, research findings have suggested that many of the abilities attributed to children at a certain age are inaccurate, and that children can demonstrate higher-level skills at earlier stages than Piaget anticipated.

Abstract thinking and problem-solving

A large amount of research has been conducted into the ability of children to problem-solve. This has shed significant light on our understanding of abstract thinking in young children. In particular, it has shown that, when tasks are designed in an age-appropriate manner, even very young children can reason in an abstract manner. One particular area of interest is children's ability to reason by analogy. This is a fundamental cognitive process, and it is used frequently in educational settings to teach children new concepts. Analogical reasoning is also used throughout life whenever a previous situation is recalled in order to deal with a new one.

Research has shown that even babies can make rudimentary analogies (Chen, Campbell and Polley 1995). In this experiment it was demonstrated that, using a simple toy acquisition problem, babies as young as 13 months could transfer their knowledge of reaching for a toy in one situation and apply the same method to a different situation. When given a higher level of perceptual support, some babies as young as 10 months demonstrated the ability to solve the problem analogically. Evidence suggests that the presence of these abilities, even in a rudimentary form in early infancy, is critical for the acquisition of knowledge and for conceptual development throughout childhood.

Abstract thinking in clinical populations

The importance of abstract thinking can best be highlighted by considering people in whom this ability is severely compromised or absent, such as individuals with obsessive compulsive disorder (Chapter 14), schizophrenia and pervasive developmental disorders.

Children and adults with social communication disorders, such as autism and Asperger syndrome (Chapter 7), have profound difficulties in abstraction. As a result their interpretation of events, rules and instructions, as well as their interpretation of language, is often very concrete. This causes significant difficulty in understanding a very abstract world full of inference, deduction and 'unwritten rules'. Just considering language alone, it is easy to see how the concrete, literal interpretation of everyday expressions might be extremely confusing. For example, saying 'my heart's in my mouth' to imply that you are nervous or afraid would cause alarm to a child with autism, who may well check that your heart was still in the right place. This lack of ability to see the 'meaning beyond the meaning' often renders their speech devoid of abstract components, such as metaphor and idioms.

Schizophrenia (Chapter 17) is a mental illness characterized by deterioration in social, cognitive and vocational functioning with a pattern of psychotic features such as thought disturbances, delusions and a disturbed sense of self. One particular area of marked impairment is executive functioning. These executive functions encompass a range of abilities, one of which is the capacity for abstraction and problem-solving. Research has since shown that individuals with schizophrenia tend to think more concretely than other people, and even more concretely than psychiatric patients suffering from other illness, such as bipolar affective disorder (Seidman *et al.* 2002). Individuals with schizophrenia were seriously impaired on a number of measures, including tests that explored abstraction abilities.

Difficulties in thinking abstractly significantly impede a full understanding of complex concepts, such as time, and also impede the ability to understand the intentions of others. This is known as 'theory of mind' (Chapter 4) which, at its simplest level, is the understanding that another person may be thinking something different to you. Research experiments have shown that developing children acquire a theory of mind around the age of 3 years but that this ability is impaired in autistic children. This has implications not only for forms of thinking but also with regard to the understanding of more abstract or inferred social behaviours that operate in a particular group or society.

SYMBOLIC THOUGHT

The philosopher Thomas Hobbes (1588–1679) argued that the beginning of rational thought is the ability to create marks, signs or symbols to represent the things that we experience. Symbolic thinking is a particular form of abstract thought, and it plays a part in virtually all types of complex communication such as art and music.

Signs and symbols

A sign has only one meaning and directly represents the thing itself, such as a road sign warning of men at work or falling rocks. It is not open to personal interpretation, and does not carry any wider implications or hidden meaning. For example, the small figures on toilet doors simply serve as a guide to identify male and female facilities. In contrast, symbols are metaphors which can have multiple and complex meanings, and which may change over time.

To be regarded as a symbol rather than a sign, an image must have at least three characteristics (Von Bertalanffy 1965). First, it needs to represent something else. A symbol is therefore a substitute for the thing it represents, and is not the actual thing itself. For example, an image of a hammer and a sickle does not evoke thoughts about farming implements (which would constitute a sign) but almost immediately brings thoughts about Communism to mind (which would constitute a symbol).

Second, symbols are not accurate reflections of reality and there may be no overt connection between the symbol chosen and the thing it represents. For example, the true layout of the London Underground is not reflected in the simple symbolic map used by commuters to represent the different routes and destinations. Instead, the curved tracks and irregular gaps between stations are symbolically represented by straight lines, uniform distances and colour coding.

Third, symbols are culturally transmitted and need to be learned. People are not born with knowledge about symbols, their meaning or their use. Instead, children come to learn how to use symbols, and what these symbols mean within their community. For example, an image of a fish may represent Christianity in one country, while the same image could represent danger or good luck in another part of the world.

The use of language is a good example of symbolic thinking, as is the capacity to think in terms of images, concepts and categories.

Development of symbolic thought

The ability to think about the world representationally (moving from Piaget's sensorimotor stage to the pre-operational stage) marks the beginning of symbolic thought or symbolic function in infants. According to Piaget, this is when infants begin to exhibit deferred imitation or the ability to imitate an action that they have seen someone perform previously, for example, children imitating their mother dusting the house when they are at nursery. This ability to imitate behaviours from the past indicates a capacity to store the image or concept in a representational form, a capacity to retrieve the representation and a capacity to use it in an appropriate context or situation.

This emerging capacity for symbolic function can also be seen in the development of symbolic play. The child learns to use objects to stand for something else, such as using an empty toilet roll to represent a telescope. However, the presence of symbolic play and the extention of symbolic function does not yet imply the advent of symbolic understanding, which will only be developed later (Tomasello, Striano and Rochat 1999).

Ongoing research has brought new insights into how children think. Meltzoff and Moore (1994) demonstrated that infants as young as 6 weeks of age were capable of generating actions on the basis of stored representations or imitating actions from memory after a delay. Another series of experiments that examined how young infants achieve success in tasks which require symbolic thinking were conducted by Younger and Johnson (2003). They found that, although some understanding of the relationship between miniature toy replicas and their 'real' counterparts began to emerge in a 14-month-old group, it was not until 18 months of age that a more sophisticated comprehension of the symbolic link between models and their real object counterparts was demonstrated.

Although there is no firm consensus as to the exact age at which symbolic thinking develops, recent research indicates that symbolic thinking may start to emerge very early in infancy. This ability to symbolize may take place at different levels, with later developments in thinking and understanding simply representing a more complex version of what is present very early on. Leslie (1987) suggests that all infants begin with a capacity to form *primary representations* that encode aspects of the world in a literal manner. However, towards the end of infancy, they acquire the ability to represent the world and themselves more symbolically. This may play an essential role in child development.

The ability to symbolize is also crucial for the development of language. Piaget suggested that, at the age of 2, children discover the symbolic nature of language when they realize that everything has a name. A number of researchers have since stressed that language is probably the 'prime symbolic medium' (Nowak-Fabrykowski 2000). In addition to the early challenge of assigning names and symbols to objects, children also have to tackle the later emergence of more complex symbolic challenges such as the use of metaphor and the expression of emotion.

Symbolism and social behaviour

The understanding of symbols as social referents or clues is critical for the emergence and development of social behaviour. Social rules are rarely made explicit, and it is invariably assumed that their symbolic meaning has been understood and taken 'as read'. However, this 'meanings beyond the meanings' of symbols within a social context requires constant evaluation and re-evaluation of factors that may influence meaning. For example, someone glancing at his or her watch may simply indicate that he or she wishes to know the time. However, in a different social context, the symbolic interpretation of this gesture could relate to boredom, stress or pressing engagements. A similar multiplicity of social meaning can be attributed to other gestures such as looking away or yawning. While these behaviours may represent something at an individual level, they are also symbolic of generally recognized social meanings at a society level.

If symbolic meaning cannot be understood as part of the interaction between people, this may have serious consequences in terms of successful social functioning. It is well-documented that individuals with social communication disorders (Chapter 7) have difficulty with interpreting social behaviours symbolically. This is demonstrated in their frequent misinterpretation of intentions and fluid social circumstances. For example, the factual and concrete interest displayed in football by a child with social communication problems will manifest itself very differently to a child who understands the symbolic significance of belonging to and supporting a team. The latter would be found supporting and cheering on the sidelines while a child with autism may instead be fascinated with match statistics or memorizing the players from the last ten years.

ABSTRACT AND SYMBOLIC THINKING IN A WIDER CONTEXT

The capacity for higher-order cognition and thinking has served an important evolutionary purpose. However, the distinctly human ability to understand and utilize abstract and symbolic thinking reaches far beyond problem-solving and basic interpretation. Human beings have cultivated an existence that values artistic expression, which embodies the principles of symbolism and abstraction. When someone plays a piece of music or reads a book, these activities may evoke emotions, ideas, further images and thoughts even in the absence of concrete form.

Religion and science also draw heavily on these abilities. Religious concepts are often abstract, and many religious groups make use of symbolism to understand these abstract concepts. Religious symbols such as the cross, the five-pointed star and the moon carry a global meaning which evokes far more understanding than the simple sign of a given faith. In science and mathematics, new understanding stems from abstract reasoning about such topics as the intricacies of quantum mechanics or the mysteries of the space–time continuum.

SUMMARY

Symbolization and abstract thinking are key aspects of development that serve to establish and extend expression and understanding. From early infancy, these abilities expand logical and factual knowledge. However, they are also the building blocks of social communication and understanding. Individuals with neuro-developmental, psychological and psychiatric difficulties may show deficits of these essential abilities, which may have profound consequences on their development and functioning. Symbolism and abstraction therefore hold a prominent place in the cultural, philosophical and scientific aspects of society. They form part of its identity, part of its history and are fundamental to its future survival.

REFERENCES

Chen, Z., Campbell, T. and Polley, R. (1995) 'From beyond to within their grasp: The rudiments of analogical problem solving in 10 and 13 month old infants.' Paper presented at the Biennal Meeting of the Society for Research in Child Development, Indianapolis.

Leslie, A.M. (1987) 'Pretense and representation: the origins of "theory of mind".' *Psychological Review 94*, 412–426.

Meltzoff, A.N. and Moore, M.K. (1994) 'Imitation, memory and the representation of persons.' *Infant Behaviour and Development 17*, 83–89.

Nowak-Fabrykowski, K. (2000) 'The role of poetry and stories of young children in their process of learning.' *Journal of Instructional Psychology 27*, 59–65.

Seidman, L.J., Kremen, W.S., Koren, D., Faraone, S.V. *et al.* (2002) 'A comparative profile analysis of neuro- psychological functioning in patients with schizophrenia and bipolar psychosis.' *Schizophrenia Research 53*, 31–44.

Tomasello, M., Striano, T. and Rochat, P. (1999) 'Do young children use objects as symbols?' *British Journal of Developmental Psychology 17*, 563–584.

Von Bertalanffy, L. (1965) 'On the definition of the symbol.' In J.R. Joyce (ed) *Psychology and the Symbol.* New York: Random.

Younger, B.A. and Johnson, K.E. (2003) 'Infants' comprehension of toy replicas as symbols for real objects.' *Cognitive Psychology 48*, 207–242.

Chapter 4

Theory of mind

Ashlee Clifford and Samuel M. Stein

INTRODUCTION

As adults, we are aware that other people have minds of their own. We appreciate that they hold personal beliefs about the world around them, and that these views may be different from our own. We also recognize that their opinion or perspective may change with time and circumstance. Whatever our beliefs, we appreciate that these will directly influence how we behave and we can similarly make assumptions about the beliefs of others by studying the way in which they behave.

'Theory of mind' is the term used to describe this understanding that other people may have thoughts, beliefs, desires and intentions that are different from our own. Theory of mind also reflects the capacity to interpret what people say, to make sense of their actions and to predict what they may do next. This is achieved through the development of a dual ability to understand both one's own state of mind and the mental states (feelings and emotions) of other people.

THEORY OF MIND

At its most basic, if children can imagine what another person thinks, and then apply this knowledge socially, they can be said to have theory of mind. This is based on their emerging capacity to understand that people have minds and mental states of their own, and that these mental states relate to their behaviour. Without a theory of mind, children cannot interpret the mental states of others or use this information to predict their subsequent actions.

This understanding of the mind and its mental operations constitutes the child's theory of mind. Even during pre-school years, children attempt to construct an understanding, not only of physical reality, but also of the human mind and such concepts as knowing, wanting, thinking, remembering and intending. Children as young as 18 to 30 months already display some evidence of theory of mind and Wellman (1990) has shown that, by the age of 3, children invariably possess a commonsense theory of mind. He found that children of this age are able to grasp the difference between states of mind and physical objects, as well as having an understanding of the relationship between the mental states of individuals and their subsequent actions.

In developing a theory of mind, children come to understand five fundamental principles (DeHart, Stroufe and Cooper 2000). The first principle, which is established even before the pre-school years, is simply that the mind exists. This becomes apparent during the toddler period when children start referring to mental states such as feelings and desires. It implies that they have already begun to grasp the notion that minds exist. The second principle is that minds have connections to the physical world. What people think, feel, know and want is unavoidably linked to the objects and events around them. A substantial improvement in this understanding occurs between the ages of 2 and 3.

The third principle is that minds are separate and different from the physical world. This new understanding of mental events makes children of 3 or more less fearful of imagined ghosts and monsters. The fourth principle can be exhibited by 4 and 5-year-old children who come to understand that minds can represent objects and events both accurately and inaccurately. The fifth and final principle in developing a theory of mind is that minds actively interpret reality and emotional experiences. Even children of up to 8 years of age may still believe that everyone who hears the same message, regardless of their age or perspective, will understand it in the same way.

Developmental psychologists therefore widely agree that children slowly acquire a theory of mind as part of normal development, based on their experiences of the world, especially their social interactions.

IMPORTANCE OF MIND-READING

Daniel Dennett, one of the theorists who has stressed the importance of mind-reading within social interactions, suggests that the easiest way to understand others is by attributing thoughts and feelings (or mental states) to them, including emotions and desires. This allows the individual to devise explanations about other people's behaviour, including a capacity to predict reliably what others might do next. Being able to mind-read is this ability to confidently but unconsciously attribute beliefs and desires to another person, and thus to understand their intentions, behaviours and social interactions (Dennett 1978).

Theory of mind is also essential for the understanding of communication, and for understanding the communicative intention of the person who is trying to speak. This is based on an awareness of the difference between concrete things and more abstract thoughts about these things as, in day-to-day conversation, people often do not say exactly what they mean. Instead, they use figurative speech, sarcasm, irony and metaphor to explain their thoughts or feelings in a more symbolic manner (Chapter 3). This is where mind-reading becomes important as, in order to understand the speaker, the individual needs to look beyond what is actually being said or the words being used. Instead, a working hypothesis or prediction must be developed about the speaker's thoughts, feelings, intentions, desires and emotions in order to understand fully what is being communicated.

Mind-reading is not only important for the listener to understand the speaker, but plays an essential role in enabling the speaker to understand the listener too. When speaking, we need to monitor what the listener may already know or not know, and then decide what additional information must still be supplied before the listener can fully understand the communicator's intention. To be confident that the communication has been understood, the speaker must also monitor the listener to ensure that the message has been received as intended. If the speaker feels that the message has not been fully understood by the listener, which reflects his or her mind-reading ability, then he or she needs to try again using different words or explanations.

Other applications of theory of mind in everyday life include deception, persuasion, empathy and self-awareness. By using mind-reading, children are often capable of displaying persuasive forms of deception from around 4 years of age (Sodian 1991). In persuasion, the realization that other people have thoughts and beliefs of their own allows for teaching and for convincing others to change their minds. Empathy, which is the ability to understand how someone may be feeling, requires a good deal of mind-reading and is often evident from the age of 3 years. The ability to mind-read also allows children to develop an awareness of their own thoughts and beliefs, and to experience some degree of self-reflection. This will enable a child to understand the reasons for his or her own behaviour, and to reflect on possible solutions to problems before trying them.

The ability to mind-read tends to develop naturally in children. However, an increasing number of studies have shown that children with social communication disorders have specific difficulty in understanding the mental states of others (Howlin, Baron-Cohen and Hadwin 1999). This may impact on their capacity to understand unwritten social rules and impair their adaptation to subtle changes in context. They also struggle to understand deceit or dissembling, and find it difficult to comprehend that other people may have their own plans, thoughts, points of view, beliefs, attitudes and emotions. It is because of this lack of understanding that children with autistic spectrum disorders (Chapter 7) are likely to have problems relating socially and communicating with other people.

SIGNS OF MIND-READING

From an early age, children are clearly able to demonstrate their developing theory of mind, and their emerging capacity to mind-read the mental states of other people with whom they come into contact.

Visual perspective-taking

The presence of visual perspective-taking serves as an early indication that children are aware that other people may see things differently to them. There are two levels of visual perspective-taking. Level 1 reflects an ability to identify what another person may be looking at. This tends to be evident in children of 2 years of age who are able to move objects out of sight and then bring them back into sight when asked. Level 2 reflects an ability to infer how the other person may view the object which he or she is looking at. This level of visual perspective-taking doesn't usually become evident until children are around 3 or 4 years of age. Thus visual perspective-taking involves the ability to predict actions on the basis of the other person's knowledge and understanding.

Seeing leads to knowing

Another aspect of theory of mind is the understanding that seeing will lead to knowing. This demonstrates the child's awareness that, in order to obtain knowledge, it is important to have access to relevant information. For example, a 3-year-old will be able to indicate which of two people would know if a toy is in a box when one of them has looked into the box while the other has merely touched it.

Pretence

Pretence is yet another mental state that seems to be understood by children from a very early age. From as young as 10 to 18 months, children are already able to participate in pretend play. Further evidence of children's capacity to differentiate pretence as being different from reality can be found in verbal children almost as soon as they can answer questions.

False belief tasks

The accepted way in which researchers investigate children's theory of mind is called the 'false belief' task. One of these approaches was designed by Wimmer and Perner (1983) to explore children's understanding of what someone wants versus what they believe.

In the false belief task, models are used to act out a story about a little boy called Maxi. Maxi puts some chocolate into a blue cupboard in front of the child participating in the research. When Maxi leaves the room, his mother lifts the chocolate out of the blue cupboard and places it into a green cupboard. When Wimmer and Perner tested 3-year-old children, they asked them to predict where Maxi would look for the chocolate on his return to the room. At this age, children would typically answer that Maxi would look for the chocolate in the green cupboard. They did not recognize that Maxi, who had left the room, could not possibly know that the chocolate had been moved from the blue cupboard to the green cupboard by his mother.

This experiment proved influential in developing the theory of mind concept. It demonstrated that children's interpretation of people's behaviour was very different to the assumptions made by adults about the same scenario. It also highlighted that developing children under the age of 4 were unable to demonstrate theory of mind. This research further showed that children with autism, and children with visual and auditory impairment, performed significantly worse on the false belief task than peers who were developing in keeping with their chronological age.

Between the ages of 3 and 4, there is a noticeable shift in performance on the false belief task by children as theory of mind increasingly emerges and continues to develop throughout childhood.

Belief–desire reasoning

Understanding desire is important in predicting another person's behaviour, and studies using the false belief task have found that desires are often understood much earlier than beliefs. Children who failed the task seemed only to consider what a person wanted or desired without recognizing what the person may believe. At the age of 2 years, children tended to attribute mental states exclusively to desire, with a focus on terms like 'want' and 'like'. Even 3-year-old children, who were beginning to understand belief–desire reasoning better, still relied heavily on desire-based reasoning when undertaking a false belief task. As a result, children in both age groups were unable to predict a person's behaviour based on theory of mind (Wellman 1990).

However, by 3 years of age, children can increasingly predict how situations affect emotions and, by the age of 4, they are able to predict how a person feels by considering both their desires and beliefs. According to Wellman (1985), the ability to acknowledge other people's mental states, and to use these mental states to predict their behaviour, relies on belief–desire strategies which are essential to the development of a theory of mind.

Emotion

A child's recognition of emotional states can be understood within the beliefs–desires model. Children as young as 2 or 3 years of age are capable of understanding happiness and sadness as a result of desires being, or not being, fulfilled (Wellman 1990). This was reinforced in a study carried out by Wellman and Bartsch (1988) who found that 4-year-old children were able to detect surprise when perceived beliefs and desires corresponded with each other. In this experiment, children were told in detail of the likes and thoughts of a character in a story. They were then shown a picture of a possible outcome, and were asked whether the character would feel surprised or not. The children were able to understand that the character would feel surprised when the outcome contradicted his or her beliefs. However, further studies found conflicting results, whereby only 5 and 6-year-olds were able to demonstrate an understanding that the character would be surprised when his or her beliefs conflicted with reality.

CAN MIND-READING BE TAUGHT?

Mind-reading tends to develop naturally throughout the early years of normal development. For those who do not display growing evidence of theory of mind as an infant, interventions have been developed to teach them the basic skills of mind-reading. Such procedures have demonstrated that, even with relatively brief treatment programmes, improvements are evident especially in children with autism (Wellman 1990). However, it can prove very difficult to teach the concept of mind-reading to children with autistic spectrum disorders as this will involve changing their fundamental understanding of the mental states of other people.

Howlin *et al.* (1999) developed intervention techniques for people with social communication problems. Their approaches were designed to teach theory of mind skills to individuals across the autistic spectrum while taking into consideration the developmental stages of theory of mind acquisition in normal children. They focused on three different mental states: emotional, informational and play. The teaching experience was designed to be as natural as possible for the child, as well as being rewarding, using play, games, pictures and computers.

Each aspect of training is carried out across five levels. These were designed not only to teach children to recognize emotions and to understand other people's beliefs, but also to help enhance the intricacy of their developmental play. The child is encouraged to participate in imaginative play which, by Level 5, is spontaneous without any encouragement from an adult.

ATTACHMENT AND THEORY OF MIND

Secure attachment is essential for the development of theory of mind as the emergence of symbolic thought is closely linked to the harmoniousness of the mother–child relationship (Fonagy 2001). For example, one of the early stages in the development of theory of mind is shared attention. Infants know, from early on, how to track their mother's gaze, and how to coordinate this with pointing towards things to which they wish to draw their mother's attention. The infant is thus aiming to influence the mother's state of mind so that the two of them can share an interest in the same object. Such shared attention implies that the infant realizes that his or her mother has a mental state of her own which he or she now wishes to align with his or her own. In this way, children soon come to understand that they share with others the capacity for intentionality, as well as sharing the mind's inherent tendency to form mental images and representations. The development of theory of mind and infant attachment are therefore closely linked.

REFERENCES

DeHart, G., Sroufe, L.A. and Cooper, R.G. (2000) *Child Development: Its Nature and Course*, 4th edn. New York: McGraw-Hill.

Dennett, D. (1978) *Brainstorms: Philosophical Essays on Mind and Psychology*. Brighton: Harvester Press.

Fonagy, P. (2001) *Attachment Theory and Psychoanalysis*. New York: Other Press.

Howlin, P., Baron-Cohen, S. and Hadwin, J. (1999) *Teaching Children to Mind-Read. A Practical Guide.* Chichester: John Wiley.

Sodian, B. (1991) 'The development of deception in young children.' *British Journal of Developmental Psychology 9*, 173–188.

Wellman, H.M. (1985) 'The child's theory of mind: Development of conceptions of cognition.' In S.R. Yussen (ed) *Developing Theories of Mind*. New York: Cambridge University Press.

Wellman, H.M. (1990) *The Child's Theory of Mind*. Cambridge, MA: Bradford.

Wellman, H.M. and Bartsch, K. (1988) 'Young children's reasoning about beliefs.' *Cognition 30*, 239–277.

Wimmer, H. and Perner, J. (1983) 'Beliefs about beliefs: Representation and constraining function of wrong beliefs in young children's understanding of deception.' *Cognition 13*, 103–128.

Chapter 5

Attachment

Sarah O'Reilly and Samuel M. Stein

INTRODUCTION

Attachment can be defined as 'an emotional tie with another person, shown in young children by their seeking closeness to the caregiver and showing distress on separation' (Myers 1998). This attachment between children and their parents (or caregivers) begins long before the actual birth of a child and proceeds long after death. Even before conception, parental imagination has already taken over with thoughts about the character of the child, what the child will be named, what the child will look like and how he or she will act. These thoughts are also accompanied by dreams and hopes for the child's future.

This chapter will focus on the origins of attachment theory, the different types of attachment and how important this attachment is with regard to relationships and character development. The impact of maternal separation and deprivation will also be discussed, and literature on developments in attachment theory over the last few decades will be examined throughout.

ATTACHMENT THEORY

Early psychoanalytical and psychological theories considered feeding as the main explanation for attachment between mother and child. Food and comfort were viewed as the primary reason for this growing link. However, in 1957, Lorenz observed that baby geese developed a strong bond towards the first moving object which they encountered after hatching. In 1958, Harlow found that monkeys who were separated from their mothers became intensely attached to their blankets and, when these blankets were taken away, the young monkeys became very distressed (Myers 1998).

John Bowlby, building on these ethological developments, combined a wide range of different perspectives into a single holistic theory of attachment. While working with juvenile delinquents, he found that some of the children had affectionless characters, which he linked to the disruption of early attachment due to separation or 'maternal deprivation'. Bowlby came to view infants and their mothers as being tied together through invisible emotional bonds, and recognized that this attachment between children and their caregivers was fundamental to normal development.

In doing so, Bowlby (1953) extended attachment theory beyond the realm of physical need, seeing it instead as a social pre-requisite. Based on the work of Freud and Blatz (Ainsworth, Bell and Stayton 1971), he identified these first attachments as crucial in providing a secure base from which the infant begins to explore and learn. Only by establishing a secure dependence on their parents can children venture into unfamiliar situations where they increasingly learn to cope on their own. This encourages development and growing independence, with these first attachments providing a blueprint for the establishment of other age-appropriate attachments as children and adolescent mature. Even in later life, attachments continue to provide a secure base, a source of support and a safeguard against stress. However, over time, the focus shifts from parents to peers and then to partners.

STAGES OF ATTACHMENT

As described by Durkin (1995), there are three stages of primary attachment. First there is an asocial stage between 0 and 6 weeks, during which time the infant will smile and cry indiscriminately without this being directed at anyone. This is followed by indiscriminate attachment, which occurs between 6 weeks and 7 months of age, during which time the infant will seek attention from both familiar caregivers and strangers. Finally, specific attachments start to form between the ages of 7 and 11 months, with the infant becoming more selective and a growing tendency to seek attention only from specific individuals.

The attachment stage at which infants learn to discriminate between familiar and unfamiliar people coincides with their increasing mobility. This presents as a growing fear of strangers, and children of this age may cling tightly to their parents when frightened or faced with a period of separation. When reunited, they respond by showering their parents with hugs and smiles. In contrast, children at this level of development will stare cautiously, withdraw, cry or even scream when confronted by strangers.

These attachment-linked behaviours exist to reduce the distance between a mother and her child. Infants instinctively realize that the closer they remain to their caregiver, the greater the level of protection which can be provided to safeguard them from harm. As described by Bowlby (1988), this could include 'any form of behaviour that results in a person attaining or maintaining proximity to some other clearly identified individual who is conceived as better able to cope with the world. It is most obvious whenever the person is frightened, fatigued, or sick, and is assuaged by comforting and caregiving.'

Along with protection, the caregiver also provides food, equips the infant with knowledge about the environment and enhances his or her ability to interact socially. Children have an innate desire to explore, and secure attachment provides them with the opportunity to do so within safe confines. It offers a balance between exploring, which is essential to growing autonomy, while allowing them to stay within a safe distance of parents and caregivers to reduce the risk of harm.

Sroufe, Fox and Pancake (1983) demonstrated how infants who were securely attached at 12 to 18 months functioned more confidently than other toddlers when re-studied as 2- to 3-year-olds. This complemented Erikson, Stroufe and Egeland's (1985) theory that securely attached children approached life with a sense of basic trust and a sense of the world as predictable and reliable. These children were therefore better equipped to deal with the world as their secure attachment helped in the development of later social competence and future relationships.

TYPES OF ATTACHMENT

Mary Ainsworth was strongly influenced by Bowlby's work, and she developed a technique for measuring attachment using the standard stranger situation (Ainsworth *et al.* 1971). In this laboratory proceedure, known as the Strange Situation, the child and his or her caregiver enter a playroom, which the child is free to explore. In a series of episodes and short separations, the child is exposed to a stranger, both with and without the mother being present, and is left alone briefly before being reunited with the mother.

Ainsworth, using this approach, identified three different types of attachment relationship, with the child's response to the Strange Situation being seen as indicative of the attachment which he or she enjoyed with the caregiver. A fourth category was later added by Mary Main. Anxious attachment was divided into Avoidant Attachment (Type A) and Ambivalent/Resistant Attachment (Type C). Disorganized/Disoriented Attachment was added as Type D, while Secure Attachment was coded as Type B (DeHart, Stroufe and Cooper 2000)

In Type A (avoidant) attachment, children readily separate from the caregiver and they tend not to cry when the mother leaves the room. Typically, they are not wary of the stranger either. However, when the mother returns, the child actively avoids her, turning away, moving away or ignoring her. He or she does not seek proximity with the mother after a separation.

In Type C (ambivalent/resistant) attachment, children are reluctant to separate from their caregiver and are quite upset when their mother leaves the room. However, they are not easily comforted upon her return, mixing a desire for proximity with a resistance to close contact. One moment they may raise their arms to be picked up, only to squirm, push away and kick out in anger.

Type A and Type C children are therefore not confident about their caregiver's availability or responsiveness, and cannot use the caregiver as a secure base for exploration and growth. This may lead to insecurities and conflicts which disrupt or inhibit their experiences and development.

Type B (secure) children show a good balance between play and exploration versus a desire for proximity with their caregiver. They separate readily from their mothers, but actively share discoveries with them. They respond positively to their mother's return, and clearly differentiate between the caregiver and the stranger. It is therefore a pattern of attachment behaviour in which the infant is confident of the caregiver's availability and responsiveness, and can use the caregiver as a secure base for exploration.

Type D (disorganized/disoriented) children cannot maintain a coherent strategy for expressing attachment. They seek proximity to the caregiver in strange ways, such as approaching the mother backwards, hiding, suddenly freezing in mid-movement or just staring into space (Main and Solomon 1990). Their response to the Strange Situation highlights contradictory features of several patterns of anxious attachment, leaving them disoriented or in a daze. Their behaviour is characterized by a motivation to approach attachment figures while feeling equally motivated to withdraw from them as a source of fear. High-risk children often fall into this category, indicating the possible presence of traumatic separation, abuse, neglect, parental psychopathology or exposure to any caregiving behaviour which is frightening or bizarre.

Ainsworth's infant attachment patterns received further support from the Adult Attachment Interview (AAI) devised by Main *et al.* (1985) which gauged caregivers' memories and representations of their own childhood attachments and emotions. They were also asked about how these early relationships had potentially influenced their own development. This approach yielded four different patterns of attachment, three (Types D, E and U) which represent insecure attachment and one (Type F) representing secure attachment.

Dismissing–Detached individuals (D) often claim that they cannot remember much about the relationship with their parents during childhood. They tend to either idealize their early caregiver experience, or are actively derogatory about it. Preoccupied–Entangled individuals (E) produce many conflicting childhood memories about attachment, but are unable to organize them into a consistent representation. This tends to emerge as either anger or passivity. Unresolved–Disorganized individuals (U) present contradictory behaviours with evidence that their early loss or abuse has yet to be resolved. In contrast,

Autonomous–Secure individuals (F) are able to give a clear and consistent account of their early attachments, irrespective of whether these experiences had been positive or negative.

Subsequent attachment research has shown a strong correlation between Strange Situation findings and AAI results. Adults who present with D or E classifications on the AAI map conceptually with Type A and Type C attachment patterns found in the Strange Situation. Similarly disorganization and lack of resolution (U) on the AAI maps closely with Type D attachment patterns found in the Strange Situation. In both approaches, secure attachment is reflected by coherence and containment of thoughts and behaviour.

DOES ATTACHMENT SHAPE FUTURE RELATIONSHIPS?

From the outset, Bowlby believed that early exposure to abuse or neglect would impact on the child when he or she emerged into adulthood. He attributed this to internal working models through which all children mentally represent their first relationships. These representations soon become part of the child's sense of self, and influence how they perceive themselves in relation to others. If the working models are based on abusive or inconsistent caregiving, then the child's later ability to form relationships may be permanently impaired. Unfortunately, such early working models are relatively stable across the lifespan, and can prove very resistant to change.

Stern (1985) found that infants, even of only a few weeks of age, can begin to develop and retain representations of the mother–child interaction which they are experiencing. This is constructed using forms of non-verbal or pre-verbal memory and, if the representations of caregiving are consistent and can be maintained, then they are likely to form an essential component of the child's sense of core self. This will include feelings of self-worth, self-esteem and self-confidence. Children who are maltreated are therefore less likely to prove securely attached to their mothers.

Unfortunately, the anxious or disorganized attachment may become internalized by the child as a working model for interacting with others. It will subsequently form a mental prototype according to which all future relationships are understood and managed. Children who experience such early insecure relationships have since been observed to be more prone to moodiness, poor peer relations, symptoms of depression, aggression, learning difficulties and poor motivation (Fonagy and Target 2003). Abused and neglected children may therefore experience long-standing problems in forming close and intimate relationships with peers, partners and even their own children. This may generate cycles of disadvantage, in which poor attachment patterns are passed from one generation to the next with reinforcement of problem behaviours and unstable relationships.

Individuals who experience early trauma may present with disordered self-perception and impoverished attachments later in life. Their early experiences may also predispose them to mental disorders in adulthood, including an increased risk of self-harming behaviour, emotional distress, depression, child abuse, sexual offending, anxiety, substance misuse, personality disorder and psychosomatic illness (Fonagy and Target 2003).

While parental stress and depression may be associated with insecure attachments, the impact which the child may have on its caregiver also needs to be acknowledged. For example, if a child has behavioural problems, it may prove more difficult for the parent to develop a secure attachment with him or her. Infants are therefore active agents within the mother–child interaction.

CONCLUSION

Attachment is a cross-cultural phenomenon. Although the nature of parent–child relationships may vary in different societies, all infants develop an intense bond with those who care for them. Attachment theory has therefore affected society, just as society continues to affect attachment theory, by providing a model for the integration of early childhood experience with later development. As a result, attachment theory has also been incorporated into psychotherapy and psychoanalysis. It has come to form an essential part of the direct work with patients based on the capacity of children with a history of secure attachments to prove more resilient, more self-reliant, more socially oriented and more empathic, with deeper relationships, higher self-esteem, lower anxiety and less hostility (Fonagy and Target 2003). However, further research clearly needs to be done with families to identify and prevent unhelpful attachment styles in order to break the negative cycles that currently exist.

REFERENCES

Ainsworth, M.D.S., Bell, S.M. and Stayton, D.J. (1971) 'Individual differences in the strange situation behaviour of one-year-olds.' In H.R. Schaffer (ed) *The Origins of Human Social Relations.* New York: Academic Press, pp.15–71.

Bowlby, J. (1953) 'Psychopathological processes set in train by early mother–child separation.' In *Proceedings of the Seventh Conference on Infancy and Childhood.* New York: Jos Macy Jnr Foundation.

Bowlby, J. (1988) *A Secure Base.* New York: Basic Books.

DeHart, G., Sroufe, L.A. and Cooper, R.G. (2000) *Child Development: Its Nature and Course,* 4th edn. New York: McGraw-Hill.

Durkin, K. (1995) *Developmental Social Psychology.* Oxford: Blackwell.

Erikson, M.F., Sroufe, L.A. and Egeland, B. (1985)' The relationship between quality of attachment and behaviour problems in a preschool high-risk sample.' *Monographs of the Society for Research in Child Development 50*, 147–166.

Fonagy, P. and Target, M. (2003) *Psychoanalytic Theories: Perspectives from Developmental Psychopathology.* London: Whurr Publishers.

Main, M. and Solomon, J. (1990) 'Procedures for identifying infants as disorganized/disoriented during the Ainsworth strange situation.' In M.T. Greenberg, D. Cicchetti and E.M. Cummings (eds) *Attachment in the Preschool Years: Theory, Research and Intervention.* Chicago, IL: University of Chicago Press, pp.121–160.

Main, M., Kaplan, N. and Cassidy, J. (1985) 'Security in infancy, childhood, and adulthood: A move to the level of representation.' In I. Bretherton and E. Waters (eds) *Growing Points of Attachment Theory and Research. Monographs of the Society for Research in Child Development 50*, 66–104.

Myers, D.G. (1998) *Psychology*, 5th edn. New York: Worth Publishers.

Sroufe, L.A., Fox, N.E. and Pancake, V.R. (1983) 'Attachment and dependency in developmental perspective.' *Child Development 54*, 1615–1627.

Stern, D.N. (1985) *The Interpersonal World of the Infant.* New York: Basic Books.

Part 2

Neuro-Developmental Problems

Chapter 6

Attention deficit hyperactivity disorder

Sharon Davies and Sue Jennings

INTRODUCTION

Attention Deficit Hyperactivity Disorder (ADHD) is a complex neuro-developmental disorder with core symptoms of inattention, hyperactivity and impulsive behaviour which are present from an early age. These symptoms are common in children but, when extreme, cause marked impairment in the individual child and are considered to be symptoms of a mental health disorder. Prevalence ranges from 1 to 5 per cent of school-age children depending on the diagnostic criteria used. However, there remains some controversy around the diagnosis and, as with many mental health problems, there is no validated diagnostic test.

ADHD usually begins early in life with impairing symptoms exhibited before 7 years of age. It can affect the individual throughout his or her lifespan, often persisting into adolescence and adulthood. Impaired peer and family relationships may result, and there is an increased risk of social isolation. Adverse outcomes include delinquency, anti-social behaviour and academic underachievement. It is therefore appropriate that ADHD is a major focus of child mental health intervention.

HISTORICAL PERSPECTIVE

The first clinical description of ADHD appeared in 1902 when it was conceptualized as a deficit in 'volitional inhibition' or 'moral control'. Between 1940 and 1960, the term 'minimal brain damage or dysfunction' (Chapter 13) was used, only to be replaced by descriptions such as hyperactivity or poor impulse control in the 1960s. The 1980s brought to the fore theories regarding primary deficits in attention and impulse control, leading to current approaches which focus on impaired self-regulation and behavioural inhibition. Cognitive models of ADHD highlight faulty information processing and executive functioning which impair appraising, selecting, initiating, allocating mental effort, monitoring, evaluating, correcting and ending. Neurobiological models of ADHD emphasize genetic influences on anatomical and biochemical impairments. Dexamphetamine, which was discovered to be a safe and effective treatment for ADHD in 1937, continues to be the mainstay of pharmacological treatment up to the present time (Bradley 1937).

PREVALENCE AND COURSE

The prevalence of ADHD is difficult to measure as its identification depends on the diagnostic criteria being used, the number of informants interviewed, sampling methods, the age of the research population and whether children live in urban or rural settings. If ICD criteria (World Health Organization 1992) are used, then 1 to 2 per cent prevalence rates are found. However, using DSM criteria (American Psychiatric Association 2000), prevalence rates range from 5 to 10 per cent. Although not widely studied, epidemiological data suggest about 2 per cent of children aged 3 to 5 years have ADHD.

Initially thought to be a transient disorder, it is now established that ADHD persists into adolescence in at least 50 per cent of affected persons, and into adulthood in at least half of adolescence cases. Outcome studies have shown a five times greater risk for the development of substance use, anti-social behaviour and psychiatric disorders such as depression and anxiety. Early academic and educational problems often persist into adolescence, and hyperactive children complete less schooling and hold lower-status jobs than non-affected peers.

A poor outcome is more likely if there are additional stressful life circumstances such as poverty, overcrowding, negative parent–child relationships or parental mental illness. Outcome is also worse if symptoms are severe, predominantly hyperactive/impulsive and if children have early conduct, language or learning disorders (Taylor *et al.* 1996).

THEORETICAL BACKGROUND

ADHD is a collection of symptoms which can be caused by a number of different pathological processes including biological, social and psychological conditions that may interact to produce the disorder. Recent research suggests that the genetic contribution to aetiology is high. Strong evidence for this genetic susceptibility to ADHD has been demonstrated by family, twin and adoption studies, and more recently by advances in molecular genetics.

Adverse factors in pregnancy have also been implicated in the aetiology of ADHD (Chapter 15). Foetal exposure to alcohol and benzodiazepines are particularly associated with ADHD. Additional perinatal factors include pre-eclamptic toxaemia, maternal smoking, low foetal heart rate during labour and small head circumference at birth. There are many other known associations with ADHD such as central nervous system conditions, psycho-social adversity, institutionalization, idiosyncratic reactions to food, recurrent otitis media and exposure to toxic levels of lead (Taylor *et al.* 1998).

However, it is important to recognize that the degree of restlessness or inattention being acted out by a child may simply be appropriate to his or her developmental age and stage.

CLINICAL PRESENTATION

ADHD presents with core symptoms of inattention, hyperactivity and impulsive behaviour. Children are considered to be hyperactive when their physical (motor) activity is excessive and inappropriate for a given situation, although this will vary according to the age and developmental stage of the child. The overactivity may manifest as fidgetiness, squirming, an inability to remain still or boisterousness. Hyperactive children also tend to be restless sleepers.

Inattention refers to the inability to sustain concentration on activities which may present as careless errors, poor organization, forgetfulness, daydreaming, failure to finish work and a tendency to lose things. Impulsivity presents as recklessness, being accident prone, not paying heed to social rules, being cheeky and frequently interrupting. However, the features of ADHD may vary within and among individual children, and behaviour may even vary from day to day and hour by hour.

Age and gender differences with regard to ADHD are well recognized. Affected boys outnumber affected girls by a ratio of approximately 4 to 1. Whereas girls are more likely to show attentional problems with less marked hyperactivity, boys are more likely to exhibit impulsive and hyperactive behaviours. Although epidemiological studies have shown similar levels of overactive behaviour across cultures and geographical regions, differences in reported prevalence rates of ADHD do exist. However, this may reflect identification bias rather than true differences in prevalence (Leung *et al.* 1996).

Children with ADHD may present with IQ scores which are lower than average, and a significant association with chronic behavioural and academic impairment has been observed. In pre-school day care settings, children with ADHD often change activities frequently and spend less time engaged in social interactions during play. Such children tend to be less socially skilled, with a greater risk of accidental injury due to their impulsive and overactive behaviour. During unstructured play, their overactivity is more evident and such children may have hoarse voices as a result of talking too much.

Box 6.1 ADHD symptom list

(DSM-IV-TR, APA 2000)

Inattention
- Careless with detail
- Fails to sustain attention
- Appears not to listen
- Does not finish instructed task
- Poor self-organization
- Avoids tasks that require sustained mental effort
- Loses things
- Easily distracted
- Seems forgetful

Hyperactivity/impulsivity
- Fidgets
- Leaves seat when should be seated
- Runs/climbs excessively and inappropriately
- Noisy in play
- Persistent motor overactivity unmodified by social context
- Blurts out answers before question completed
- Fails to wait turn or queue
- Interrupts conversation or games
- Talks excessively

ADHD characteristics tend to be pervasive across different situations and persistent over time. These may include features such as defiance, aggression, antisocial behaviour and problems with social relationships. Children with ADHD can be rude and disinhibited, and their impulsivity and failure to think through actions may lead to rule-breaking behaviour. Such children may be easily influenced by others, and may well be noticed more in class leading to an escalation of conduct difficulties. With increasing age, the symptoms of ADHD tend to have a greater impact in all areas of functioning, affecting academic performance, peer relations and family life. Parents of young children with ADHD tend to have greater levels of parenting stress, and subsequently exhibit more problematic parent–child interactions. Later, during adolescence, some of these ADHD features may be masked by delinquent behaviour, drug misuse and risk-taking behaviour.

ASSOCIATED FEATURES AND CO-MORBIDITY

A number of other conditions may be confused with ADHD, or even present together with ADHD. Such co-morbidity is common, including behavioural disorders, conduct disorders and oppositional defiant disorders. Other co-morbidity may include learning difficulties, emotional disorders, autistic spectrum disorders, language disorders, tic disorders and substance misuse.

Mood disorders such as depression, mania and anxiety can all mimic ADHD as they present with inattention, lack of concentration, restlessness and agitated behaviour. Less severe autistic spectrum disorders may not have been diagnosed, and it is therefore important to acquire a detailed developmental history, as well as assessing social and communication skills. Hyperactivity is also more common when there is developmental delay, and young children who have experienced disrupted early parenting with poor attachment relationships can present with similarities to ADHD.

Conduct disorder is also characterized by impulsiveness, and these children may appear restless and inattentive within classroom situations. The differentiating question is whether there are any activities during which attention can be sustained. Hyperactivity in only one setting is more indicative of a situational cause which may include specific learning difficulty, exposure to domestic violence or child abuse. However, caution must be exercised and a careful exploration of any additional psychological and social factors may be necessary.

Case example: Peter, a younger child with ADHD

Peter, a 6-year-old boy, was taken to the GP surgery by his mother. He immediately started climbing onto the examination couch and pushing over equipment without concern. His mother tried to hold him, but he started struggling and screaming. Peter seemed to quieten a little when she distracted him with a favourite toy but, after a few minutes, he was pulling at the blind and tangling the string. It was difficult for the GP to begin a conversation without constant interruptions from Peter, and his mother frequently needing to attend to his behaviour.

His mother said that there had been increasing problems at school, and that she had been asked to take him home on a number of occasions. The main difficulties were his inability to do as he was told or remain seated for more than a few minutes. She added that Peter did not have any friends and that he engaged frequently in fights, particularly when participating in turn-taking games. The school responded by developing an educational plan and by providing one-to-one support, both of which resulted in some improvement in his behaviour. They also asked Peter's mother to have him assessed for possible ADHD.

The history provided was of an active child, who had been like this from the word go. Peter did not need as much sleep as his siblings, and was always getting into mischief. He also did not listen long enough to take in commands. His mother had been patient and spent a great deal of time helping him at home. However, the school was proving less able to manage, and was considering excluding Peter from lessons. This was not helped by his tendency to say the first thing that came into his head and, as Peter left the surgery, he said 'Bye Rathead'.

Case example: Simon, an older child with ADHD

Simon, who is 16, had been in intermittent contact with the local Child and Adolescent Mental Health Service since he was 10. He was the eldest son of Greek parents but was born in the United Kingdom. The original referral was prompted by Social Services as Simon's father had been hitting him because he would not do as he was told. His parents did not know how to manage his restless behaviour, and his mother was often in tears. Simon was apparently always on the go, never being able to sit still for more than a few minutes.

Family therapy had been provided when he was younger, and Simon's behaviour had improved a little. However, at secondary school he began to experience increasing difficulties. Having been assessed for a statement of special educational needs, he was found to have an IQ of 90 which placed him well within the average learning range for his age. In spite of this, Simon was unable to attend in class, even with extra help, and he was eventually excluded from school for getting in fights and being abusive to teachers.

Simon then attended a special educational unit for over two years. He still proved difficult to manage and would often not attend class. Instead, he was spending time with older boys, some of whom had criminal records. A trial of medication produced some improvement in his behaviour.

However, Simon was upset about being seen as 'mad' and disliked the effect which the tablets had on him. He therefore refused to take them, with an ongoing decline in his ability to function. At 16, he left school without qualifications and with the ambition to be a butcher.

Unfortunately, with no structure to his days and an absent father to set firm boundaries, he came to the notice of the local police when, together with some friends, he was caught breaking into an office building. Simon received a supervision order with a condition to attend Child and Adolescent Mental Health Services for treatment. His attendance was initially sporadic but, over time, he became increasingly compliant with his medication and managed to successfully complete a college course with support.

ASSESSMENT AND INVESTIGATION

An assessment may be carried out within a multi-disciplinary specialist clinic or by an individual clinician, usually a paediatrician or a child psychiatrist. More than one session may be required to establish the symptomatology and history. As a minimum, this information should be obtained from both parents and from the school. Other individuals, such as child minders or grandparents, may also prove a useful source of information. There is a strong genetic component to ADHD and a detailed family history of similar behaviour problems in parents and other relatives is essential.

It is important to ask the parents to describe in detail the behaviours which they are concerned about. A description of a typical day could include activities such as dressing, meal-times, sleep routines and interactions with other children. This can help to provide a full picture of the difficulties, and identification of the specific situations in which the behaviour is most problematic. It is also important to understand when the parents first noticed any difficulties as children with ADHD typically have symptoms from early infancy. Associated areas of developmental concern may include problems around birth complications, temperament, developmental milestones, motor clumsiness, specific learning difficulties, social development and medical problems such as epilepsy.

Direct observation of the child is essential but it should be noted that children with ADHD can often present without symptoms in new and unfamiliar situations. Thus, if the history and assessment questionnaires suggest hyperactivity, then a single observation of a settled child does not exclude the diagnosis. As well as multi-informant history taking and observation, the use of validated rating scales is essential. The Connors' Questionnaires are a useful instrument for assessing behaviour in both school and home situations (Connors 1973). The

Strengths and Difficulties Questionnaire (SDQ), which is available for download free on the internet (www.sdqinfo.com), is available in young person, parent and teacher versions (Goodman 2001).

TREATMENT

The main elements of treatment for ADHD include:

- psycho-education
- medication
- behavioural interventions at home and at school
- child-focused work to teach strategies for managing symptoms.

Psycho-education

After the diagnosis of ADHD has been made, the family should be provided with an opportunity to ask questions and express concerns about the condition, its outcome and the available treatment options. It is recommended that parents are given written information about ADHD symptoms, medication and behavioural management which can be shared with the school and others involved in the child's care. A list of self-help organizations, websites and other literature can prove helpful too. Parents often find it reassuring to have an explanation of their child's behaviour, and to learn that it is not the child or the parents' fault. However, it is still important to ensure that appropriate boundaries for behaviour are set and consistently applied. Some parents are reluctant to be given a diagnosis for their child for fear of labelling. However, many parents find that the diagnosis provides a useful way forward in better understanding their child's difficult behaviour. Parents may have very different views regading the various therapeutic options available, and their engagement in the treatment plan is essential to any intervention.

Medication

It is well established that stimulants improve the behavioural symptoms of ADHD. The major effects are a reduction in fidgetiness, fewer interruptions and an increase in concentration. At home, medication may lead to improved parent–child interactions and compliance with instructions. In social settings, it may improve peer relationships and attention during sporting activities. Even in the presence of co-morbidity, a reduction of core ADHD symptoms may be achieved.

Before starting a trial of medication, the child should have a formal diagnosis of ADHD. He or she should also be of an age suited to the use of stimulant medication as this treatment should not be prescribed to children under 4. Information should be given to parents about dosage regimes, safety and side-effects as parents may have concerns about addiction, long-term effects and the length of treatment. Physical examination is essential, including baseline measurements of both height and weight. It is important to assess the attitude of both the child and his or her carers with regard to the use of stimulant medication and, before prescribing medication, it is always helpful to ascertain if the school will cooperate with its implementation and monitoring.

A number of different medications are available for the treatment of ADHD. The most common choice remains short-acting methylphenidate. Some clinicians may use slow release methylphenidate as first choice since a dose does not need to be administered at school. Whatever the choice, the dose should be titrated against symptom relief, academic and social achievement, and the presence of side-effects. Frequent side-effects include loss of appetite, nausea and sleep disturbance. Other less frequent side-effects include headaches, irritability, tearfulness, anxiety, tics, excessive drowsiness and, rarely, hallucinations. Age will potentially influence the response to medication and pre-school children in particular need close monitoring due to frequent side-effects (American Academy of Child and Adolescent Psychiatry 2001). It is therefore essential, prior to starting medication, to establish if there are any contraindications to its use.

Unfortunately, there is no proven threshold of ADHD symptoms that predict a positive treatment response. It is therefore important that medication is reserved for children whose symptoms are moderate or severe, and where there has been a significant impairment of functioning in academic, family and social areas. A good response to stimulant medication is more likely if symptoms are present both at home and at school, and where co-morbid emotional symptoms are absent.

Cognitive and behavioural interventions

Cognitive and behavioural approaches may prove effective for milder cases of ADHD. However, they need to be applied consistently over a sustained period of time. With children whose behaviour has been difficult to manage over a long period, and where negative parental attitudes to the child are evident, such approaches may be hard to put into practice. However, for motivated parents who are keen to avoid the use of or minimize medication, it is a useful starting point.

Behavioural management techniques focus on the parents rather than on the child. They utilize basic parental strategies, such as praise and reward, in response to desired behaviours by the child rather than resorting to criticism and arguments in response to adverse behaviour. However, it is important for parents to have realistic expectations of anticipated behaviour and positive reinforcement should also be clear and immediate. Cognitive strategies, such as stopping and thinking before acting, can be helpful but are more likely to benefit older motivated children.

It is important to involve the school at an early stage since they can be invaluable in monitoring responses to medication and possible side-effects. In addition, there are well-established strategies for managing the symptoms of ADHD and school-based learning difficulties. A teaching assistant may be able to facilitate the use of such structured behavioural techniques, and close liaison with education departments is desirable to ensure adequate support for classroom teachers. Research has shown that home/school reward-based systems and contingency management programmes are effective. However, academic targets must be achievable and praise should be given for their completion. Individual work tailored to the child's needs can take place outside of lessons with a focus on improving concentration, social skills, self-awareness and anger management.

In the past, common practice was to provide behavioural management prior to the introduction of medication. There is now strong evidence for the effectiveness of stimulant medication, and recent research suggests that a tailored medication regime is more effective than a behavioural regime. Research has also shown that combined treatment may have no benefit over medication alone (MTA 2001). However, clinical practice suggests that behavioural management techniques may work well in the presence of medication.

CONCLUSION

ADHD is a common disorder among children. There is increasing evidence that, for some, it may prove to be a life-long illness. If untreated, there can be severe consequences with an increased risk of developing further psychiatric disorder, poor academic achievement, poor peer group relations and low self-esteem. If there is associated conduct disorder or oppositional behaviour, then the outlook is even less favourable with associated criminality, and substance misuse. On the positive side, with appropriate treatment before secondary impairments such as delinquency and drug misuse become entrenched, the outlook for children with ADHD is relatively good.

REFERENCES

American Academy of Child and Adolescent Psychiatry (2001) 'Summary of Practice Parameters of the Use of Stimulant Medications in the Treatment of Children, Adolescents and Adults.' *Journal of the American Academy of Child and Adolescent Psychiatry 40*, 1352–1355.

American Psychiatric Association (2000) *Diagnostic and Statistical Manual of Mental Disorders*, 4th edn (DSM-IV Text Revision). Washington, DC: American Psychiatric Association.

Bradley, C. (1937) 'The behaviour of children receiving benzedrine.' *American Journal of Orthopsychiatry 15*, 577–585.

Connors, C.K. (1973) 'Rating scales for use in drug studies with children.' *Psychopharmacology Bulletin: Special Issue on Pharmacotherapy with Children 9*, 24–84.

Goodman, R. (2001) 'Psychometric properties of the strengths and difficulties questionnaire.' *Journal of the American Academy of Child and Adolescent Psychiatry 40*, 1337–1345.

Leung, P.W.L., Luk, S.L., Ho, T.P., Taylor, E. *et al.* (1996) 'The diagnosis and prevalence of hyperactivity in Chinese schoolboys.' *British Journal of Psychiatry 168*, 486–496.

The MTA Cooperative Group (2001) 'ADHD Comorbidity: Findings from the MTA Study: Comparing Comorbid Subgroups.' *Journal of the American Academy of Child and Adolescent Psychiatry 40*, 147–158.

Taylor, E., Chadwick, O., Heptinstall, E. and Danckaerts, M. (1996) 'Hyperactivity and conduct problems as risk factors for adolescent development.' *Journal of the American Academy of Child and Adolescent Psychiatry 35*, 1213–1226.

Taylor, E., Sergeant, J., Doepfer, M., Gunning, B. *et al.* (1998) 'Clinical guidelines for hyperkinetic disorder.' *European Child and Adolescent Psychiatry 7*, 184–200.

World Health Organization (1992) *International Statistical Classification of Diseases and Related Health Problems*, 10th revision (ICD-10). Geneva: World Health Organization.

Chapter 7

Autistic spectrum disorders

Alex Horne

INTRODUCTION

In 1943, Leo Kanner, an American child psychiatrist, described 11 children with an 'inability to relate themselves in the ordinary way to people and to situations from the beginning of life', associated with a failure to use language for communication. He also described two additional features: 'an anxiously obsessive desire for the maintenance of sameness' and a preoccupation with particular objects. He named this condition Infantile Autism (Kanner 1943).

In 1944, Hans Asperger, an Austrian physician working independently of Kanner, described a group of children with broadly similar difficulties. He identified these problems across a wide range of individuals, from those with overt neurological conditions to those with near normal development. He termed the common difficulty which they all experienced Autistic Psychopathy (Asperger 1944).

Kanner's work became internationally recognized much earlier than Asperger's, but both accounts have since been used as the basis for formulating and classifying the developmental disorders in which social communication is the main impairment. Kanner's original description is still recognizable within the diagnostic criteria listed under Pervasive Developmental Disorders in both DSM-IV (American Psychiatric Association 1994) and ICD-10 (World Health Organization 1992).

Asperger's work was not well known within the UK before the 1980s when Lorna Wing reassessed his original work and coined the term 'Asperger's Syndrome' (Wing 1981). Ironically, Asperger's original cases, as he described them, would probably not be given the diagnosis of Asperger syndrome today. The term Asperger syndrome (AS) is currently used to describe those individuals with autism who have normal to above average intelligence. The term High-Functioning Autism (HFA) is also used to describe these cases. However, there is ongoing debate as to the possible differences between high-functioning autism and Asperger syndrome, as well as discussion about the qualitative difference between Asperger syndrome and more profoundly affected individuals with autism.

Although Asperger described a broadly similar group of people to Kanner, his description included milder forms of the disorder. This has led to increasing recognition that they were probably describing related but different conditions. What is most likely is that we are dealing with a spectrum of symptoms related to impairments in social communication with textbook cases of autism and classic presentations of AS falling at the extreme ends of the spectrum.

Box 7.1 Pervasive developmental disorders (PDD)

Autism
- Deficits in sociability and empathy
- Deficits in communicative language
- Deficit in cognitive flexibility
- Delay with speech development
- Detectable before the age of 3

Asperger syndrome
- Poor social skills, lack of insight
- Behavioural inflexibility
- Narrow range of interests
- IQ over 70
- No delay with speech
- Motor clumsiness

PDD Not Otherwise Specified
- Applies to less severely affected children who do not meet the criteria for either autism or Asperger syndrome

---

CLINICAL PRESENTATION

Qualitative impairment in social interaction

Children with these deficits demonstrate poor eye contact, poor use of gestures and limited understanding of facial expressions. They also find sharing difficult, lack interest in forming social relationships with peers, do not join in with group activities and struggle to recognize the effect of their behaviour on others.

Qualitative impairment in communication

This includes delay in speech, and the misinterpreting of others' use of speech. These children take things very literally, and cannot comprehend more abstract communications such as idioms, sarcasm and jokes. They also show poor use of speech, poor understanding of non-verbal gestures and limited use of non-verbal communications such as pointing.

Restrictive and repetitive patterns of behaviour and activity

These patterns present as an overwhelming interest in a specific topic, to the extent that the child talks excessively and exclusively on this theme. The source of fascination may seem unusual, such as traffic lights, telegraph poles or number plates. The children will also become anxious if unable to perform specific rituals, and dislike any interruptions to routine and everyday life.

Language development

For a diagnosis of autism, the child must show overt delay of language development and individuals with Autistic Spectrum Disorders (ASDs) will all show substantial impairment in language skills. About 70 per cent of children with diagnosable autism will have an IQ of below 70, and one-third will present with unprovoked epileptic seizures by the time they reach adolescence.

PREVALENCE

Recent studies have found a prevalence rate of 20 to 40 per 10,000 (Chakrabarti and Fombonne 2001). However, if broader diagnostic criteria are used, the prevalence may be as high as 60 per 10,000. The ratio of males to females is 4 to 1 for autism, and 10 to 1 for Asperger syndrome.

AETIOLOGY

Early theories exploring the causes of autism suggested that the way in which children were raised could produce the problem. For example, the hypothesis of the so called 'refrigerator mother' grew out of a recognition that some parents were finding it as difficult to relate to their children as their children were finding it to relate to them. Although this theory is no longer accepted as a cause of autism, clinical practice still highlights the difficulties experienced by a minority of parents in interacting with their children. However, we would now interpret this problem as an expression of their own inherited social disabilities. Such observations point towards the interconnectedness of genetic inheritance, and how it plays itself out in the complex world of human relationships. Nature supports, or otherwise, the processes of nurture.

Genetics

The role that genetics play in the aetiology of ASDs is clearly shown in twin studies. The identical twin of an affected individual is likely to have autistic features in 69 per cent of cases compared with 0 per cent in non-identical twins. It has been estimated that there is a heritability of 91–93 per cent for the liability of autism (Bailey *et al.* 1995). Despite this high heritability, autism has a heterogeneous aetiology with multiple genes and chromosomal regions likely to be involved.

Neurology

Imaging techniques such as magnetic resonance imaging (MRI) and positron emission tomography (PET) are beginning to reveal regions of the brain that may be affected in autism (Schultz and Klin 2002). These include the brain regions responsible for emotional and social functions, regions involving face recognition and social–cognitive systems involved in understanding the intentions of others. Neurotransmitters (such as serotonin) are also thought to be involved in neuro-development, particularly in areas of the brain critical to emotional expression and social behaviour (Anderson 2002). However, the functional significance of these observations is not as yet clear as the neural circuitry supporting social understanding and its related language functions is still being unravelled.

Psychological theories

There are three main psychological theories used to explain what may be going on in the minds of children with ASDs.

The theory of mind (Chapter 4) strand began in 1985 when Baron-Cohen, Leslie and Frith queried whether autistic children were able to have a 'theory of mind'. They asked if these children could understand other people's thoughts, feelings and intentions by mentally putting themselves in the other person's shoes. Their resulting hypothesis was that a difficulty in coming to know another person's mind explained the presenting features of autism. However, even in the original studies, around one-fifth of children tested showed an ability to appreciate other people's mental states or viewpoint, even though they remained autistic in their overall presentation.

An underlying deficit in executive function has also been suggested. These are the cognitive (thinking) processes used when planning a task, monitoring how the task is being executed, modifying behaviour in the light of performance and so on. Executive function is therefore the term used to describe being able to attend, being able to hold a number of ideas in memory, being able to plan sequences of activity and being able to shift attention between different levels or aspects of a problem. Autistic children find it particularly difficult to shift their attention from specific details to a more global appreciation of the situation (set shifting). These are all related functions, which are involved in everyday tasks across a wide range of daily activities. Executive function deficits are also hypothesized to lie behind the presentation of ADHD (Chapter 6) and Tourette syndrome (Chapter 18).

A third hypothesis, put forward by Frith in 1989, suggests that autistic children have difficulty in extracting meaning from different sources of information. She termed this a problem with central coherence, which can be simplified as an ability to remember the gist but forget the details. Autistic children are particularly sensitive to detail as a source of fascination but this also leads to upset if their specific routines or arrangements are disturbed. Given this attention to detail, they find it difficult to understand and take on board the overall meaning of a situation based on a summation of all the different contributing details.

These three approaches seem to be looking at the same autistic picture but from three different vantage points. To extract meaning from diverse sources of information requires the ability to shift attention from the detailed to the global, and an ability to understand the overall context of a situation is needed in constructing a theory of mind. This ability to appreciate contextual experiences flexibly will enhance an understanding of what may be going on in someone else's mind. These deficits have led to the notion of 'mind blindness' as a catch phrase which captures the essence of what is missing in autistic children.

ASSESSMENT

There is still ongoing debate as to which autistic features are truly primary to the condition, and which are more secondary. Some features might be better thought of as adaptations to the adverse consequences of the primary difficulties. For example, repetitive behaviours can be understood as ways of reducing anxiety or as the consequence of not being able to function easily within the social world.

Similarly, hand flapping in response to anxiety helps the child to calm down. In effect, the diagnosis of autism is therefore a positive diagnosis based on the characteristic way in which a child either does not relate, or relates with difficulty, to those around him or her.

Although there is, as yet, no cure for ASDs, there are two main reasons for undertaking extensive assessment of each child. First, parents may be relieved to know exactly what is wrong with their child, how this can be understood and that it has a name. It may reduce any feelings of guilt, and provide a context in which to explain why their child is behaving in odd and socially unacceptable ways. Diagnosis may also help parents to accept their child's difficulties, even allowing them to grieve for lost hopes and come to terms with the child as he or she is. Second, essential resources within schools and the community may be mobilized by the relevant statutory bodies to meet the child's needs, now and for the future.

To elicit whether the features of autism are present, a broad-based assessment should explore the following areas:

- The child's developmental history.

- Observations of the child in structured and semi-structured situations. (In the structured situation the clinician can observe how readily the child accepts another initiating and extending activities with the child. In semi-structured situations, where other children are present, observations of the child's level of interest and ability to initiate interactions can be observed).

- Assessment of cognitive level as many autistic children may have a co-existing learning difficulty, which could further compromise their cognitive processes.

- Assessment of problem behaviours.

- Speech and language therapy assessment – this can be extremely valuable.

- Audiology and sight tests if indicated.

- Physical investigations, which may be specifically indicated in some cases.

- Chromosomal screening if needed although there is still debate as to whether these investigations should be performed routinely given the low yield of positive results.

- A number of formalized interview schedules have been developed to aid accurate diagnosis by either eliciting the features of autism through a history of the child's development or through direct observation of the child in interaction with others and on his or her own.

CO-MORBIDITY

There are a wide range of behavioural presentations which may reflect a lack of social understanding, as well as reflecting problems relating to overall cognitive ability and levels of development. Clinical presentation can therefore prove quite complex, hence the need for multi-disciplinary assessment and extended observations over time and in different settings. This would allow all the potential difficulties to be recognized. In formulating a diagnosis of autism, the following conditions should be excluded as the main cause of any social difficulties:

- Learning disability
- Speech and language disorders
- Social anxiety disorder
- Selective mutism
- Obsessive compulsive disorder
- Rett syndrome
- Epilepsy
- ADHD
- Tourette syndrome.

Case example: Andrew

Andrew is a 7-year-old boy who lives with his mother and two siblings. He attends a mainstream infant school, and was referred for assessment as his classroom behaviour was becoming increasingly disruptive. For example, he would disappear under the desk and refuse to come out if he did not like a lesson. He was also frequently in altercations with other children, during which time he would hit out aggressively. Even after episodes in which he had injured peers, Andrew would deny that he had done anything wrong and showed no empathy or remorse. On reflection, his teacher recognized that all of his behaviour, whether odd or not, took place without regard to how it affected either herself or other children.

As a result, Andrew never quite fitted in. He did try to make friends and, on occasion, had been uncharacteristically upset about not having anyone to play with. While he would often attribute friendship to different children, this usually involved picking a particular child for a few days and becoming obsessed with him or her. He would then hug the child indiscriminately, squeeze him or her too tightly and try to kiss him or her, whether a boy or girl. He would also copy this child's behaviour, much to his or her annoyance. In contrast, in one-to-one situations with adults, he presented as a pleasant and likable child, rather passive socially, and apparently happy just to sit with people. His mother reported that Andrew never wanted other children to visit him at home, and he had never been invited to a birthday party. His siblings would often try to encourage him to play with them, but this was only successful if he was not expected to take an active part in the game.

Andrew has well-developed language skills, with good vocabulary and grammar. He is able to learn facts, and can be engaged in conversations about the different things which he has learned. However, these interactions have a stilted quality as he simply recounts facts in endless detail rather than contributing to the conversation. Andrew also tends not to ask questions or show any curiosity about the other person. It is as if he is not aware, or does not care, that the other person may not be interested in what he is saying, or is bored by the excessive detail. Instead, he talks as if not expecting a response, in stark contrast to his peers who are full of questions when someone new enters their classroom.

Although Andrew had recently been on holiday with his family, he struggled to describe his experiences. When asked about what he had enjoyed, he talked at length about the practicalities of a bus journey to the beach. However, all of his accounts had a literal two-dimensional quality to them, and there was no reference to his feelings or other people. In a similar way, although he does have an imagination, the content of Andrew's stories is stilted and even gruesome scenes are related in a flat, cold way.

At assessment, Andrew was able to hold good eye contact, saying 'hello' in response to being greeted. He was quite happy to accompany the therapist into the interview room where he sat patiently, but expressionlessly, without obvious inattention, upset or odd behaviour. He seemed to be waiting for the therapist to take the lead and, after some basic opening questions, it became clear that his ability to actively take part in conversation was limited. Although he answered many questions, in an appropriate if factual way, there was no sense of a relationship being formed. He showed no curiosity, and there was no evidence that he was either enjoying or not enjoying the interaction. However, he did show a tendency to switch off and focus on lines and patterns instead.

Andrew is often late for school, and does not seem to recognize that all children are expected to arrive on time. Although he can tell the time, and knows the difference between morning and afternoon, he arrives according to his own schedule. Also, while generally compliant with his teacher at school, at home Andrew can be very stubborn. He often refuses to change out of his school uniform, leading to arguments with his mother. She increasingly feels that he resists everything asked of him, yet he always wants to be in the same room and is unhappy if left alone. However, even when he is with her, Andrew does not interact directly and will simply loll against her and suck his thumb.

Although Andrew had met his developmental milestones for language, toileting and other independence skills, from the nursery onwards he was often seen as an odd boy. His mother had not been too worried when he was younger but now there were increasing problems both at home and at school. She had recently seen a programme on television about autism, and had recognized numerous similarities with Andrew. His teachers were also able to give many examples of Andrew's difficulties in relating to his peers, and his inability to understand fully what was expected of him. In spite of this, he had made academic progress although there were concerns about him underachieving.

The history from his mother, and the descriptions of daily behaviour in class, coupled with direct conversational contact with Andrew, confirmed a diagnosis of Asperger syndrome.

MANAGEMENT

Autism is not curable but each child has the potential to develop new skills within his or her range of ability. However, until relatively recently, it was difficult to assess the effect of different treatments and interventions. A review of these psychological and educational approaches has been provided by Howlin (1998), although it remains important to be inquisitive and critical of any therapies boasting success.

Improving the child's educational situation remains one of the most important interventions. This should focus on learning basic social, communication and cognitive skills in a safe setting throughout the school year. More specific behavioural problems may need to be looked at closely to identify possible precipitants and contributing factors. But, before either teachers or other professionals can select appropriate targets for intervention, they need to come to know the individual child as a person in his or her own right.

Behavioural approaches need to be consistent with the child's age and level of ability, recognizing that difficult and challenging behaviour may reflect the child's reduced ability to communicate. Using play activities, individually or in groups, can encourage a child's social interaction skills. Visual clues, in the form of line drawings or photographs, may also help with communicating, sequencing of activity, information sharing and reducing anxiety.

There are no drugs available for improving the core features of ASDs and most anecdotal accounts have not been supported by empirical studies. However, there have been encouraging trials on the use of medication for reducing aggressive and self-injurious behaviour.

The task for parents involves coming to terms with the loss of their hoped-for child, and developing an ability to see their child as he or she really is. This will have to replace their anticipated parent–child relationship, given the constant need to work on the relationship with their child. More time needs to be spent on 'holding' and nourishing the relationship as the interaction will simply not take place spontaneously. Also, any approach is likely to be more effective if it includes the parents, making them co-workers in the intervention process and providing them with some understanding of what is being worked on. For example, a teenager with Asperger syndrome who was worrying about the world ending at the stroke of midnight found that walking the dog for his father around this time could banish the thoughts completely. Parental support groups can also provide much needed support and reassurance.

PROGNOSIS

Outcome generally depends on IQ and language development. While there may be improvement in language after the pre-school years, most individuals continue to show impairments in social skills and communication over time. Asperger syndrome is associated with a better prognosis due to a relatively greater IQ. However, teenagers may be vulnerable to developing depression and self-injurious behaviour, particularly if bullying and teasing are a problem.

Clinical experience has shown that children who grow up in families that can accept their disability and meet their needs, sympathetically and with the least fuss, have far greater self-esteem and confidence than those children from families where the difficulty in relating becomes the focus of arguments and tension. Self-esteem and confidence may also be a key factor in determining later independence and employment.

REFERENCES

American Psychiatric Association (1994) *Diagnostic and Statistical Manual of Mental Disorders*, 4th edn (DSM-IV). Washington, DC: American Psychiatric Association.

Anderson, G. (2002) 'Genetics of childhood disorders: autism, Part 4: Serotonin in autism.' *Journal of American Academy of Child and Adolescent Psychiatry 41*, 1513–1516.

Asperger, H. (1944) 'Die "autistischen Psychopathen" im Kindesalter.' *Archiv für Psychiatrie und Nervenkrankheiten, 117*, 76–136.

Bailey, A.J., Le Couter, A., Gottesman, I.I., Bolton, P. *et al.* (1995) 'Autism is a strongly genetic disorder. Evidence from a British twin study.' *Psychological Medicine 25*, 63–78.

Baron-Cohen, S., Leslie, A.M. and Frith, U. (1985) 'Does the autistic child have a theory of mind?' *Cognition 21*, 37–46.

Chakrabarti, S. and Fombonne, E. (2001) 'Pervasive developmental disorders in preschool children.' *JAMA 285*, 3093–3099.

Frith, U. (1989) *Autism: Explaining the Enigma.* Oxford: Basil Blackwell.

Howlin, P. (1998) 'Practitioner review: Psychological and educational treatments for autism.' *Journal of Child Psychology and Psychiatry 39*, 307–322.

Kanner, L. (1943) 'Autistic disturbance of affective contact.' *Nervous Child 2*, 217–250.

Schultz, R. and Klin, A. (2002) 'Genetics of childhood disorders: autism, Part 2: Neural foundations.' *Journal of the American Academy of Child and Adolescent Psychiatry 41*, 1259–1262.

Wing, L. (1981) 'Asperger's syndrome: a clinical account.' *Journal of Psychological Medicine 11*, 115–129.

World Health Organization (1992) *International Statistical Classification of Diseases and Related Health Problems*, 10th revision (ICD-10). Geneva: World Health Organization.

Chapter 8

Behavioural phenotypes

Christopher Roberts

INTRODUCTION

Behavioural phenotypes have been defined as the specific and characteristic sets (repertoires) of behaviour that are exhibited by patients with specific genetic or chromosomal disorders (Flint 1998). Skuse extended this definition of behaviour further to include cognitive processes and social interaction styles (Skuse 2002). The concept has therefore evolved and developed due to an increasing recognition that genetic disorders may have specific and identifiable behavioural manifestations, in addition to the more observable physical characteristics (physical phenotypes) and anatomical features (dysmorphology) of the condition. However, variability of expression (the finding that individuals with the same condition will not always be equally affected) is seen as much in the study of behaviour as it is in the study of physiology and anatomy. This variability in the presentation of genetic and chromosomal conditions can add to the difficulties of differential diagnosis in children with emotional and behavioural problems.

Difficulties regarding the definition of behavioural phenotypes have been explored by Einfeld and Hall (1994) and Skuse (2000, 2002). Both point out that there is no consensus around the definition, and that Flint's approach can be seen as too restrictive. The resultant uncertainty has led to frequent changes with regard to which syndromes should or should not be included within the field. For example, until recently, the position of Rett syndrome as a behavioural phenotype has been unclear. While a genetic aetiology had long been assumed, the condition was only deemed to have met the definition of a behavioural phenotype since the discovery of a specific gene mutation.

It is important for child psychiatrists and other child mental health professionals to have a working knowledge of behavioural phenotypes, as clearly summarized by Moldavsky, Lev and Lerman-Sagie (2001). A child's behaviour is often the reason for referral and, if behavioural patterns are recognized as matching a particular genetic syndrome, not only can a more accurate diagnosis be made but the implications for siblings or future pregnancies can also be addressed. Early intervention and specific therapeutic strategies (if available) can be set in motion too. Parents often describe a sense of relief at having received a 'medical' explanation for the behavioural problems, and parents can be reassured that the behaviours are 'neither their fault, nor caused by wilfulness on the part of the child' (Skuse 2000). Parents can also be advised about specific support groups.

Skuse (2002) gives a fascinating vignette of a behavioural phenotype which meets all aspects of the definition. He cites the study by Gray *et al.* (1997) showing that carriers of the gene for Huntington's chorea who are not (yet) clinically affected were found to have a highly selective deficit in the ability to recognize the facial expression of disgust. The specific part of the brain that processes the emotion of disgust is known to medical science from imaging studies, and it is also known that this area of the brain is affected by Huntington's chorea. Thus a known genetic cause or aetiology can be shown to produce a subtle but discrete phenotypic feature (characteristic presentation) with a behavioural manifestation or presentation.

The aim of this chapter is to give an overview of the more common behavioural phenotypes, all of which are rare. The following summaries describe the characteristic behaviours for a range of clinical conditions, which have been selected on the grounds of clinical interest and likelihood of being seen in practice. However, the list is by no means exhaustive. Each summary includes some brief epidemiological data and descriptions of the behavioural, cognitive and physical features associated with the condition. Further details of the non-behavioural phenotypic manifestations are described in detail in Moldavsky *et al.* (2001) and Udwin and Dennis (1995). The behaviours associated with mental health diagnoses such as attention deficit hyperactivity disorder (ADHD) (Chapter 6), autism (Chapter 7), obsessive compulsive disorder (Chapter 14), schizophrenia (Chapter 17) and Tourette syndrome (Chapter 18) are described elsewhere as they lack the specificity demanded and do not, at present, meet the definition of behavioural phenotypes.

PRADER–WILLI SYNDROME (PWS)

First described by Prader, Labhart and Willi in 1956.

Frequency

- 1 in 16,000 to 1 in 25,000.

Behavioural features

- Commonest syndromal cause of human obesity.

- Neonates show decreased arousal and feeding problems, often leading to failure to thrive.

- Young children are often placid, with excessive daytime sleepiness, with or without sleep apnoea, and depressed motor activity.

- Older children can be stubborn, irritable, impulsive and aggressive with labile mood and low self-esteem.

- A small percentage meet the diagnostic criteria for ADHD.

- Hyperphagia (excessive eating) and obesity are caused by a lack of satiation, beginning between 1 and 6 years of age.

- Food-related behaviours includes food-seeking, hoarding and stealing.

- Obsessional, compulsive and repetitive behaviours are characteristic and around 50 per cent of children meet criteria for obsessive compulsive disorder.

Cognitive features

- Average IQ of 70.

- Mild to moderate learning disability is common.

- Children may show cognitive strengths in areas of visual–spatial integration.

Physical features

- Children with PWS have a typical facial appearance with a flat face, prominent forehead, almond-shaped eyes and thin down-turned lips.

- They also present with short stature, hypogonadism (reduction in size and development of ovaries and testes, and reduction in the hormones which they produce), hypotonia (reduced tone of skeletal muscles), small hands and small feet.

- There is an increased prevalence of orthopaedic problems such as scoliosis (curvature of the spine) and osteoporosis.

TURNER SYNDROME

First described by Turner in 1938.

Frequency

- 1 in 2000 live female births.

Behavioural features

- Poor visuo–spatial awareness and visual–motor skills.
- Social relationship problems.
- There appears to be increased severity of psychiatric and cognitive impairments when the problematic chromosome is of maternal origin.
- Emotional disturbance is common.

Cognitive features

- Intelligence is usually within the normal range, with mental retardation in only 5 per cent of typical cases.
- Specific learning disabilities in mathematics.
- Deficits in social cognition.

Physical features

- These children present with short stature, a webbed neck, cubitus valgus (a deformity of the elbow) and a broad chest with widely spaced nipples.

FRAGILE X SYNDROME

First described by Martin and Bell in 1943.

Frequency

- 1 in 4000 males.
- This is the commonest form of inherited mental retardation.

Behavioural features

- 70 per cent of cases meet ADHD criteria, and 15 per cent meet diagnostic criteria for autism.

- Hyperactivity, distractibility and labile mood are common.
- These children present with poor eye contact and hypersensitivity to tactile, visual and auditory stimuli.

Cognitive features

- Mild to severe mental retardation.
- Difficulties with abstract thinking, processing, short-term memory and visual–motor coordination.

Physical features

- Children present with a long face, prominent ears, a prominent jaw and an arched palate.
- They also present with macro-orchidism (enlargement of the testes).
- Hyperextensible finger joints and flat feet are evident.

TUBEROUS SCLEROSIS
First described by Bourneville in 1880.

Frequency

- 1 in 7000.

Behavioural features

- Obsessive and ritualistic behaviours.
- Sleep problems.
- Occasionally self-injurious behaviour.

Cognitive features

- Mental retardation of varying severity.

Physical features

- Epilepsy and mental retardation.
- Characteristic facial lesion – facial angiofibromas (adenoma sebaceum).

- Hamartomatous tumours affecting the skin, brain, kidney and heart.

- Skin has areas of thickening known as 'shagreen' patches.

VELO-CARDIO-FACIAL SYNDROME
First described by Murphy and Owen in 1996.

Frequency
- 1 in 5000.

Physical features
- Cleft lip anomalies and congenital heart defects.

- Thymus hypoplasia or aplasia (underdevelopment of thymus gland which may affect healthy immune system).

- Hypocalcaemia (low serum calcium concentration).

- Characteristic facial features include a long face, a narrow palpebral fissure (opening between the eye lids), a prominent tubular nose with a bulbous nasal tip, a small mouth and ear anomalies.

Behavioural features
- Increased risk of psychiatric illness, especially psychoses such as schizophrenia and bipolar disorder.

- Increased association with ADHD and depression.

- Poor motor coordination.

Cognitive features
- Language problems.

- Poor numeracy skills.

- Poor reading and spelling.

- Learning difficulties.

- Difficulty with abstract thinking.

KLINEFELTER SYNDROME (47XXY)

First described by Klinefelter, Reifenstein and Albright in 1942.

Frequency

- 1 in 500 to 1 in 1000 males.

Behavioural features

- Awkward and clumsy with motor deficits.
- Introverted, quiet and less assertive.
- Anxious and dependent.

Cognitive features

- IQ is within the normal range but 20 per cent have an IQ below 90.
- Speech and language problems.

Physical features

- Tall, often much taller than their parents.
- May have small testes, gynaecomastia (abnormal enlargement of the breasts) and infertility.

WILLIAMS SYNDROME

First described by Williams, Barratt-Boyes and Lowe in 1961.

Frequency

- 1 in 10,000.

Physical features

- 'Elfin-like' face with epicanthal folds (skinfold from upper eyelid to side of nose), flat nasal bridge, a short upturned nose, a long philtrum (area between nose and upper lip) and full lips.
- Medical history includes aortic stenosis, hypertension and hypercalcaemia.

Behavioural features

- Over-friendly to strangers.
- Autistic features.
- Hyperactivity.
- Anxious and obsessively wary about the future.
- Very sensitive to noise.

Cognitive features

- Mild learning difficulties.
- Higher verbal IQ than performance IQ.
- Tend to use stereotypic adult social phrases or 'cocktail party talk'.

NEUROFIBROMATOSIS TYPE 1 SYNDROME (NF1)

First described by Von Recklinghausen in 1882.

Frequency

1 in 3000.

Behavioural features

- Attention deficit hyperactivity disorder.
- Speech and language problems.
- Clumsiness and poor coordination.

Cognitive features

- 10 per cent have learning difficulties.
- Problems with reading and writing.
- Poor visuo-spatial skills.
- Poor verbal memory.

Physical features

- Two or more of the following features are required for a diagnosis: six or more café-au-lait (light brown) skin lesions; two or more fibromas or one plexiform neurofibroma (types of tumour); axillary freckles; lisch nodules; optic glioma; a bony lesion characteristic of NF1; or a first-degree relative with NF1.

REFERENCES

Bourneville, D.M. (1880) 'Sclerose tubereuse des circonvolutions cerebrales: Idiotie et epilepsie hemiplegique.' *Archives de Neurologie (Paris) 1*, 81–91.

Einfeld, S.L. and Hall, W. (1994) 'When is a behavioural phenotype not a phenotype?' *Developmental Medicine and Child Neurology 36*, 463–470.

Flint, J. (1998) 'Behavioural phenotypes: Conceptual and methodological issues.' *American Journal of Medical Genetics 81*, 235–240.

Gray, J.M., Young, A.W., Barker, W.A, Curtis, A. *et al.* (1997) 'Impaired recognition of disgust in Huntington's disease carriers.' *Brain 122*, 2015–2032.

Klinefelter, H.F., Reifenstein, E.C. and Albright, F. (1942) 'Syndrome characterised by gynecomastia, aspermatogenesis without A-Leydigism, and increased excretion of follicle-stimulating hormone.' *Journal of Clinical Endocrinology 2*, 615–627.

Martin, J.P. and Bell, J. (1943) 'A pedigree of mental defect showing sex-linkage.' *Journal of Neurology and Psychiatry 6*, 154–157.

Moldavsky, M., Lev, D. and Lerman-Sagie, T. (2001) 'Behavioral phenotypes of genetic syndromes: A reference guide for psychiatrists.' *Journal of the American Academy of Child and Adolescent Psychiatry 40*, 749–761.

Murphy, K.C. and Owen, M.J. (1996) 'Schizophrenia, CATCH 22 and FISH.' *British Journal of Psychiatry 168*, 397–398.

Prader, A., Labhart, A. and Willi, H. (1956) 'Ein Syndrom von Adipositas, Kleinwuchs, Kryptorchismus und Oligophrenie nach myatonieartigen Zustand im Neugeborenenalter.' *Schweizerische Medizinische Wochenschrift 86*, 1260–1261.

Skuse, D.H. (2000) 'Behavioural phenotypes: What do they teach us?' *Archives of Disease in Childhood 82*, 222–225.

Skuse, D.H. (2002) 'Behavioural phenotypes.' *Psychiatry 1*, 98–102.

Turner, H.H. (1938) 'A syndrome of infantilism, congenital webbed neck, and cubitus valgus.' *Endocrinology 23*, 566–574.

Udwin, O. and Dennis, J. (1995) 'Psychological and behavioural phenotypes in genetically determined syndromes: A review of research findings.' In G. O'Brien and W. Yule (eds) *Behavioural Phenotypes*. London: MacKeith Press.

Von Recklinghausen, F. (1882) *Über die Multiplen Fibroma der Haut und ihre Beziehung zu den Multiplen Neuromen.* Berlin: A. Hirschwald.

Williams, J.C.P., Barratt-Boyes, B.G. and Lowe, J.B. (1961) 'Supravalvular aortic stenosis.' *Circulation 24*, 1311–1318.

Chapter 9

Developmental dyspraxia

Sydney Chu

INTRODUCTION

Over time, a wide range of different terms have been used to describe children with problems relating specifically to motor control or motor organization. These concepts, such as Clumsy Child Syndrome, Minimal Brain Dysfunction (Chapter 13) or Developmental Coordination Disorder, were invariably used to describe motor dysfunction in children with an average intellectual capacity. Unfortunately, inconsistencies in the use of these diagnostic terms created a great deal of confusion, impeding differential diagnosis and the application of appropriate intervention programmes.

Within the UK, a general consensus has been reached that the term Developmental Coordination Disorder (DCD) should be used as an umbrella description for children with difficulty in movement skills that are not primarily due to general intellectual impairment, primary sensory impairment or motor neurological impairment (Cermak, Gubbay and Larkin 2002). Developmental Dyspraxia is a sub-type of DCD, and refers to deficits in the conceptualization, planning and execution of motor acts or motor organization.

HISTORICAL PERSPECTIVE

The description of subtle motor difficulties in children, not associated with frank neurological deficits, dates back to the early 1900s. Over the last three decades, significant attempts have been made to differentiate the various forms of motor dysfunction and establish a formalized classification. In ICD-10 (World Health Organization 1992), the category of 'Specific Developmental Disorder of Motor Functions' was introduced and, in DSM-IV (American Psychiatric Association 1994), the term 'Developmental Coordination Disorder' (DCD) was used to describe children with specific motor difficulties.

'The London Consensus' Statement (Fox and Polatajko 1994) provided a clearer, more descriptive definition of DCD. Minimal requirements for assessment, identification and intervention were discussed. It also highlighted that DCD was multi-factorial in origin, and that there were probably a number of sub-types of children with DCD. In 1998, professionals from around the world attended a subsequent meeting in London and concluded that the term developmental coordination disorder (DCD) should be used as an umbrella term, with developmental dyspraxia constituting one of the sub-types of DCD.

Unfortunately, the term developmental dyspraxia continues to be used loosely by different professionals and organizations, and confusion regarding this specific childhood disorder therefore continues.

THE CONCEPT OF PRAXIS

The term dyspraxia is derived from the Greek word 'praxis', which means 'doing, acting, deed and practice', while the term 'dys' describes any malfunction which can be improved by appropriate intervention. The word 'developmental' indicates that the problems begin early in the child's life, and may affect his or her subsequent growth and development.

Praxis is considered to be a specific human skill requiring conscious thought and 'enabling the brain to conceptualize, organize and direct purposeful interaction with the physical world' (Ayres, Mailloux and Wendler 1987). Through positive integration with other perceptual and cognitive processes, this enables the individual to interact successfully with people and objects in his or her environment. It serves as an important foundation for the organization of behaviour in daily activities, and also with regard to social interaction and communication.

Ayres (1985) described three key components of praxis. *Ideation* is the ability to formulate and grasp an idea or concept to allow purposeful interaction with the environment (i.e. knowing what to do). *Motor planning* or *programming* is the ability to plan and structure a sequence of actions to produce a purposeful and adaptive response. It entails knowing how to move, how to sequence and how to predict end results (i.e. knowing how to do it). *Execution* is the ability to carry out a task using a planned sequence of actions combined in a smooth process (i.e. knowing how to complete it successfully).

Cermak (1991) later defined dyspraxia as a difficulty in planning and carrying out skilled, non-habitual motor acts in the correct sequence. As such, dyspraxia represents a problem with integrating information rather than a problem with motor function. The deficit lies in formulating ideas and then developing plans to set purposeful tasks into action. Ideation and motor planning can therefore be used to distinguish dyspraxia from other sub-types of DCD.

Although execution is unlikely to be a major source of difficulty in children with dyspraxia, it is mainly through the execution of a motor act that the quality of ideation and motor planning can be observed.

PREVALENCE OF MOTOR DYSFUNCTIONS

In the USA, the prevalence of DCD is estimated to affect 6 per cent of the population and affect more males than females (APA 1994). In the UK, it is believed to affect around 10 per cent of the general population, with 4 per cent having significant difficulties. However, these figures include all children with any form of motor dysfunction and the percentage of children who have developmental dyspraxia alone has yet to be determined.

CLINICAL FEATURES

It is important to differentiate between the primary underlying deficits which constitute a diagnosis of developmental dyspraxia (Box 9.1) and the secondary behavioural features which may arise as a consequence of these difficulties (Box 9.2). Clinicians should use the primary presentation as a basis for making the diagnosis as the constellation of secondary behavioural features can be caused by a wide range of other factors.

Because of the regular episodes of failure, teasing and social rejection which many children with dyspraxia may experience, they are particularly susceptible to developing emotional and behavioural difficulties. This may manifest as low self-esteem, or as avoidant behaviour when faced with situations in which motor planning and skills are essential.

Children with dyspraxia may also present with the following clinical features: minimal delays in attainment of early developmental milestones; difficulties with fundamental motor skills associated with poor postural–motor control (e.g. hopping, skipping, riding a bicycle, ball skills); soft neurological signs; behavioural problems; minor neurological deficits (e.g. mild tightness of muscles or tendons) and over-reactivity and sensitivity to sensory inputs.

Box 9.1 Primary underlying deficits of developmental dyspraxia

Essential criteria

- Poor praxis, especially in the process of ideation and motor planning, which in turn leads to poor motor execution.
- Performance IQ lower than verbal IQ, not explained by other conditions, in the presence of average general intellectual capacity.
- Immaturity of body scheme and awareness, which is a poor understanding of body parts, their relationship to each other and their orientation in the physical world.

May have one or more of the following features

- Visual–perceptual and auditory–perceptual dysfunctions, with difficulties in interpreting and using visual and auditory information for learning and daily activities.
- Poor spatial skills in 2-dimensional and 3-dimensional orientation.
- Poor perceptual–motor integration, with impaired visual–motor skills, reduced auditory–motor skills, limited rhythm and deficits in temporal awareness.
- May have poor postural–motor functions, with weak muscle tone, poor postural control and poor bilateral integration.
- Delay in the development of laterality/dominance with inconsistent use of left and right sides of the body (e.g. hand, foot, eye and ear).
- Poor fine motor skills, includes poor in-hand manipulations and two-handed coordination.
- Speech and articulation deficits.

DIAGNOSTIC CRITERIA

Although clinicians use the classifications described in ICD-10 and DSM-IV, there are still no universal diagnostic criteria for identifying children with developmental dyspraxia. Instead, exclusionary criteria tend to be used, based on the absence of primary deficits in other sensory, motor or cognitive functions. Current approaches emphasize that the child's motor dsyfunctions must be significantly below the level expected on the basis of his or her age and general intelligence. Also, the dysfunctions must significantly interfere with academic achievement and activities of daily living. Unfortunately, this approach does not

Box 9.2 Secondary behavioural patterns of developmental dyspraxia

These behavioural difficulties may result from the primary underlying deficits of developmental dyspraxia, but it is important to identify a pattern of behaviour rather than isolated and individual features.

- Clumsy or awkward in movement, frequently bumping into things, dropping things, tripping and falling.
- Difficulties in learning new motor skills which require motor planning and sequencing functions (e.g. ball skills, team games).
- Constantly needing to think about planning movements, with moments of hesitation in between tasks.
- Difficulties in organizing approach to tasks, and analysing task requirements and components needed, when preparing actions.
- May be viewed as disorganized, lazy or having poor work habits.
- Difficulties in learning new and unfamiliar tasks.
- Unable to generalize newly learnt tasks to similar situations.
- Difficulties following daily routine and sequences of verbal instructions.
- Use of verbalization (talking through) to assist in planning actions.
- May need to watch others in order to understand what to do and to model the plan of action.
- Delays in acquiring skills in different activities of daily living, especially those requiring motor planning, perceptual analysis and fine motor manipulation (e.g. tying shoelaces, scissor skills).
- Difficulties in developing mature, efficient manual handwriting skills.

give any indication of possible aetiological factors, nor are different sub-types of dysfunction identified.

There has been ongoing debate regarding the use of Intelligence Quotient (IQ) as a criteria for the diagnosis of developmental dyspraxia. Gubbay (1975) argued in favour of a significantly lower performance IQ score than verbal IQ score, usually considered to be a 15-point discrepancy, on the revised Wechsler Intelligence Scale for Children (see Chapter 21). However, clinical experience indicates that not all children with dyspraxia will meet this definition, and there is general consensus that children with developmental dyspraxia will demonstrate average intellectual capacity on testing.

DIFFERENTIAL DIAGNOSIS

A number of childhood conditions produce signs and symptoms that may superficially mimic clinically significant developmental dyspraxia. It is therefore important to differentiate out other motor dysfunctions as this may reflect aetiology and impact on treatment options. The differential diagnoses include:

- postural–motor dysfunctions in which the problem lies with motor control (or execution) rather than with ideation and motor planning.

- minor neurological deficits such as the presence of mild hypertonicity (with mild tightness on certain muscle groups).

- benign congenital hypotonia which presents with extremely weak but non-progressive muscle tone.

- hypermobility or increased joint laxity.

- motor impairment linked to specific perceptual–motor dysfunctions.

- poor motor skills as part of global developmental delay.

- decreased motor functions related to progressive muscle disease (e.g. early-onset muscular dystrophy).

- motor incoordination associated with serious medical conditions.

- motor problems resulting from deficits in the central nervous system (e.g. cerebral palsy).

CO-MORBIDITY

Many other conditions can co-exist with a primary diagnosis of developmental dyspraxia. Children with severe dyspraxia tend to overlap with children who have Attention Deficit Hyperactivity Disorder (ADHD) (Chapter 6). Up to 52 per cent of children with ADHD have poor motor coordination (Barkley, DuPaul and McMurray 1990), while about 50 per cent of children with DCD have moderate to severe symptoms of ADHD (Kadesjö and Gillberg 1999). Children with Tourette syndrome (Chapter 18) may have deficits in fine motor dexterity, visuo-motor skills, spatial skills and executive functioning (Bornstein and Yang 1991). Approximately one-third of autistic children (Chapter 7) have significant visuo-motor dyspraxia (Jones and Prior 1985), and 50–90 per cent of children and adults with Asperger syndrome have problems with motor coordination (Attwood 1998). Children with mild to moderate dyspraxia may also present with concomitant specific learning difficulties (Chapter 11) and specific language disorders (Chapter 16).

ASSESSMENT

Early identification and management of developmental dyspraxia may prevent later difficulties and long-term problems from emerging. The assessment process, which focuses on attributes that contribute to the successful motor organization of a child, is therefore important for excluding differential diagnoses, in identifying co-morbid conditions and for selecting the most appropriate treatment approaches.

Developmental history

The signs and symptoms of dyspraxia vary according to the child's age, and will manifest differently throughout the course of his or her development. Reviewing the birth and developmental history may help to illuminate any potential factors that may have contributed to motor organization difficulties. As an infant, the dyspraxic child usually achieves motor milestones within normal limits, albeit in the low average range. In the pre-school years, problems become more evident and the child often has difficulty with activities of daily living, especially those which require motor learning such as fastening buttons or blowing their nose. The child may also have difficulty with puzzles, cutting, colouring, pasting and with playground equipment.

In the early school years, previously unrecognized problems may become evident and the child may have continued difficulty with dressing tasks, handwriting, cutting, colouring, pasting and assembling. Play skills such as riding a bicycle, using a skipping rope and ball activities are performed with difficulty. In school, the child may struggle as organized sports become increasingly important. As a result, he or she may not be picked for any team games and become isolated in the playground.

Observational assessment

Observing the child in natural environments (e.g. playgroup or school) can assist in gathering information on the child's behavioural patterns and performance levels in different daily and learning tasks. The three components of praxis should be observed. Ideation can be assessed by observing the way in which a child plays with toys, especially with regard to spontaneity and creativity. The child may have a clear idea of what he or she wants to do, and be able to express this verbally, yet not be able to organize his or her body to execute the action effectively. A child with motor planning dysfunction will have difficulties in performing similar tasks in different situations, and deficits in execution, such as abnormal muscle tone or involuntary movements, need to be excluded. The therapist may also gain important information from parents and teachers. In addition to medical and educational records, it may prove helpful to obtain reports from any other professionals who may have already been involved in the child's care. Information gathered in this way may help to provide a baseline for subsequent evaluation and guide clinical decision-making.

Clinical assessment

Skilled motor behaviour can be assessed at two levels. Task-oriented approaches explore the different tasks or activities that constitute a repertoire of motor skills. In contrast, process-oriented approaches consider the various processes which underlie motor behaviour and are commonly used by occupational therapists. For example, tying a shoelace requires two-handed coordination, fine finger manipulation, motor planning function and spatial orientation skills. If a child cannot tie his or her shoelace at the expected age, the therapist may assess the function of the different underlying processes in order to identify the causes.

Process-oriented tests are based on underlying models of motor function, and on theories that causally link sensory, perceptual and cognitive deficits to motor dysfunction. The Sensory Integration and Praxis Tests (SIPT) is one of the most comprehensive investigations of sensory integrative and practic dysfunction. Other standardized tests focus on task-oriented approaches, such as Bruininks–Oseretsky Test of Motor Proficiency (BOTMP) and the Movement Assessment Battery for Children (MABC). However, these tests do not include specific measures of praxis and the therapist needs to make an observational assessment and interpret the information with respect to the concepts of praxis and developmental dyspraxia.

TREATMENT

The primary goal of all treatment approaches for children with developmental dyspraxia is to improve their practic functions, their performance in different activities of daily living and their academic skills. Research studies indicate that children with developmental dyspraxia will not simply grow out of their problems, and that early intervention is important. After confirming the diagnosis, the intervention that will best fit the child's underlying dysfunctions and presenting difficulties needs to be identified. Specific treatment objectives should be established as stepping stones in achieving long-term goals. However, the objectives selected should be achievable, observable, measurable and prove to be important from the child's perspective.

As different sub-types of developmental dyspraxia have different aetiological factors, it is important to select appropriate treatment approaches depending on the nature of the child's motor dysfunctions. Process-oriented approaches, such as sensory integrative therapy, psychomotor therapy, perceptual–motor programming and kinesthetic training, aim to improve the processes which underlie motor behaviour. Task-oriented approaches aim to improve the performance of a particular task or certain motor skill. Examples are teaching of functional skills, coaching on specific motor skills and developing certain visual–motor skills. These approaches can be implemented according to the child's level of neurological information processing.

Bottom-up interventions aim to improve sensory and perceptual processing functions in order to facilitate an ability to formulate ideas and motor plan for different motor behaviours. Most process-oriented approaches are bottom-up in nature. Top-down approaches focus on the performance difficulties that children experience by assisting them to identify, develop and utilize cognitive strategies to manage daily tasks more effectively. Examples of top-down approaches are task analysis and problem-solving strategies.

Therapeutic activities should be selected and integrated into the child's daily routine, within different natural environments, such as school and home. These interventions should be holistic, family-centred, multi-faceted and individualized to meet the unique needs of each child. The therapist should set the goals of treatment with parents, teachers, other involved professionals and, where appropriate, with the child.

Case example: Steven

Steven is a 7-year-old boy with average intellectual capacity. His parents described him as awkward and clumsy, with poor coordination in different daily tasks. He falls down, bumps into things, and has difficulty in judging body position. Steven also trips when climbing the stairs and generally has difficulty in organizing himself. Buttoning shirts, tying shoelaces and doing up zippers are all very difficult, and he has difficulties in following and implementing sequences of verbal commands. At school, Steven has average reading skills but handwriting is a particular problem and he has great difficulty in keeping up with written work.

His mother reported that both pregnancy and delivery were normal but that Steven's early motor milestones were slightly delayed. She also said that he was an irritable young child who had difficulty in settling. He received speech and language therapy input at 3 years of age, when it was noted that Steven had difficulties in his attention control and an inability to stay seated. Steven has a 5-year-old younger sister who is more advanced in all areas of development, and Steven becomes very frustrated when he cannot complete tasks as well as her.

An evaluation was carried out using appropriate tests and the results indicated poor discrimination of tactile and kinesthetic information, poor praxis functions, moderate deficits in postural control, difficulties with bilateral integrative and sequencing functions, problems in different gross and fine motor skills, and difficulties in certain self-care skills. The overall interpretation of the data suggested that Steven has sensory-integrative based dyspraxia which affects his motor organizational ability, performance in different learning and daily activities, and social interaction with his peers within school.

An occupational therapy programme with stated goals and objectives was planned in conjunction with Steven's parents and teachers. The programme included remedial approaches to enhance Steven's ability to discriminate tactile and movement information, body awareness, postural–motor control, bilateral integrative functions, motor planning and sequencing functions. Functional approaches integrated structured therapeutic activities into his daily routine in order to improve his gross motor skills, fine motor skills, handwriting and fastening skills. Compensatory and adaptive approaches included chairs and tables of appropriate size and height, the use of a sloped tabletop to provide better position for handwriting tasks and the the use of four-lined papers for proper positioning of letters. Maintenance approaches included participation in non-competitive physical activities after school.

After 6 months, Steven's parents and teacher reported that his motor coordination and planning function had improved. He was more confident about participating in team games. He was also more motivated when taking on different routines and new activities. He was more able to organize himself in the morning. Steven also demonstrated better social interactions in the playground. Further occupational therapy input would serve to concentrate on generalizing and extending these gains into different environments and into demanding situations.

REFERENCES

American Psychiatric Association (1994) *Diagnostic and Statistical Manual of Mental Disorders*, 4th edn (DSM-IV). Washington, DC: APA.

Attwood, T. (1998) *Asperger's Syndrome: A Guide for Parents and Professionals.* London: Jessica Kingsley Publishers.

Ayres, A.J. (1985) *Developmental Dyspraxia and Adult Onset Apraxia.* Torrance, CA: Sensory Integration International.

Ayres, A.J., Mailloux, Z. and Wendler, C.L. (1987) 'Developmental dyspraxia: is it a unitary function?' *Occupational Therapy Journal of Research* 7, 93–110.

Barkley, R.A., DuPaul, G.J. and McMurray, M.B. (1990) 'A comprehensive evaluation of attention deficit disorder with and without hyperactivity.' *Journal of Consulting and Clinical Psychology 58*, 775–789.

Bornstein, R.A. and Yang, V. (1991) 'Neuropsychological performance in medicated and unmedicated patients with Tourette's Disorder.' *American Journal of Psychiatry 148*, 468–471.

Cermak, S.A. (1991) 'Somatodyspraxia.' In A.G. Fisher, E. Murray, and A. Bundy (eds) *Sensory Integration – Theory and Practice*. Philadelphia, PA: F.A. Davis Co.

Cermak, S.A., Gubbay, S.S. and Larkin, D. (2002) 'What is developmental coordination disorder?' In S.A. Cermak and D. Larkin (eds) *Developmental Coordination Disorder*. Albany, NY: Delmar.

Fox, A.M. and Polatajko, H.J. (1994) 'Children and clumsiness: A Disability in Search of Definition.' International Consensus Meeting. Canada, 11th–14th October.

Gubbay, S.S. (1975) *The Clumsy Child*. New York: W.B. Saunders.

Jones, V. and Prior, M.R. (1985) 'Motor imitation abilities and neurological signs in autistic children.' *Journal of Autism and Developmental Disorders 15*, 37–46.

Kadesjö, B. and Gillberg, C. (1999) 'Developmental coordination disorder in Swedish 7-year-old children.' *Journal of the American Academy of Child and Adolescent Psychiatry 38*, 820–828.

World Health Organization (1992) *International Statistical Classification of Diseases and Related Health Problems*, 10th revision (ICD-10). Geneva: World Health Organization.

Chapter 10

Deficits in attention, motor control and perception (DAMP)

Christopher Gillberg

INTRODUCTION

The concept of DAMP (Deficits in Attention, Motor Control and Perception) has been used clinically in Scandinavia for about 20 years. DAMP is diagnosed on the basis of concomitant Attention Deficit Hyperactivity Disorder (ADHD) (Chapter 6) and Developmental Coordination Disorder (Chapter 9) in children who do not have severe learning disability or cerebral palsy. In a clinically severe form, it affects about 1.5 per cent of the general population of school-age children although other children will be affected by more moderate variants of the condition. Boys are over-represented, but girls are probably under-diagnosed. There are many co-morbid conditions and associated problems, including conduct disorder, depression/anxiety and academic failure. Of particular interest is the strong link with autistic spectrum disorders (Chapter 7) in severe DAMP. Two community-based studies suggest that familial factors and perinatal risk factors (Chapter 15) account for much of the variance. Psycho-social risk factors appear to increase the risk of marked psychiatric abnormality in DAMP, and outcome in early adult age was psycho-socially poor in almost 60 per cent of unmedicated cases. There are effective interventions available for many of the problems encountered in DAMP, and it is hoped that with earlier diagnosis and better support, particularly during the school years, many individuals with DAMP should be able to achieve a considerably better outcome than appears currently to be the case.

HISTORICAL BACKGROUND

It is more than 100 years since George Still (1902) drew the medical community's attention to children with a combination of attentional, motivational, motor control and learning deficits – a set of problems later variously referred to as Minimal Brain Dysfunction (Chapter 13), Attention Deficit Disorder/ Hyperkinetic Disorder/ADHD or DAMP. Since Still's early writings, on what he believed to be a syndrome of moral dyscontrol, these clinically heterogeneous conditions have undergone changes in basic conceptualization, delineation and diagnostic criteria but the core notion of a crucial dysfunction of attention and activity control has remained relatively unshaken.

Attention deficits, inappropriate overactivity and problematic impulsiveness are still common symptoms of concern among school-age children and ADHD has become the internationally dominant concept in the field given its strong empirical basis (Barkley *et al.* 2002). Nevertheless, controversy regarding its prevalence, aetiology, treatment and outcome often pervades the media and, to a lesser extent, scientific debate. Also, while the frequent co-occurrence of psychiatric problems in ADHD has gradually been acknowledged, the high rate and clinical significance of co-existing developmental incoordination problems, motor control dysfunction, speech/language dysfunction and reading/writing disorders have been neglected.

In Scandinavia, the DAMP concept was developed in the 1970s in an attempt to operationalize the syndrome of Minimal Brain Dysfunction (MBD) well before ADHD appeared in a formalized fashion for the first time. Bengt Hagberg (1975) initiated a large-scale empirical study of MBD, out of which the concept of DAMP gradually emerged to become rooted in everyday clinical practice and parlance, particularly in Denmark and Sweden (Airaksinen *et al.* 1991).

DEFINITION

In the first longitudinal study, DAMP was defined as the combination of (1) cross-situational impairing attention deficit with or without impairing hyperactivity/impulsivity, and (2) an impairing deficit in at least one of the following areas: gross motor function, fine motor funtion, perception or speech/language in the absence of clear mental retardation, cerebral palsy or other major neurological disabilities. Severe DAMP was diagnosed in cases showing attention deficit in combination with all of the other deficits (Gillberg *et al.* 1983). In later reports, given that children with perceptual abnormality virtually always had some impairing motor control problems, DAMP was defined as the combination of ADHD and Developmental Coordination Disorder (Kadesjö and Gillberg 2001) and constitutes a sub-group of ADHD which is conceptually similar but not clinically identical to the concept of Hyperkinetic Disorder (World Health Organization 1992).

Box 10.1 Diagnostic criteria for DAMP

A.   ADHD as defined in the DSM-IV (American Psychiatric Association 1994)

B.   DCD as defined in the DSM-IV

C.   Condition not better accounted for by cerebral palsy

D.   Not associated with severe learning disability (IQ about 50)

E.   Other diagnostic categories often apply (e.g. autistic spectrum disorder, depression) but are not required for diagnosis of DAMP

PREVALENCE

DAMP in severe form occurs in 1.2 to 2.0 per cent of all 7-year-olds. It is always clinically impairing and invariably leads to attendance at paediatric, child psychiatry or speech/language clinics before 10 years of age with concerns regarding ADHD, conduct disorder or autistic spectrum problems (Kadesjö and Gillberg 1998). An additional 4 to 6 per cent of the general population in that age group will have milder variants of the disorder and specialist evaluation and intervention is common, but often at a later age, due to concerns about depression, anxiety or academic failure. Most DAMP studies have reported a male:female ratio of 3–5:1, which is similar to ratios found in other neuro-developmental disorders. However, it is possible that girls with DAMP are often misdiagnosed as suffering from emotional problems such as depression or anxiety (Kopp and Gillberg 2003).

CO-MORBIDITY AND OVERLAPPING PROBLEMS

About half of all cases with ADHD will meet criteria for DAMP due to the presence of Developmental Coordination Disorder (DCD). Conversely, ADHD occurs in about half of all cases of DCD (Kadesjö and Gillberg 1999). DCD in its severe or moderate form occurs at similarly high rates in both severe and moderate forms of ADHD. According to Kadesjö and Gillberg (2001) this is very different from the overlap pattern of ADHD with Oppositional Defiant Disorder (ODD), which might signal a more robust overlap of ADHD with DCD.

DAMP was demonstrated, in the early 1980s, to overlap with a number of other diagnostic entities (Gillberg 1983). At 7 years of age, about 1 in 3 DAMP children with a combination of ADHD and DCD met criteria for a depressive disorder, and one in ten qualified for a diagnosis of conduct disorder. These problems occurred in children with severe and mild–moderate variants alike. In those with severe DAMP, autistic features were extremely common, amounting to an autistic spectrum disorder in no less than two-thirds of cases. Several of the cases in this sub-group – constituting about 0.7 per cent of the general population of Swedish 7-year-olds in the mid-1970s – met full operationalized criteria for Asperger syndrome (Gillberg and Gillberg 1989). Altogether 65 per cent of individuals with DAMP (severe and mild–moderate variants) had some kind of 'marked psychiatric abnormality' by the age of 7.

Learning problems, including mathematical and reading/writing disorders, were present in 65 to 80 per cent of DAMP cases both at age 10 years, and later at age 13. Speech and language disorders, such as Semantic–Pragmatic Disorder (Chapter 16), were present in half of all individuals with DAMP. In severe DAMP, all children presented with speech/language disorders whereas, in those with mild–moderate variants, about one in four children had such disorder. Two in three children with DAMP met diagnostic criteria for psychiatric disorders other than ADHD and DCD, or fulfilled the diagnostic criteria for personality disorder at 16 years of age. A similar proportion met such criteria at age 22, including diagnoses of anti-social personality disorder, substance use disorder and bipolar disorder. Tic disorders (Chapter 18) are also commonly encountered in ADHD with and without DCD (Kadesjö and Gillberg 2001).

NEURO-PSYCHOLOGY OF DAMP

Although DAMP was originally only diagnosed in cases without learning disability, it has now become clinically acceptable to diagnose the condition in children with mild mental retardation. A population study of DAMP demonstrated that a non-verbal IQ of under 70 occurred in about one in six cases of ADHD with DCD. This is similar to the proportion of individuals with DAMP who, in spite of not testing in the retarded non-verbal range on school entry, attended classrooms for pupils with learning disability for some period during their first nine years of school.

Similarly, children with ADHD (including the sub-group with DAMP) have an average IQ of 5 to 8 points lower than that of the general population (Jensen 2000). The neuro-psychology of DAMP is therefore similar to that encountered in ADHD, and executive dysfunction is almost universal (as in most other neuro-developmental disorders). One sub-group with DAMP (about half of all cases) have typical troughs on two or more of the four WISC-subtests (see Chapter 21) and another sub-group show depressed scores on most, if not all, subtests. It has therefore been argued that DAMP could represent 'misunderstood' subnormal intelligence and that a child with serious learning disability, if submitted to all the demands of mainstream school, would show attention deficits, motor clumsiness and perceptual problems.

RISK FACTORS FOR THE DEVELOPMENT OF DAMP

Familial factors play an important role in the aetiology of DAMP, and are evident in about one-third of cases (Gillberg and Rasmussen 1982). Roughly one in two children with the condition have a sibling or parent similarly affected, although the severity of symptoms may vary considerably across family members. A combination of both familial and prenatal/perinatal factors are common, and various risk factors are over-represented in DAMP. Low birthweight and premature birth, which are associated with ADHD, have also been implicated in DAMP. Maternal alcohol abuse in pregnancy is associated with an increased risk of DAMP, and smoking in pregnancy probably has a similar effect on the developing child.

Psycho-social risk factors are also over-represented in DAMP. However, while they do not actually account for the condition, they may contribute to many of the co-morbid psychiatric, behavioural and emotional problems. For example, highly inconsistent patterns of rearing on the part of parents do not contribute to the severity of DAMP, but strongly predict 'marked psychiatric abnormality' both in DAMP and non-DAMP cases.

DIAGNOSTIC ASSESSMENT

All children with severe DAMP will need diagnostic appraisal at some point during development, often by a multi-disciplinary team of developmental paediatricians, child psychiatrists, clinical psychologists, speech/language therapists, physiotherapists, occupational therapists and special education teachers. Many of those with moderate and milder variants of the condition will also need evaluation, but these may be appropriately dealt with in primary care or at school.

Basic evaluation in all cases should consist of a thorough developmental history from one of the parents focusing on symptoms of inattention, hyperactivity, impulsivity, autistic spectrum problems, tics, conduct problems, motor control dysfunction, speech/language problems, academic failure and depression. An individual examination of the child, including a brief neuro-developmental battery, is required in all cases as outlined below.

INTERVENTIONS

School-age children with severe DAMP are in need of comprehensive evaluation, intervention and even long-term treatment programmes provided by a multi-disciplinary team of professionals. Many with moderate, and some of those with mild, problems will need similar interventions.

Box 10.2 Diagnostic assessment and evaluation in DAMP

All cases

- Detailed developmental history from primary carer
- ADHD-R interview
- Co-morbidity questionnaire, e.g. Child Behaviour Checklist (Achenbach and Edelbrock 1983)
- Brief neuromotor examination, e.g. Medical Motor Examination
- General physical examination including height, weight, head circumference, vision and hearing, and screen for multiple minor physical anomalies

Severe cases

As above plus, as appropriate:

- EEG (in cases raising any suspicion of seizures or absences)
- Genetic testing
- Targeted DNA analysis
- Brain imaging in some cases

Psycho-education

All families with a child afflicted by DAMP will need psycho-educational interventions. Parents and carers need information about the condition, which can be imparted both with the child present and separately, should they have information which they do not want to share with the child. However, it is appropriate to inform the child about his or her condition as soon as a definite diagnosis has been made. Everything that has a name is less frightening than the unmentionable, and even young children with DAMP are aware that something is amiss. They already know that their attention deficits, clumsiness and learning difficulties are major problems, and may respond well to having a label to account for these difficulties. However, it is important to convey that neither the child, nor anyone else, can be blamed for the condition. Educating everyone involved, including siblings and teachers, about the neuro-developmental nature of the condition is essential as psycho-education is the first and most important part of any intervention plan.

Special educational needs

Most children with DAMP will need some adjustment in their school setting. This can often be accomplished merely by informing the teacher about the nature of the child's problems. Attending a special classroom may be indicated for part or all of the school day. A high ratio of teachers to children is almost always necessary for the child with DAMP to progress academically. Keeping on task is difficult without interested and well-informed teachers to keep the child 'on track'. Most children with DAMP will manage school work more efficiently if they are allowed extra time to complete the tasks, but they also need to have regular brief breaks to maintain concentration. Having a 'coach' to guide the child through everyday activities, particularly in the school setting, is often one of the best ways to address the many-faceted problems faced by children suffering from DAMP.

Motor control interventions

About half of all individuals with DAMP need special programmes for the treatment/alleviation of motor control problems. It is essential to inform physical education teachers about the child's difficulties, and physical education in a small group of 'like-minded' children may often solve the problem. Children with DAMP currently comprise the largest sub-group of all those who do not want to participate in physical education. A physiotherapist or an occupational therapist may also need to make a detailed evaluation of gross and fine motor functions, and to prescribe specific training programmes for muscle strength, body posture, body image and fine motor dysfunction. Motor control problems are a sadly neglected area of clinical attention, yet training in these areas may actively benefit the child.

Speech and language therapy and dyslexia programmes

Speech/language problems and dyslexia in DAMP are intimately linked, and children with impaired speech/language or with severe dyslexia will need an intervention programme specifically aimed at addressing such problems. There is often a failure to recognize language and reading/writing problems in affected children, and the DAMP diagnosis makes more explicit demands on the clinician to look out for these very common co-morbid problems.

Psychopharmacology

Stimulant medication can ameliorate basic symptoms of ADHD (inattention, hyperactivity, impulsivity) and also affect some of the associated problems (fine motor dysfunction and conduct problems). Longer-term studies indicate remaining positive effects of stimulants after one and two years of continued treatment (Gillberg *et al.* 1997) and there is increasing scientific support for other psychopharmacological agents in the treatment of ADHD/DAMP. While the exact role of these substances remains unclear at the present time, it is likely that there will be more diverse options when opting for psychopharmacological treatment of ADHD/DAMP in the future.

It is my view that drugs should not be used in the treatment of DAMP unless other avenues of intervention have been entered first. In extreme cases, and particularly if change of school or dwelling has been seriously discussed, or if admission to hospital has been raised as a real issue, it would be appropriate to discuss stimulant treatment even at the 'first' evaluation, after the diagnosis of DAMP has been settled. Otherwise, it would seem prudent to go for other interventions for a period of six months or so, before one opts for stimulant treatment as an addition to other interventions.

Psychotherapies

Psychotherapy may not, in itself, prove superior to non-specialized community treatment as young children, and even many adolescents, with DAMP cannot concentrate sufficiently on individual or family work. However, some individuals with DAMP may, in late adolescence and adult life, develop secondary emotional problems for which psychotherapy may be considered a necessary intervention. Even in such cases, it is important for the therapist to be well versed in issues relating to ADHD and DAMP.

THE COURSE OF DAMP

Children diagnosed as having DAMP at an early age have a high risk of persistent problems throughout childhood and adolescence, and well into adulthood. Almost 60 per cent of those with a diagnosis of DAMP at the age of 7 years had a 'very poor outcome' at age 22 in the Gothenburg longitudinal study. They were either receiving a full sick pension, suffering from severe persistent personality or psychiatric disorder (depression not included), misusing substances or had committed serious criminal offences. The proportion of very poor outcomes was more than four times that of the general population without DAMP.

Motor clumsiness tends to become much less marked with increasing age. By 10, obvious motor clumsiness (which was present in all cases around age 7) is only evident in less than half of all cases. This proportion drops to about one in three by the early teens, but DCD can still be diagnosed in 30–35 per cent of the DAMP cases at the ages of 16 and 22 years. Thus, there is an impression of improved motor skill control in the DAMP group over time. However, this could reflect the crudeness of later diagnostic evaluation rather than any real improvement. Nevertheless, DCD does not appear to have the same clinical impact on adults as it does at younger ages.

Attention deficits tend to persist into adulthood in the vast majority of DAMP cases. However, only about one in two will meet the full criteria for ADHD around 22 years of age. The overt symptoms of overactivity and impulsivity tend to decline in frequency and impact over the years, even in those cases that show persistent impairing attention deficits well into their twenties. It may merit mention that none of the cases in the longitudinal prospective controlled follow-up study of DAMP in Gothenburg, Sweden had ever received treatment with stimulant medication, although some 60 per cent had consulted specialists at one or other point during childhood or adolescence.

Attempts to tease out the contribution of background factors to the very poor psycho-social early adult outcome in untreated cases of DAMP have not been very successful. Preliminary data indicate that DCD in boys may constitute a much more handicapping problem with regard to psycho-social well-being than currently appreciated, and research in progress shows that boys with motor control problems have particularly poor self-esteem (Landgren *et al.* in progress). There are also stronger links to autistic spectrum disorders and academic failure in ADHD cases with concomitant DCD.

The natural outcome in the longer-term perspective (say into the thirties and middle age) of DAMP is not known. However, retrospective studies currently being undertaken in Sweden have shown that DAMP exists and can be reliably diagnosed even beyond age 50 years.

CONCLUSION

DAMP is a sub-group of ADHD with the concomitant condition of DCD, and has been validated in several Scandinavian studies. All those with severe DAMP will need evaluation and intervention at early school age, whereas the needs of those with more moderate DAMP are less predictable. The ADHD component of DAMP needs the kind of interventions generally agreed on for that condition. However, the addition of DCD and other co-morbidities needs to be addressed in their own right. DCD remains a 'black sheep' in the history of ADHD even though it is perhaps the most common overlapping condition. The concept of DAMP has helped draw attention to the clinical importance of DCD in ADHD, and some families may be more at ease with the DAMP concept than a diagnosis of ADHD. DAMP has also provided a historical link between ADHD and autistic spectrum disorders, which may become a heated topic of debate in the next few years.

REFERENCES

Achenbach, T.M. and Edelbrock, C. (1983) *Manual for the child behaviour checklist and revised child behaviour profile.* Burlington, VT: Queen City Printers.

Airaksinen, E., Bille, B., Carlström, G. (1991) 'Barn och ungdomar med DAMP/MBD.' *Läkartidningen 9*, 714.

American Psychiatric Association (1994) *Diagnostic and Statistical Manual of Mental Disorders,* 4th edn (DSM-IV). Washington, DC: American Psychiatric Association.

Barkley, R., Cook, E.H., Dulcan, M., Campbell, S.B. *et al.* (2002) 'International consensus statement of ADHD.' *European Child and Adolescent Psychiatry 11*, 96–98.

Gillberg, C. (1983) 'Perceptual, motor and attentional deficits in Swedish primary school children.' *Journal of Child Psychology and Psychiatry 24*, 377–403.

Gillberg, C., Carlström, G., Rasmussen, P. and Waldenström, E. (1983) 'Perceptual, motor and attentional deficits in seven-year-old children. Neurological screening aspects.' *Acta Paediatrica Scandinavica 72*, 119–124.

Gillberg, C., Melander, H., von Knorring, A.-L., Janols, L.-O. *et al.* (1997) 'Long-term stimulant treatment of children with attention-deficit hyperactivity disorder symptoms. A randomized, double-blind, placebo-controlled trial.' *Archives of General Psychiatry 54*, 857–864.

Gillberg, C. and Rasmussen, P. (1982) 'Perceptual, motor and attentional deficits in seven-year-old children: background factors.' *Developmental Medicine and Child Neurology 24*, 752–770.

Gillberg, I.C. and Gillberg, C. (1989) 'Asperger syndrome – some epidemiological considerations: A research note.' *Journal of Child Psychology and Psychiatry 30*, 631–638.

Hagberg, B. (1975) 'Minimal Brain Dysfunction – vad innebär det för barnets utveckling och anpassning.' *Läkartidningen 72*, 3296–3300.

Jensen, P.S. (2000) 'ADHD: Current concepts on etiology, pathophysiology, and neurobiology.' *Child and Adolescent Psychiatric Clinics of North America 9*, 557–572.

Kadesjö, B. and Gillberg, C. (1998) 'Attention deficits and clumsiness in Swedish 7-year-old children.' *Developmental Medicine and Child Neurology 40*, 796–811.

Kadesjö, B. and Gillberg, C. (1999) 'Developmental coordination disorder in Swedish 7-year-old children.' *Journal of the American Academy of Child and Adolescent Psychiatry 38*, 820–828.

Kadesjö, B. and Gillberg, C. (2001) 'The comorbidity of ADHD in the general population of Swedish school-age children.' *Journal of Child Psychology and Psychiatry 42*, 487–492.

Kopp, S. and Gillberg, C. (2003) 'Swedish child and adolescent psychiatric out-patients: A five year cohort.' *European and Child and Adolescent Psychiatry 12*, 30–35.

Still, G.F. (1902) 'The Coulstonian lectures on some abnormal psychical conditions in children.' *Lancet 1*, 1008–1012.

World Health Organization (1992) *International Statistical Classification of Diseases and Related Health Problems,* 10th revision (ICD-10). Geneva: World Health Organization.

Chapter 11

Dyslexia

Kerry Bennett

INTRODUCTION

Dyslexia, derived from the Greek 'dys' (inadequate) and 'lexis' (words), can be defined as a difficulty with language that is neurologically based and runs in families. Behavioural, cognitive and biological definitions have all been explored with different levels of description and complex interactions between them. However, there remains great variation in how the terminology is used, and the definition alone has caused a great deal of controversy. Frith (1999) describes what she calls the paradoxes of the definition of dyslexia, and defines dyslexia as a 'neuro-developmental disorder with a biological origin and behavioural signs which extend far beyond problems with written language'.

Dyslexia is increasingly described as a 'difference in learning' rather than a 'learning disability'. This change in terminology recognizes that the brains of individuals with dyslexia may differ anatomically and functionally from those of non-dyslexic individuals. There is increasing evidence that the characteristics which accompany dyslexia are the result of a difference in brain structure and function, and clear differences in the activation of specific parts of the brain have been observed. To avoid confusion, and for the purposes of this chapter, the following definition will be used: 'Dyslexia is an inherited different kind of mind that causes a difference in learning.'

CHARACTERISTICS OF DYSLEXIA
Primary characteristics

Dyslexia can occur at any level of intellectual ability, and the primary characteristics are:

- lack of phonological awareness (sounds)
- difficulty with decoding words (reading)

- difficulty with encoding words (spelling)

- difficulty with handwriting

- poor short-term memory

- poor visual and/or auditory memory

- poor sequencing of numbers or letters in words, when read or written (b–d, sing–sign, left–felt, soiled–solid, 12–21)

- difficulty with mathematics (often related to sequencing of steps or the language of mathematics)

- confusion about directions in space or time (right/left, early/late)

- difficulties with comprehension and understanding

- difficulty expressing thoughts in written form

- difficulty in expressing thoughts verbally.

It is a common misconception that all people with dyslexia can neither read nor spell. While many may have difficulties in these areas, some may read very well. Instead, their main difficulties may present in terms of sequencing, memory skills and mathematics. However, it would be very rare for any one dyslexic child to have all of the above characteristics, and the number and type of difficulties with which a dyslexic child may present can vary significantly within the population.

The severity of dyslexia can also vary from borderline to very severe, being measured by the difference between potential and performance. For example, a child whose chronological age is 10 years, but who is performing at the level of a 9-year-old, would appear to be only one year behind. However, if his or her IQ suggests that he or she should be performing at the level of a 12-year-old, then he or she is actually three years behind. Therefore, if a child's IQ and age are known, it is possible to predict his or her expected reading skill. Children who are found to be operating significantly below their expected level can be said to have specific reading difficulties or 'dyslexia'.

Secondary characteristics

The primary characteristics of dyslexia may have social implications. Personality, economic background, culture, social background, parenting and schooling are fundamental factors in how dyslexia may present. Thus, there are many confounding variables, which makes dyslexia very individual. These secondary characteristics may manifest as behavioural problems including:

- frustration leading to disruptive and/or aggressive behaviour

- poor self-esteem

- low self-confidence
- poor motivation
- withdrawal
- depression.

PREVALENCE

Dyslexia occurs among all groups of people irrespective of age, race or social class. According to Sally and Shaywitz (1998), dyslexia is the most common and carefully studied of the learning disabilities, affecting 80 per cent of all those identified as learning disabled. Depending on the data source, the percentage of the population that are potentially dyslexic ranges from 4 to 15 per cent, which is reflective of variations in the definitions being used.

Dyslexia is said to affect 10 per cent of the Western world (Sims 1998) and the National Institute of Child Health and Human Development reports that there are 10 million American children (1 in 5) with dyslexia. There is some variability regarding the estimated incidence of dyslexia in British school children, ranging from 3 to 10 per cent. However, both the United Kingdom Dyslexia Institute and the British Dyslexia Association state that 10 per cent of the population have some degree of language difficulty, while 4 per cent of the population have severe dyslexia.

There are further discrepancies in the prevalence of dyslexia between the sexes. Although some studies have shown that the incidence of dyslexia is approximately four times more prevalent in males than in females (Grigorenko *et al.* 1997), it is now more widely accepted that there is no significant difference between the sexes. Instead, it would seem that boys tend to be more efficiently recognized and identified than girls.

BRAIN ABNORMALITIES IN DYSLEXIA

Recent neuro-imaging studies, using positron emission tomography (PET) and functional magnetic resonance imaging (fMRI), have shown that there are clear differences in patterns of brain activation between those with dyslexia and those without (Rumsey *et al.* 1997; Shaywitz *et al.* 2002). The differences occur mainly in the left cerebral hemisphere, which is the side of the brain most concerned with language processing and generation. The sites of dysfunction in dyslexic individuals can be localized to the temporo-parietal junction (Wernicke's area), the inferior frontal gyrus (Broca's area), the angular gyrus and the insula. Other studies have suggested that there are deficits in the cerebellum, which may explain the motor deficits seen in people with dyslexia (Eden and Zeffiro 1998; Nicolson and Fawcett 1999).

Some studies have pointed to abnormalities in the visual system, and Stein and Fowler (1993) have suggested that people with dyslexia may experience words moving around on the page because they have deficient ocular motor control. The brain areas which help to control eye movement are affected, as well as those areas responsible for passing information to the visual cortex. Lovegrove, Martin and Slaghuis (1986) also highlight abnormalities with the visual system, suggesting that people with dyslexia have low-level impairments of the transient visual system which can be exerienced as blurring of print.

Language is a complex, multi-faceted skill that encompasses the formation of sounds, the understanding of sophisticated rules, vast quantities of meaning, the significance of information and development of memory. Language processing and formation therefore requires a number of specific brain regions and pathways, but it also relies on the accuracy with which visual and/or auditory information (hearing) is received and processed. Thus, a difference in the structure and function of any of these areas would result in a difficulty in being able to process language in the conventional manner. This could explain why no one specific focus in the brain has yet been identified as the specific cause of dyslexia.

It would seem fair to surmise that dyslexia is not solely the result of impairment in one of the language areas, and there is no consistency among dyslexic individuals pointing to one specifically affected area of the brain. It therefore follows that the characteristics with which a dyslexic individual may present will relate directly to the personal language area that is affected. For example, an abnormality in Broca's area might characteristically lead to difficulty in expressing thoughts verbally because this area is associated with the structure and form of words and articulation. Equally, an impairment in Wernicke's area could lead to difficulty in decoding words since this area deals with the understanding of communication. However, characteristics such as confusion between left and right, and difficulties with handwriting, are more likely to be the result of deficits in the cerebellum.

GENETICS

According to Darwin, variation within species is the result of natural selection and the influence of environment on particular characteristics over time. A gene is only conserved within evolution if its impact is essential to life. Therefore, if a particular gene that codes for a life-supporting system is altered, and the resulting phenotype/characteristic is dysfunctional (see Chapter 8), that life will not survive and the defective genes will not be passed on to subsequent generations. However, genetic variations may arise which are not essential for life.

It is probably fair to assume that dyslexia is the result of such genetic variation. The ability to communicate through written language is unique to human beings but this ability is not essential to life. Therefore, the genes that code for the development of language areas within the brain, and the pathways between them, are open to mutation and thus variation. These changes may be readily passed on to subsequent generations via genetic coding. Studies have already revealed that, if one parent is dyslexic, then there is a 50 per cent chance of any of his or her children also being dyslexic.

As language processing requires multiple brain regions and pathways, there is an equal multiplicity of genes needed to code for these developments. This not only increases the probability of mutation and variation, but it also increases the number of different changes or permutations that could potentially cause difficulties with language. This reflects the number of different brain regions which have been implicated to date, and would explain why some dyslexics inherit certain characteristics but not others. It would also suggest that the number of mutations, and/or the degree of mutation, would be directly responsible for the degree of severity. However, it is equally important to note that, while genetic make-up gives an indication of risk, environmental and other factors will also influence how dyslexia may manifest according to nature and nurture theories.

Recent advances in molecular genetics involving linkage studies in families (where more than one family member is affected) and twin studies (where at least one twin is affected) have implicated chromosomes 1, 6, 15 and 18 as possible sites for a gene locus. Chromosome 1 was analysed in a father and his two sons who presented with dyslexia, writing problems, reading difficulties and severely delayed speech development (Froster *et al.* 1993). With regard to chromosome 6, Smith, Kimberling and Pennington (1991) revealed a linkage to human leucocyte antigen (HLA), a defect of which could lead to possible autoimmune disorders, and subsequent studies have established a potential link between auto- immune disorders and developmental learning problems (Kaplan and Crawford 1994). Goei *et al.* (1998) further recognized chromosome 6 as a genetic locus for schizophrenia, juvenile myoclonic epilepsy and dyslexia, which they refer to as neuro-behavioural disorders.

Grigorenko *et al.* (1997) observed a linkage between chromosome 6 and phonological awareness, and also a linkage between chromosome 15 and single-word reading. In 2002, the Wellcome Centre for Human Genetics in Oxford scanned children from 208 British and American families in which at least one child had dyslexia. Having tested the reading skills of all the other children in these families, researchers were able to pinpoint a region on chromosome 18 with a gene that has a likely link to dyslexia (Fisher *et al.* 2002).

PSYCHOLOGICAL ASSESSMENT

Formal assessment by an educational psychologist or specialist teacher is the recognized procedure currently being used within the UK to identify dyslexia in children from 5 years of age through to adulthood. As discussed previously, the manifestation of dyslexia is the result of behavioural, cognitive and biological factors. Personality, culture, social background, parenting and schooling all need to be considered and may be helpful in allowing the psychologist to form an accurate cognitive profile of the individual. For this reason, often prior to assessment, the psychologist may request completion of family and school questionnaires. At assessment, further exploration of background issues may take place with the parents or carers who accompany the child. As dyslexia is inherited, it is essential to determine whether similar difficulties exist within the extended family.

The initial assessment may take up to two and a half hours. During this time, the psychologist will assess everything from single word recognition to problem-solving skills. The procedures which are administered are diagnostic and attainment tests, and tests of general ability. From these data, a full cognitive profile of an individual's strengths and weakness can be formulated. Both a verbal and a non-verbal score are obtained, as well as an overall IQ score.

Any discrepancies between performance and ability will become very apparent. Generally, if individuals are dyslexic, there will be a gap between their potential, the level of their IQ and how they actually perform on specific tasks. Dyslexic individuals are more likely to underachieve in areas that are characteristic of dyslexia such as reading, spelling, sequencing and memory. Based on this testing, the individual characteristics of dyslexia will become apparent. The educational psychologist will also be able to assess the severity of the dyslexia, which will be reflective of the gap between ability and performance.

Following assessment, the psychologist should be able to give a conclusive evaluation of an individual's specific difficulties and whether these are the result of being dyslexic. This should include a full report, which would include not only the test results but also a list of recommendations to help the individual perform to the optimum level of his or her ability.

SPECIALIST TUITION

Specialist tuition is an internationally recognized intervention, and one that has been proven to be of help to individuals of any age with dyslexia. Specialist tuition recognizes that dyslexic people acquire and process information in different ways to non-dyslexic individuals. However, rather than trying to force the dyslexic person to learn in conventional ways, the teacher changes the way in which he or she teaches so that it is appropriate to the skills and needs of the individual. This form of tuition should be provided by specially qualified teachers.

The tuition should also be structured, cumulative and multisensory. The teacher needs to utilize the information gained from the psychology assessment to implement a strategic teaching plan applicable to that particular individual's needs. This should take into serious consideration both strengths and weaknesses.

Specialist tuition deals with the primary characteristics of dyslexia, and aims to help individuals in overcoming their primary difficulties. This may simultaneously prove very effective in resolving any secondary characteristics of dyslexia, such as problems with behaviour and self-confidence. Once individuals with dyslexia come to realize that they are capable, and that they can achieve their aims and goals, there is a marked improvement in confidence and a reduction in frustration and difficult behaviour.

EARLY INTERVENTION

It is imperative that dyslexia is recognized early as, if the problem is not addressed, then the individual will almost certainly continue to underachieve over time in spite of his or her natural potential. Once the problem has been addressed, and the specific details of individual difficulties and strengths is known, then it becomes possible to apply appropriate and beneficial strategies. This will also help to minimize the later development of the behavioural problems that are so common in dyslexic children whose difficulties are not recognized, or whose difficulties are recognized too late.

THE GIFT OF DYSLEXIA

West (1991) describes the talents of some famous people who suffered from dyslexia. In spite of their difficulties, dyslexic individuals may prove to be very creative and artistic. They are often good lateral thinkers, with efficient problem-solving skills. Dyslexic people have often been reported as having an all-round view rather than using step-by-step analytical approaches. This lends itself to an intuitive and untaught understanding of how things work and it is for these reasons that dyslexic people often make good architects, designers, engineers, IT experts or surgeons. It could be argued that these skills are acquired as a compensatory measure, perhaps related to the patterns of overactivation in the brain that have been observed. However, it may equally represent a gift, reflective of the different kind of mind that dyslexic people have.

SUMMARY

Dyslexia is an inherited condition with a neurobiological foundation. It is a polygenic disorder because of the large number of potential genes involved, and because its manifestation may be the result of environmental factors. There is a great deal of variation in the difficulties that are inherited and, combined with the individual's environment, this results in a way of learning that is unique to that individual. Even though dyslexia is biological in nature, it is not a disease. Instead, it can be described more accurately as 'a different kind of mind that causes a difference in learning'.

REFERENCES

Eden, G.F. and Zeffiro, T.A. (1998) 'Neural systems affected in developmental dyslexia revealed by functional neuroimaging.' *Neuron 21*, 279–282.

Fisher, S.E., Francks, C., Marlow, A.J., MacPhie, L. *et al.* (2002) 'Independent genome-wide scans identify a chromosome 18 quantitative-trait locus influencing dyslexia.' *Nature Genetics 30*, 86–91.

Frith, U. (1999) 'Paradoxes in the definition of Dyslexia'. *Dyslexia: An International Journal of Research and Practice 5*, 4, 192–214.

Froster, U., Schulte-Korne, G., Hebebrand, J. and Remschmidt, H. (1993) 'Cosegregation of balanced translocation (1;2) with retarded speech development and dyslexia.' *Lancet 342*, 178–179.

Goei, V.L., Choi, J., Bowlus, C.L., Raha-Chowdhury, R. *et al.* (1998) 'Human gamma- aminobutyric acid B receptor gene: complementary DNA cloning, expression, chromosomal location and genomic organisation.' *Biological Psychiatry 44*, 659–666.

Grigorenko, E.L., Wood, F.B., Meyer, M.S., Hart, L.A. *et al.* (1997) 'Susceptibility loci for distinct components of developmental dyslexia on chromosome 6 and 15.' *American Journal of Human Genetics 60*, 27–39.

Kaplan, B.J. and Crawford, S.G. (1994) 'The GBG model: Is there more to consider than handedness?' *Brain Cognitive 26*, 219–299.

Lovegrove, W., Martin, F. and Slaghuis, W. (1986) 'The theoretical and experimental case for a visual deficit in specific reading disability.' *Cognitive Neuropsychology 3*, 225–267.

Nicolson, R.I. and Fawcett, A.J. (1999) 'Developmental dyslexia: The role of the cerebellum.' *Dyslexia 5*, 155–177.

Rumsey, J.M., Nace, K., Donohue, B., Wise, D. *et al.* (1997) 'A positron emission tomographic study of impaired word recognition and phonological processing in dyslexic men.' *Archives of Neurology 54*, 562–573.

Sally, E. and Shaywitz, M.D. (1998) 'Dyslexia.' *The New England Journal of Medicine 338*, 307–312.

Shaywitz, B.A., Shaywitz, S.E., Pugh, K.R., Mencl, W.E. *et al.* (2002) 'Disruption of posterior brain system for reading in children with developmental dyslexia.' *Biological Psychiatry 52*, 101–110.

Sims, J. (1998) 'Making sence of dyslexia.' *Mensa Magazine*, June, 13–14.

Smith, S.D., Kimberling, W.J. and Pennington, B.F. (1991) 'Screening for multiple genes influencing dyslexia.' *Reading and Writing 3*, 285–298.

Stein, J.F. and Fowler, M.S. (1993) 'Unstable binocular control in children with specific reading retardation.' *Journal of Research in Reading 16*, 30–45.

West, T. (1991) *In the Mind's Eye*. London: Prometheus Books.

Chapter 12

Epilepsy

Frank M.C. Besag

INTRODUCTION

Some disorganized children may have major underlying brain problems that also predispose to epilepsy. In these cases, the epilepsy is neither a cause nor a consequence of the disorganized behaviour. Instead, both the epilepsy and the disorganized behaviour have a common source, namely the brain damage or dysfunction. However, in other cases, the epilepsy or factors relating specifically to the epilepsy may be responsible for the disorganized performance of the child. While there is no single causal relationship, there are many possible causes for disorganized behaviour or performance in a child with epilepsy.

As is the case for behavioural disturbance of any type in children with epilepsy, a systematic approach is needed (Besag 1995, 2002). The aim should be to find the cause or causes of the disorganized behaviour or performance in an individual child so that a carefully planned and appropriate management strategy can be adopted. Some of the causes of disorganized behaviour and performance in children with epilepsy may only affect the child for short periods of time, whereas others may continue for long periods or until a suitable intervention is made. Both the short-term and the long-term causes, as described in Box 12.1, will be discussed.

EPILEPSY ITSELF
Peri-ictal changes

Peri-ictal episodes may include prodrome, aura, automatism and post-ictal changes.

Prodrome is a period typically lasting a few minutes or hours, but sometimes lasting days, before a seizure or cluster of seizures occur. During this time mood, and consequently behaviour, is disturbed and, because of the mood disturbance, the child's activities may become seriously disorganized. Parents are often acutely

Box 12.1 Possible causes of disorganized behaviour and performance in a child with epilepsy

1. The epilepsy itself

(i) Peri-ictal changes

- Prodrome
- Aura
- Automatism
- Post-ictal changes
  - confusion
  - disinhibition
  - paranoid or affective states
  - post-ictal states resulting from nocturnal seizures
  - epileptiform activity

(ii) Inter-ictal psychoses

- Schizophreniform
- Affective

(iii) Focal discharges

- Temporal
- Frontal
- Hemispheric
- Other

(iv) Frequent generalized discharges/absence seizures

2. Treatment of the epilepsy

3. Reactions to the epilepsy

4. Associated brain damage/dysfunction

5. Causes equally applicable to children without epilepsy

aware of when their child is about to have a seizure because of these characteristic changes. The situation resolves when the seizure manifests, but there is some evidence that prodromal behavioural changes may sometimes occur without an ensuing seizure. Histories from parents of children who experience a marked prodrome confirm this concept. It happens when the changes that normally precede a seizure occur but, at the point at which the seizure would have started, the seizure threshold is too high, and the prodrome may then occur without the following seizure. This can lead to diagnostic confusion and parents, teachers and carers should be extremely aware of possible prodromes. To punish a child for prodromal mood or behaviour changes would prove unhelpful, and the situation should instead be managed with sensitivity and understanding, knowing that the prodromal changes will resolve when the seizure occurs.

Auras are simple partial seizures, implying that they take place in full consciousness. They occur as the result of very localized epileptiform discharges in the brain. The aura may mimic the function served by the part of the brain in which the abnormal discharge occurs, but this function may be distorted. For example, experiencing odd sensations, smelling an odour that is not there or having very unpleasant feelings in the abdomen or head are typical. Sometimes flashing lights are perceived and, rarely, fully formed visual hallucinations may occur. But, because only a relatively small part of the brain is involved, the child is fully conscious and may consequently find the experience very distressing. Taking a careful history from the child, asking specifically about odd perceptions, funny smells, flashing lights or strange feelings in any part of the body, may help both to determine the cause of the behaviour and provide the first step towards reassuring the child. Repeated auras may occur within a single day, proving very anxiety-provoking and leading to very disorganized behaviour. Unfortunately, anxiety further lowers seizure threshold, making more auras likely. Benzodiazepines remain the treatment of choice for multiple auras, given as required, not as an anxiolytic but as anti-epileptic medication.

Automatisms are actions that do not appear to arise from the will. Epilepsy-associated automatisms often occur in relation to complex partial seizures. Awareness is impaired during these seizures, and the person usually has no recollection of the action afterwards, although a considerable degree of consciousness may be retained. Typical automatisms include lip-licking, lip-smacking, swallowing, grasping, rubbing or climbing movements. A variety of other actions can occur which, given that they may appear highly disorganized, can easily be misinterpreted. They may also lead to teasing at school because the behaviours appear very peculiar to other children. Careful diagnosis, followed by explanation and education, are the key elements of management. The education should include the child, the family, friends, staff and other pupils at school. The apparently disorganized behaviours are likely to be very short-lived as automatisms usually last for only a few minutes. However, if the child is teased, this may affect already impaired behaviour through a lowering of self-esteem.

While *post-ictal changes* are very obvious in most cases, they may prove less apparent in a number of different situations. First, if a child regularly has several seizures a day, he or she may not have time to recover from one seizure before having another. The child therefore remains in a constant post-ictal state, and his or her disorganization and other poor cognitive or coping skills may be attributed to more permanent intellectual deficits. Instead, these are a direct result of the seizures and reducing the seizure frequency will allow the child to emerge from the constant post-ictal state and to perform to his or her true ability. Paranoid or mood states may occur as a form of post-ictal psychosis in adults and teenagers, and diagnostic confusion may occur because there is often a lucid interval between the seizures and the onset of the psychosis. Both schizophreniform and affective psychoses can result in gross disorganization. If the psychosis is mild and short-lived, treatment may not be necessary. However, in some cases, neuroleptic medication is required. The phenomena of post-ictal psychoses have been reviewed by Logsdail and Toone (1988).

The second situation in which post-ictal changes may not be obvious is the child who is having frequent nocturnal seizures. These can easily be missed by a casual observer. However, if the seizures are very frequent, they may have an adverse effect on the child's daytime performance, both through direct post-ictal effects and because of broken sleep. If a child has variable daytime performance, then consideration should be given to overnight electro-encephalogram (EEG) monitoring, preferably together with video recording, to exclude the possibility of frequent nocturnal seizures.

The third situation is a child who has electrical status epilepticus of slow wave sleep (ESES). The classical model is the Landau–Kleffner syndrome of acquired epileptic aphasia in which children lose the ability to understand speech. Sometimes visuo-spatial skills can be affected, leaving language skills intact, and some children may present with an autistic-like picture. These difficulties can lead to frustration and disorganized behaviour. Between a quarter and a third of these children do not have obvious seizures and, unless an overnight EEG is performed, the diagnosis of ESES may be missed. The importance of early treatment cannot be over-emphasized (Robinson *et al.* 2001).

Inter-ictal psychoses

Inter-ictal psychoses may be schizophreniform or affective (linked to mood). They bear no particular time relation to the seizures, and may commonly occur many years after the seizures have resolved (Slater and Beard 1963). In practice, they may occur in later teenage years or in adulthood. While a more accurate term for these mental disorders would possibly be 'post-epilepsy psychoses', the term 'inter-ictal psychosis' has become the accepted terminology for this condition. True inter-ictal psychoses, which occur between seizures but bear no obvious time relationship to them, can also occur in teenagers. Both schizophreniform and affective inter-ictal psychoses can result in gross disorganization and neuroleptic medication, such as risperidone or olanzapine, may be required for a period of time.

Focal discharges

Frequent temporal discharges can be associated with poor language function and feelings of anxiety, leading to frustration and aggressive behaviour. Such emotions can cause disorganized or even violent behaviour (van Elst *et al.* 2000). *Frequent frontal discharges* can also result in disinhibited behaviour and removing the source of the discharges surgically can significantly improve behaviour.

An extreme example of *other focal discharges* is provided by the child who has an abnormal hemisphere resulting in frequent epileptiform discharges. These children classically have epileptic seizures that are very resistant to medical treatment and often present with behavioural problems. Surgery, in carefully selected cases, may result in freedom from seizures and bring a marked improvement in behaviour, suggesting that the 'brain storm' of frequent epileptiform discharges were impinging on overall brain function (Goodman 1986). When the source of the discharges is removed, the child is transformed from someone who was disorganized and poorly behaved, with badly controlled seizures, to a seizure-free child who is well-behaved and able to organize their actions appropriately.

Another specific example of the association between disorganized behaviour and epilepsy is provided by the child with hypothalamic hamartoma (a rare benign brain tumour). The classical presentation is with gelastic or laughing seizures, precocious puberty, overactivity and an attention deficit disorder. Management of these children can present a considerable challenge, but it is interesting to note that the source of the epileptiform discharges appears to be the hamartoma itself rather than the effect of pressure on surrounding brain tissue. Surgical removal has been undertaken in some centres, transforming an overactive child into one who no longer presents with disorganized behaviour.

Frequent generalized discharges/absence seizures

Some children have not only hundreds but thousands of absence seizures daily (Besag 1994). These can fragment thought processes, resulting in major disorganization. The language produced by children in this state can also resemble the 'word salad' of schizophrenia. However, these children are not psychotic and the disorganized language is a result of the very frequent interruptions of brain function by epileptiform discharges. These children may present as being highly overactive, inattentive, distractible and excitable. This can mimic Attention Deficit Hyperactivity Disorder (ADHD) (Chapter 6). However, the first priority for treatment in these children is not stimulant medication but anti-epileptic medication.

Generalized or focal discharges can also lead to transitory cognitive impairment. Children who are not having obvious absence seizures, or obvious seizures of any type, may nevertheless have impaired performance because of frequent epileptiform discharges. If these occur in the dominant hemisphere, language function is liable to be affected and, if they occur in the non-dominant hemisphere, non-verbal skills are likely to be impaired (Aarts *et al.* 1984). While the cognitive impairment may be transitory, the resulting frustration may be longer-lasting. The child becomes aware that his or her thinking processes may be disorganized by the frequent discharges, and this frustration can lead to more enduring bad behaviour.

TREATMENT OF THE EPILEPSY

Some anti-epileptic drugs can result in very disruptive and disorganized behaviour, which can mimic ADHD. Phenobarbitone, benzodiazepines and vigabatrin can all cause this type of disturbance (de Silva *et al.* 1996; Besag 2001). The child is very disorganized, overactive, inattentive, distractible and excitable. The temptation may be to treat with stimulant medication whereas correct management is a review of the anti-epileptic medication, cautiously tailing off the drug that is causing the disorganized behaviour. If necessary, this can be implemented after the introduction of a better-tolerated anti-epileptic drug. Surgery is the other main form of anti-epileptic treatment and, while the outcome of surgery tends to be favourable in terms of behavioural measures, it can sometimes result in a worsening of behaviour rather than an improvement (Lendt *et al.* 2000).

Children and, in particular, teenagers generally like to be part of a group. Anything that singles the child out as being different may prove very disturbing for the individual. Children with epilepsy may therefore be teased or bullied at school, and then react with emotional or behavioural disturbance. The feeling of loss of control during seizures, and the unpredictability of the attacks, may make the situation even worse. Body-conscious teenagers may be very despondent about having seizures, especially if these are associated with incontinence in the presence of peers, and negative feelings may be profound. Teachers and other pupils may also have irrational fears about epilepsy, making life even more difficult for the child with the condition. Some of the attitudes of teachers, other pupils and parents of other pupils are well illustrated in the study by Pazzaglia and Frank-Pazzaglia (1976).

REACTIONS TO THE EPILEPSY

Reactions to the epilepsy are unlikely to lead to disorganized children but they can certainly result in disruptive behaviour. The child who is suddenly prevented from carrying out activities that have been part of daily life and greatly enjoyed, such as climbing trees or going swimming unsupervised, may respond by feeling very low in self-esteem. These emotions can affect the child in many different ways, including withdrawal or displays of aggressive behaviour.

ASSOCIATED BRAIN DAMAGE/DYSFUNCTION

In children for whom brain damage is a cause or a consequence of epilepsy, this brain damage can be a major cause of disorganized behaviour and performance. For example, prolonged seizures can cause permanent brain damage with many aspects of brain function being affected. In some cases, a single prolonged seizure can cause profound learning disability, overactivity and major behaviour problems. Frontal lobe damage can also result in overactivity, disinhibited and disorganized behaviour.

Other specific areas of brain damage/dysfunction can cause deficits resulting in disorganized behaviour, and the frustration and violent episodes that result from dominant hemisphere dysfunction have already been discussed. Epilepsy can also directly cause very fragmented thought processes. Some children with epilepsy may present with a picture of overactivity, inattentiveness, distractibility and excitability that is indistinguishable from ADHD and these children often respond to stimulant medication. This may represent an example of both the epilepsy and the disorganized behaviour resulting from underlying brain damage or dysfunction. It would be reasonable to surmise that any brain damage or dysfunction responsible for disorganized behaviour in children might lead to a higher risk of developing epilepsy. For example, children with frontal lobe damage or global cerebral damage are liable to exhibit disorganized behaviour and are also at greater risk of developing seizures (Airaksinen *et al.* 2000).

Studies of children with epilepsy attending specialist centres highlight that the two types of behaviour that are most prominent are autistic spectrum disorders and overactivity/attention deficit disorders. While some children with epilepsy and ADHD respond to stimulant medication, some do not and it might be tempting to suppose that those who do not respond are more likely to have epileptiform discharges. However, children who do have epileptiform discharges may nevertheless respond to stimulant medication, and dual therapy with anti-epileptic medication and stimulant medication may be required in order for children to perform at their optimal level. Epilepsy should therefore not be viewed as a contra-indication to the prescription of stimulant medication, although each case should be assessed carefully (Besag 2002). While methylphenidate might lower the seizure threshold in children who have an abnormal EEG, it probably does not precipitate seizures in others and will not precipitate seizures in those with well-controlled epilepsy (Gross-Tsur *et al.* 1997). It has even been suggested that dexamphetamine might have an anti-epileptic effect.

CAUSES EQUALLY APPLICABLE TO CHILDREN WITHOUT EPILEPSY

Epilepsy does not make the child immune from other causes of disorganized behaviour and performance, and the epilepsy may be purely coincidental. However, as described earlier, both the epilepsy and the disorganized behaviour are likely to result from a common underlying cause of brain damage/dysfunction.

MANAGEMENT OF THE DISORGANIZED CHILD WITH EPILEPSY

The first step in managing the disorganized child who has epilepsy is to carry out a careful assessment. It is essential to take a full history, which should cover aspects of development as well as the specific timing of any onset or worsening of disorganization. A full seizure history is also essential as it may be possible to link the occurrence of seizures and the presentation of disorganization in time. However, children with epilepsy may present with behavioural problems before the epilepsy becomes evident, suggesting that some subtle seizure activity may have been responsible in the early stages of the development of behavioural problems (Austin 2001). Assessment should also include a full physical examination, including a careful neurological examination.

Each child needs to be assessed individually, and detailed psychometric assessment can prove invaluable. This may reveal some of the specific deficits referred to earlier or identify a degree of frontal lobe dysfunction as a cause of the disorganized behaviour. EEG investigations are recommended and, in some cases, overnight monitoring may be necessary. Once the cause or causes of the disorganized behaviour have been identified, specific management strategies can be instituted. The programme of intervention should be determined not only by the organic cause of the disorganization but also by the individual characteristics and response of the child. Careful assessment of the disorganized child with epilepsy enables the development of specific management strategies that can transform the life of the child.

REFERENCES

Aarts, J.H., Binnie, C.D., Smit, A.M. and Wikins, A.J. (1984) 'Selective cognitive impairment during focal and generalized epileptiform EEG activity.' *Brain 107*, 293–308.

Airaksinen, E.M., Matilainen, R., Mononen, T., Mustonen, K. *et al.* (2000) 'A population-based study on epilepsy in mentally retarded children.' *Epilepsia 41*, 1214–1220.

Austin, J.K., Harezlak, J., Dunn, D.W., Huster, G.A. *et al.* (2001) 'Behavior problems in children before first recognized seizures.' *Pediatrics 107*, 115–122.

Besag, F.M.C. (1994) 'Lamotrigine in the management of subtle seizures.' *Reviews in Contemporary Pharmacotherapy 5*, 123–131.

Besag, F.M.C. (1995) 'Epilepsy, learning, and behavior in childhood.' *Epilepsia 36*, S58–S63.

Besag, F.M.C. (2001) 'Behavioural effects of the new anticonvulsants.' *Drug Safety 24*, 513–536.

Besag, F.M.C. (2002) 'Childhood epilepsy in relation to mental handicap and behavioural disorders.' *Journal of Child Psychology and Psychiatry and Allied Disciplines 43*, 103–131.

de Silva, M., MacArdle, B., McGowan, M. Hughes, E. *et al.* (1996) 'Randomised comparative monotherapy trial of phenobarbitone, phenytoin, carbamazepine, or sodium valproate for newly diagnosed childhood epilepsy.' *Lancet 347*, 709–713.

Goodman R. (1986) 'Hemispherectomy and its alternatives in the treatment of intractable epilepsy in patients with infantile hemiplegia.' *Developmental Medicine and Child Neurology 28*, 251–258.

Gross-Tsur, V., Manor, O., van der Meere, J., Joseph, A. *et al.* (1997) 'Epilepsy and attention deficit hyperactivity disorder: Is methylphenidate safe and effective?' *Journal of Pediatrics 130*, 670–674.

Lendt, M., Helmstaedter, C., Kuczaty, S., Schramm, J. *et al.* (2000) 'Behavioural disorders in children with epilepsy: Early improvement after surgery.' *Journal of Neurology, Neurosurgery and Psychiatry 69*, 739–744.

Logsdail, S.J. and Toone, B.K. (1988) 'Post-ictal psychoses. A clinical and phenomenological description.' *British Journal of Psychiatry 152*, 246–252.

Pazzaglia, P. and Frank-Pazzaglia, L. (1976) 'Record in grade school of pupils with epilepsy: An epidemiological study.' *Epilepsia 17*, 361–366.

Robinson, R.O., Baird, G., Robinson, G. and Simonoff, E. (2001) 'Landau–Kleffner syndrome: Course and correlates with outcome.' *Developmental Medicine and Child Neurology 43*, 243–247.

Slater, E. and Beard, A.W. (1963) 'The schizophrenia-like psychoses of epilepsy, V: Discussion and conclusions.' *Journal of Neuropsychiatry and Clinical Neurosciences 7*, 372–378.

van Elst, L.T., Woermann, F.G., Lemieux, L., Thompson, P.J. *et al.* (2000) 'Affective aggression in patients with temporal lobe epilepsy: A quantitative MRI study of the amygdala.' *Brain 123*, 234–243.

Chapter 13

Minimal brain dysfunction

Samuel M. Stein

INTRODUCTION

The concept of 'minimal brain damage' was introduced in the 1940s based on the observation that behavioural disorders seemed to occur more frequently in children with mild cerebral dysfunction. It suggested that minor, even clinically undetectable, degrees of brain damage could serve as a non-specific cause of disturbed behaviour. The term Minimal Brain Damage/Dysfunction therefore came to denote a separate and specific clinical syndrome. This was conceptualized as a combination of problems relating to attention, activity regulation, impulse control, motor control, learning problems, perceptual abnormalities and speech and language difficulties (Clements 1966).

Minimal brain dysfunction was perceived as a psycho-physiological disorder, with the diagnosis being triggered by an accumulation of various symptoms. The presentation was viewed as having multiple potential causes, and clinical profiles were developed for individual patients by collating their specific symptoms. An understanding of this multi-dimensional spectrum of aetiologies and symptoms was seen as important for the implementation of treatment plans. However, while the diagnosis of minimal brain dysfunction carried with it implications for treatment, the prognosis was not entirely benign as the presentation overlapped with other more serious childhood conditions such as learning disorders and hyperkinetic syndromes.

As a result of these developments, a growing number of children were labelled as having minimal brain dysfunction. The attraction may have lain in the way it shifted responsibility for child and adolescent disturbance from family or school to innate constitutional factors, and it also served a practical usefulness in the communication of symptoms and presentations between different disciplines (Rutter and Hersov 1985). However, although the use of this concept became widespread, it engendered an increasingly critical reaction in the 1980s, after which the term fell from favour and was gradually discarded.

HISTORICAL PERSPECTIVE

Although concerns about neurological deficits and subsequent behaviour patterns had featured in the professional literature for many years, the concept of 'minimal brain damage or dysfunction' was first put forward by Strauss and Lehtinen in 1947. Strauss, a paediatric neurologist, described a constellation of clinical features including overactivity, inattention and conduct disorder, along with perceptual and learning problems not otherwise explained by intellectual deficit in brain-damaged children (Rutter and Hersov 1985). This term gained widespread support between 1940 and 1960, and was almost universally employed in child psychiatry and developmental paediatrics from the 1950s onward.

However, in the 1970s and 1980s, there was a move to divide such overarching concepts into individual and more accurately described units comprising specific groups of symptoms. This led to widespread changes in the perception of minimal brain dysfunction and its use in clinical practice. Instead, evidence-based mental health conditions such as ADHD have since superseded these early, but less precise, attempts to understand children with behavioural problems and possible neuro-developmental deficits.

THEORETICAL BACKGROUND

The theory of minimal brain dysfunction suggested that sub-clinical damage to the brain could lead to psychological symptoms. This was supported by observations that minor or 'soft' neurological signs, as well as non-specific EEG changes, were found more often in children with learning and behaviour problems than in control groups (Rutter and Hersov 1985). It was also noted that individuals who experienced perinatal brain hypoxia constituted a population at risk for minimal brain dysfunction, and that children attending psychiatric clinics often presented with illnesses or perinatal complications of a sort known to be associated with neurological brain damage (Handford 1975). Similar behavioural observations were made by Ounsted (1955) among children with temporal lobe epilepsy, by Ingram (1956) in a group of children with cerebral palsy and by Laufer and Denhoff (1957) among children with a variety of neurological problems (Rutter and Hersov 1985).

While minimal brain dysfunction was seen as a possible consequence of perinatal or illness-related damage to the nervous system, the actual aetiology and pathology remained uncertain (Leary 1976). However, child health professionals continued to believe that such brain injury could be inferred from the presence of certain behaviours and symptoms even in the absence of corroborating neurological evidence (Rutter and Hersov 1985). These neurologically based dysfunctions were held responsible for anxiety, social withdrawal, hyperactivity, disruption of drive levels, distorted perception, problems with basic language structure and patchy cognition. Minimal brain dysfunction was also considered as a constitutional cause of distorted early object relations and impaired attachment, although social and environmental factors were considered to play an important role too.

The inability to demonstrate overt neurological damage in minimal brain dysfunction was attributed to the nature of the underlying pathology, and also to the limited ways available to measure such changes or problems (Rutter and Hersov 1985). However, subsequent research has shown that hyperactivity and inattention may occur in the absence of neurological dysfunction, and that they do not necessarily occur in its presence. Hyperactivity and inattention have also not been shown as systematically associated with neurological soft signs, and an epidemiological survey by Rutter and colleagues did not identify any relationship between brain injury and specific psychiatric conditions. They felt that imprecise terminologies such as 'minimal' or 'dysfunction' conveyed too simplistic a notion of the extremely complex nature of both brain function and the determinants of behaviour (Rutter and Hersov 1985). At best, minimal brain dysfunction may now be considered as a diffuse cerebral dysregulation which, due to delays in neurological maturation, may impact on the connections between different regions of the central nervous system.

EPIDEMIOLOGY AND PREVALENCE

It has been suggested that minimal brain dysfunction can be found in 2 to 20 per cent of school-aged children (Leary 1976; Levy 1976). Other studies have highlighted a higher prevalence of minimal brain dysfunction in rural areas, and lower rates in the families of scientific/technical professionals and those with higher education. Minimal brain dysfunction was more common in boys (16%) than in girls (12%). Prematurely delivered children were also shown to exhibit a higher frequency of minimal brain dysfunction (20%), with children born in breach presentations being affected too (14%) (Fianu and Joelsson 1979).

Children suffering from minimal brain dysfunction were found to improve as they grew older. However, although free of psychiatric disorder, 80 per cent had various types of personality disorder and 14 per cent were borderline psychotic. Global measures of outcome were also unsatisfactory in 80 per cent, especially when associated with impaired intelligence, behavioural problems, neuro-psychological findings, learning disability, special educational placement and initial classification of an organic brain syndrome (Milman 1979).

CLINICAL PRESENTATION

Minimal brain dysfunction was characterized by neuro-developmental immaturity. It was invariably identified during attendance at school, although the way in which it presented and the timing of the symptoms often varied considerably. However, the core features all related to behavioural and educational deficits (Levy 1976).

From a behavioural perspective, children with minimal brain dysfunction often presented with a history of uncontrollable rage, dating from early childhood, occurring with little or no provocation. Other presenting features included hyperactivity, problems with fine motor coordination, learning disabilities and soft neurological signs (Leary 1976). Children labelled with minimal brain dysfunction also struggled to understand emotional clues and demonstrated high levels of arousal, especially within very stimulating environments. In addition, these children presented clinically as less adaptable, less persistent and more negative than control populations (Carey, McDevitt and Baker 1979).

From an educational perspective, children with minimal brain dysfunction often presented with difficulties in remembering, an inability to maintain attention, poor concentration and a susceptibility to fatigue even when motivated to perform well. Their specific learning disability involved the communicating skills needed in reading, writing and mathematics. However, they also struggled with planning, with orienting themselves in space, with visual–spatial tasks, with complex perceptual motor activities, with auditory discrimination and with an inability to skilfully blend the auditory and visual functions essential in language performance (Levy 1976). In particular, boys with minimal brain dysfunction scored lower on psychometric testing, especially in regard to information processing. They were also off task more frequently, and for a longer duration. As a result, their academic progress was poorer than expected relative to their perceived abilities, with a greater risk of being in trouble at school.

The symptoms of minimal brain dysfunction proved less conspicuous as children grew older and matured, and the condition proved difficult to recognize during adolescence. As expected in other young people, these adolescents also presented with lowered self-esteem, feelings of powerless, persecutory ideas, identity issues, a desire for autonomy, authority problems and a higher frequency of delinquent behaviour. This raised doubt about the advisability of diagnosing minimal brain dysfunction on the basis of adolescent behaviour alone, especially as the symptoms could also be reflective of interactions within their social environment. An overlap with difficult temperament was instead suggested, with outcome often being determined by the importance of the disorder, the environment, intelligence, tolerance of relatives, peer relationships and other significant items of personal history.

CO-MORBIDITY

Minimal brain dysfunction, which itself served as an overarching condition, did not lend itself to co-morbid diagnoses. However, overlaps were recognized with motor control dysfunction, psychiatric problems, developmental incoordination, episodic dyscontrol, speech/language dysfunction and reading/writing disorders. Complex partial seizures also occurred in 34 per cent of patients with minimal brain dysfunction, although the seizures were often not recognized as epileptic because of their subtle form and rare occurrence. In addition, minimal brain dysfunction predisposed sufferers to becoming problem drinkers, and clinical experience showed that many patients diagnosed as having a borderline personality structure had a history of minimal brain dysfunction as children.

ASSESSMENT

The symptoms of minimal brain dysfunction were often far from obvious, and were unlikely to be uncovered by a superficial medical history or neurological examination. Even traditional psychological examinations failed to indicate organic deficits. However, more specialized neuro-psychological evaluation produced evidence suggestive of subtle cerebral dysfunction. Medical evaluation therefore had a role in revealing neurological soft signs, with working procedures for treating and assisting affected children. Educational appraisal frequently indicated a wide scatter in testing scores, with a marked discrepancy between evaluated potential and actual classroom achievement (Levy 1976). As no specific screening method for the early diagnosis of minimal brain dysfunction was developed, its identification in both children and adults remained subject to the limitations of traditional assessment health and education strategies.

TREATMENT

As with all neuro-developmental diagnoses, minimal brain dysfunction benefited from preventative measures, early intervention, multi-disciplinary treatment approaches and sustained follow-up. Therapists therefore needed to act as a scientific source of guidance on the plethora of therapies directed towards the child with learning disorders. These included family work, counselling, remedial education, psychotherapy and medication.

Skilled classroom teaching was the mainstay of successful management, with specific approaches developed for educating children with minimal brain dysfunction (Leary 1976). These remedial efforts provided both early detection and generic advice about educational resources. It also led to adjustment of the children's educational environment with due consideration of their individual talents and weaknesses. This provided relief from academic pressures, as well as from unjust punishment by teachers and ridicule from peers (Levy 1976). The psychotherapeutic influencing of parents with regard to their child with minimal brain dysfunction was essential, and parents were counselled regarding the development and maintenance of adverse family interactions. These programmes did much to prevent children and adolescents from developing severe personality maladjustment, delinquent behaviour and emotional illness in later life (Levy 1976).

The judicious use of medication to prolong attention span and improve neuro-developmental maturity was supported in the treatment of minimal brain dysfunction, with CNS stimulants being the agent of choice (Levy 1976). Small amounts of methylphenidate appeared to have a salutary effect on symptoms such as irritability, moodiness, restlessness and poor concentration (Packer 1978). Both methylphenidate and dextroamphetamine were significantly better than placebo, but not significantly different from each other (Arnold *et al.* 1978). Children with minimal brain dysfunction who received stimulant medication for four weeks showed improved handwriting, improved behaviour and enhanced fine motor coordination (Lerer, Lerer and Artner 1977). Both pemoline and methylphenidate, when compared with a placebo, produced improvements in children with minimal brain dysfunction. The effects of pemoline persisted both at home and school, whereas patients receiving methylphenidate tended to regress to their baseline levels sooner (Conners and Taylor 1980). However, a comparison of sustained release versus standard methylphenidate in the treatment of minimal brain dysfunction showed no consistent significant changes, nor were there significant improvements over pre-treatment measures for either group (Whitehouse, Shah and Palmer 1980). Anti-depressant, anti-convulsant, anti-anxiety and anti-psychotic agents were also all found to be less desirable than CNS stimulants for treatment since they did little to decrease distractibility or increase attention span.

MINIMAL BRAIN DYSFUNCTION IN LATER LIFE
Minimal brain dysfunction was initially considered as a disorder limited to childhood. However, a number of longitudinal and adoption studies suggested that the presentation could persist into adult life. This version of minimal brain dysfunction in adults was thought to exist either alone or in combination with a variety of other psychiatric syndromes. Unfortunately, the underlying neuro-developmental pathology was often concealed by the application of different diagnostic labels. Adults who had minimal brain dysfunction as children were therefore felt to constitute a distinct diagnostic entity.

CONCLUSION

Contemporary diagnostic systems are focused on particular functions which are either reduced or impaired by a disorder. Recent analysis of both ICD (World Health Organization 1992) and DSM (American Psychiatric Association 1994) classifications showed an increasing specification with regard to the various clinical entities which were previously included in the overarching complex of minimal brain dysfunction. There was also evidence of common symptoms which overlapped with other conditions which present with impaired activities and behaviour during childhood based on probable damage of the central nervous system. Minimal brain dysfunction should therefore not be used as a psychiatric diagnosis as these problems are better seen as a non-specific vulnerability to disorder, which reflects immaturity rather than pathology, instead of being considered as a separate and pathognomonic symptoms pattern (Rutter and Hersov 1985).

REFERENCES

American Psychiatric Association (1994) *Diagnostic and Statistical Manual of Mental Disorders*, 4th edn (DSM-IV). Washington, DC: American Psychiatric Association.

Arnold, L.E., Christopher, J., Huestis, R. and Smeltzer, D.J. (1978) 'Methylphenidate vs dextroamphetamine vs caffiene in minimal brain dysfunction.' *Archives of General Psychiatry 35*, 463–473.

Carey, W.B., McDevitt, S.C. and Baker, D. (1979) 'Differentiating minimal brain dysfunction and temperament.' *Developmental Medicine and Child Neurology 21*, 765–772.

Clements, S.D. (1966) 'Minimal brain dysfunction in children: Terminology and identification.' *Monograph 3*, NINDB.

Conners, C.K. and Taylor, E. (1980) 'Pemoline, methylphenidate and placebo in children with minimal brain dysfunction.' *Archives of General Psychiatry 37*, 922–930.

Fianu, S. and Joelsson, I. (1979) 'Minimal brain dysfunction in children born in breech presentation.' *Acta Obstetricia et Gynecologica Scandanavica 58*, 295–299.

Handford, H.A. (1975) 'Brain hypoxia, minimal brain dysfunction and schizophrenia.' *American Journal of Psychiatry 132*, 192–194.

Leary, P.M. (1976) 'Minimal brain dysfunction' *South African Medical Journal 50*, 784–786.

Lerer, R.J., Lerer, M.P. and Artner, J. (1977) 'The effects of methylphenidate on the handwriting of children with minimal brain dysfunction.' *Journal of Pediatrics 91*, 127–132.

Levy, H.B. (1976) 'Minimal brain dysfunction/specific learning disability: A clinical approach for the primary physician.' *Southern Medical Journal 69*, 642–653.

Milman, D.H. (1979) 'Minimal brain dysfunction in childhood: outcome in late adolescence and early adult years.' *Journal of Clinical Psychiatry 40*, 371–380.

Packer, S. (1978) 'Treatment of minimal brain dysfunction in a young adult.' *Canadian Psychiatric Association Journal 23*, 501–502.

Rutter, M. and Hersov, L. (1985) *Child and Adolescent Psychiatry: Modern Approaches*, 2nd edn. Oxford: Blackwell Scientific Publications.

Whitehouse, D., Shah, U. and Palmer, F.B. (1980) 'Comparison of sustained release and standard methylphenidate in the treatment of minimal brain dysfunction.' *Journal of Clinical Psychiatry 41*, 282–285.

World Health Organization (1992) *International Statistical Classification of Diseases and Related Health Problems*, 10th revision (ICD-10). Geneva: World Health Organization.

Chapter 14

Obsessive compulsive disorder

Uttom Chowdhury and Samuel M. Stein

INTRODUCTION

Obsessive Compulsive Disorder (OCD) is a distinctive and frequently disabling condition characterized by unwanted thoughts or images (obsessions) and unwanted repetitive acts and rituals (compulsions). While many children may present with mild obsessions and compulsions at some time, this is entirely normal, especially in the face of anxiety or stress. However, a diagnosis of OCD needs to be considered when the obsessions and compulsions cause severe discomfort and distress to the child, and interefere with academic functioning, social activities and relationships. Unfortunately, although OCD is a common problem, many people with OCD symptoms are reluctant to seek help or share their concerns for fear of being ridiculed or stigmatized.

It used to be thought that OCD was a condition that affected adults only. However, studies over the last 15 years have shown that the condition is prevalent in children too, although it is still debatable as to whether OCD in childhood is exactly the same condition as that in adulthood. They are similar in that both age groups share roughly the same clinical phenotype (or characteristics) and both respond to the same pharmacological interventions. In terms of differences, childhood OCD has a unique age of onset and a distinct pattern of co-morbidity with Attention Deficit Hyperactivity Disorder (ADHD) (Chapter 6) and Tic Disorders (Chapter 18).

CLINICAL FEATURES

Obsessions and compulsions are not simply excessive worries about real-life problems. OCD symptoms fall into four main groups: checking and ruminations; symmetry and ordering; fear of contamination; and hoarding.

Common obsessions include worries about germs and illness, concerns that something bad will happen to a member of the family, aggressive images or preoccupation with one's own body. Obsessions may also relate to food, and can lead to irregular and unusual eating habits. It is important to note that obsessive thoughts may vary with the age of the child, and may also change over time. These unwanted thoughts or images are recognized as unrealistic, and children with OCD symptoms are often aware that their thinking is different to that of their friends and family. This may result in them feeling silly, ashamed or embarrassed. As a result, people with OCD try hard to stop themselves from thinking about or doing these things, but then feel frustrated and anxious unless they can finish them. Children and adolescents with OCD are usually able to see that these thoughts are irrational, and that they arise from within their own minds. This distinguishes obsessions from delusions (see Chapter 17), although it can prove difficult for younger children to conceptualize the difference. Compulsions (unwanted repetitive acts and rituals) include excessive washing, checking, counting and repeating things.

In order to meet criteria for a clinical diagnosis, there needs to be some degree of impairment in terms of time consumed with OCD symptoms, and distress or interference in daily functioning. In other words, do the obsessions and compulsions seriously affect the child, and do they interfere with the child's everyday life? OCD symptoms may take up a great deal of time and energy, making it difficult to complete everyday tasks such as homework. Children may feel a need to undertake their rituals exactly right each morning, or stay up late into the night because of unwanted thoughts and images. As a result of their symptoms, children with OCD often feel anxious, pressured and stressed. They may also present as irritable, with angry outbursts, especially when their parents are unwilling to comply with OCD-related demands.

As well as impacting on families, OCD affects young people at school. Friendships and peer relationships may prove very stressful for those with OCD because they often try to conceal their thinking and rituals from peers. Even where OCD symptoms are not severe, friendships can be adversely affected by the amount of time the child or adolescent spends preoccupied with his or her obsessions and compulsions. Self-esteem can be negatively affected, and children with OCD are particularly prone to stress-related illnesses such as headaches or stomach upsets.

EPIDEMIOLOGY AND PREVALENCE

In a population study looking at 10,000 healthy children, Heyman *et al.* (2001) identified 25 children with a formal diagnosis of OCD. However, other studies have found prevalences ranging from 0.06 per cent to 4 per cent. Recent research has shown that childhood OCD is associated with a unique bimodal age of onset with peaks at 10 and 21 years of age (Geller *et al.* 1998). In the early-onset age group, there is a male preponderance and a distinct pattern of co-morbidity with other neuro-developmental disorders. Evidence is therefore emerging that the OCD which begins in childhood may be different from the OCD that begins in adulthood.

AETIOLOGY

OCD was once thought of as a psychological disorder based on unconscious defence mechanisms. However recent genetic, immunological and brain imaging studies indicate growing evidence of central nervous system dysfunction (Rosenberg and Hanna 2000). Structural neuro-imaging studies show increased size of the basal ganglia structures in the brain, and regional cerebral blood flow studies demonstrate increased metabolic activity in both the pre-frontal cortex and the basal ganglia.

There is little doubt that OCD runs in families, with strong familial associations of up to four times the rate of OCD in relatives of patients. If one parent has OCD, the likelihood that a child will be affected is about 2–8 per cent. Individuals with childhood-onset OCD also appear more likely to have blood relatives that are affected with the disorder than those whose OCD appears in adulthood. In addition, tic disorders and OCD may cluster in the same families, suggesting that these disorders may sometimes reflect the same underlying genes.

However, genes are only partly responsible for causing the disorder. There is also an ethological suggestion that compulsions are fixed action patterns related to grooming and cleaning that are not suppressed by 'higher centres' in the brain. Once initiated, the rituals persist because of their anxiety-reducing effect. It is interesting to note that animals, for example cats, can suffer from OCD symptoms such as excessive grooming which result in 'bald patches' on their skin. Some studies have shown that pets may show an improvement in their symptoms when given similar medication to those used in humans with OCD.

ASSESSMENT

There are a number of international guidelines and protocols which highlight evidence-based practice in relation to the assessment and management of children with OCD. These include the American Academy of Child and Adolescent Psychiatry's practice parameters for the assessment and treatment of children and adolescents with obsessive compulsive disorder (1998) and a practioner review by Rapoport and Inoff-Germain (2000).

It should be remembered that young children go through a developmental phase which includes behavioural rituals between the ages of 2 and 6 years. These childhood rituals differ from OCD in that they are not associated with obsessional thoughts and they are easily circumvented by distraction. They are also unlikely to be pervasive, and anger rather than anxiety usually results when obsessive or compulsive responses are thwarted.

As well as detailed questioning about symptoms of OCD, clinicians should recognize and ask about co-morbid conditions that occur with OCD, such as tic disorders and depression. The prevalence of co-morbid mood disorders ranges from 20 per cent to 73 per cent (Geller *et al.* 1990; Flament, Koby and Rapoport 1990). Other psychiatric conditions that may frequently occur along with OCD include anxiety disorders, ADHD, learning difficulties, trichotillomania (hair pulling) and body dysmorphic disorder.

It is also good practice to use established rating scales to assess the presence and severity of OCD symptoms. These include the children's version of the Yale Brown Obsessive Compulsive Disorder Scale (Scahill *et al.* 1997) and the children's version of the Leyton Obsessional Inventory (Berg, Rapoport and Flament 1986). Not only do these questionnaires provide a measure of severity, but they can also act as a baseline from which to monitor progress should treatment commence.

DIFFERENTIAL DIAGNOSIS

- Normal childhood rituals
- Undifferentiated emotional disorders
- Rituals occuring in autistic spectrum disorders
- Tourette syndrome
- Depression
- Anorexia Nervosa
- Schizophrenia/psychosis.

INTERVENTION
Psycho-education

This is an important part of the treatment offered, as families need to learn about OCD and about how to help their child combat it. The more that children and their families know about OCD, the more they are likely to feel in control of the presenting problems. Hence a brief explanation of the biological basis for OCD is valuable. This helps to stop the child being labelled as 'naughty' by parents or teachers. In some cases, the child and family are sufficiently reassured within the first session by a full explanation of OCD and require no further intervention.

Family interventions

Children develop within the context of a family, and any OCD treatment packages should reflect this. Family members often get caught up in the rituals and routines surrounding OCD, and may inadvertently contribute to the maintenance of symptoms (Waters, Barrett and Marsh 2001). Family-focused interventions concentrating on psycho-social factors are therefore likely to be more effective and durable than interventions that target the identified child only. It has also been shown that high levels of hostility and criticism are associated with poor treatment outcome and relapse in adults (Chambless and Steketee 1999).

Another reason for involving the family is that rates of OCD in family members is higher than within the general population. Helpful interventions for the symptomatic individual may therefore have secondary benefits for other potentially vulnerable members of the family. Family interventions include: exploring the effect of OCD on the family, improving coping strategies, improving communication skills, psycho-education, reducing parental involvement in the symptoms and increasing positive family interactions. The family is also encouraged to become part of the 'expert team' that helps the child to fight OCD, and this can prove to be a useful source of support away from the clinic.

Individual work with children and adolescents

Many children with OCD will respond positively to behavioural or cognitive therapy, and the aim of treatment is to teach young people how to be in control of their problem. Children and young people therefore need to be actively involved in the design, planning and implementation of any treatment approaches.

A good example of individual work with a child is described in protocols developed by March and Mulle in their book *OCD in Children and Adolescents: A Cognitive-Behavioural Treatment Manual* (1998). Their techniques for individual work include:

- externalization of OCD (seeing OCD as separate from the child, thus avoiding any blame)

- development of cognitive tactics and coping strategies (a cognitive 'toolkit') to assist with exposure–response prevention

- increasing self-efficacy

- generating a hierarchy of obsessions and compulsions which need to be tackled

- use of exposure–response prevention on targets chosen by the child, usually with some support from parents.

Medication

Medication may help at least 70 per cent of people with OCD to get better. Unfortunately, many of the people who improve on medication may become unwell again when the treatment is stopped. The aim is therefore to use the smallest amount of medication necessary for controlling the OCD symptoms effectively. Selective serotonin re-uptake inhibitors (SSRIs) such as sertraline (recently licensed for use in children with OCD) and fluoxetine are the drugs of first choice. However, it is important to discuss potential side-effects that may occur with the child and the family so that they do not lose trust in the use of medication should these occur.

Liaison with schools and other services

OCD can often have an adverse impact on the child's functioning in the class-room and with homework. For instance, children with checking rituals will often re-read a line in a textbook several times until it is 'just right', or they may need to perform a counting ritual in the classroom before they can sit down. If the child's education is being affected, it may be helpful, with the agreement of both the child and the parents, to talk to the teacher and give a brief explanation of the possible difficulties. Writing letters to examining boards, again with child and parent consent, asking for the child's condition to be taken into account during examinations, can also prove very helpful.

These interventions will help to prevent the child from being unfairly treated by either teachers or peers, especially as children with OCD are extremely vulnerable to being bullied. If there is associated depression, then the consequences of such victimization may prove devastating for the child. Addressing these issues with teachers, and ensuring that schools implement their anti-bullying policies, are essential as teachers and other educationalists can prove particularly helpful in successfully integrating young people with OCD into life at school or college.

Support groups for children

Support groups for children with OCD may be a valuable way of increasing awareness and education on all aspects of OCD. It can also provide much needed psycho-social support to the often-isolated individual and his or her family. Given the level of support that is often needed for the child and family, it is also useful to provide details of voluntary organizations such as OCD Action, a UK national charity which provides information and support for families suffering from OCD (see the Useful information section).

Evidence-base

The clinical evidence-base in relation to cognitive-behavioural therapy (CBT) and medication in children is small. At present, the majority of clinical practice seems to rest on extrapolations from adult research which supports work based on exposure and response prevention (Hollander 1997).

Case example: Rachel

Rachel, a 14-year-old schoolgirl, became worried about germs after seeing a news programme on infected meat in the food industry. She slowly became more and more preoccupied with the thought that she would catch 'mad cow disease' because she had eaten hamburgers in her childhood. Rachel subsequently refused to eat meat products and became a vegetarian. Her family accepted this, initially thinking that it was a 'fad' which she was going through. However, she soon started insisting on preparing all of her own food and would wash any vegetables and fruit several times before eating. She also refused to eat any other prepared food in case this was already infected.

Prior to eating, Rachel would wash her hands several times but would never dry them on a towel. Her hands became red and sore, which led her to believe that she was more likely to pick up germs. This, in turn, caused her greater anxiety. At this stage, Rachel was also struggling in school since she was often tired. She refused to enter the science building because it contained chemicals, and she feared that she might inadvertently come into contact with them. At first, her school was accommodating and allowed her to miss science lessons. Unfortunately, she then started missing other lessons and spending increasing amounts of time on her own in the library.

Rachel's social life suffered as she withdrew from her friends. She was petrified of accidentally touching one of them, and picking up a new strain of virus or bacteria. Rachel also started seeking reassurance from her parents that she was going to be 'OK' in spite of what she might have eaten. In addition, she developed a number of counting and touching rituals, which she believed would prevent her from catching any illnesses. If she did not act out these rituals, then Rachel would become extremely anxious. Eventually, she was referred by her GP to the local Child and Adolescent Mental Health Clinic.

A child psychiatrist and a clinical psychologist assessed Rachel and a diagnosis of OCD was confirmed. Her symptoms were so severe and worrying that the clinicians initially suggested starting medication immediately. However, because of her fears of germs, Rachel was convinced that the tablets would cause her more harm than good. The clinical psychologist therefore started individual cognitive-behavioural therapy (CBT) with her. A list of rituals which needed to be tackled was drawn up, and Rachel was encouraged to try to resist the least worrying ritual first. However, after four weeks, her condition had deteriorated to the extent that she was beginning to refuse food altogether. It was suggested that, if there was no improvement within the next few days, then Rachel would need to be admitted to hospital.

This achieved a significant change in her symptoms as Rachel's determination that she was not going into hospital was partly driven by the anxiety that she would catch more germs there. Instead, she reluctantly accepted sertraline medication and also became more active in her own CBT programme. After a month, it was noticeable that Rachel was more relaxed than previously and her rating scale scores (Y-BOCS) (Goodman *et al.* 1989) had come down. She was still experiencing severe problems with obsessional thoughts but the rituals, such as handwashing, had begun to decrease in frequency and intensity. After six months of medication and once-weekly CBT, Rachel was back in full-time education and had challenged most of her beliefs regarding germs. She was enjoying socializing again, and could remain in the science lessons although there was some slight, but not troublesome, discomfort. She remained a vegetarian, but her OCD symptoms were markedly diminished.

REFERENCES

American Academy of Child and Adolescent Psychiatry (1998) 'Practice parameters for the assessment and treatment of children and adolescents with obsessive-compulsive disorder.' *Journal of the American Academy of Child and Adolescent Psychiatry 37* (Supplement 10), 27S–45S.

Berg, C.J., Rapoport, J.L. and Flament, M. (1986) 'The Leyton Obsessionality Inventory – Child Version.' *Journal of the American Academy of Child and Adolescent Psychiatry 25*, 84–91.

Chambless, D.L. and Steketee, G. (1999) 'Expressed emotion and behaviour therapy outcome: A prospective study with obsessive-compulsive and agoraphobic patients.' *Journal of Consulting and Clinical Psychology 67*, 658–665.

Flament, M.F., Koby, E. and Rapoport, J. (1990) 'Childhood Obsessive Compulsive Disorder – a prospective follow up study.' *Journal of Child Psychology and Psychiatry 31*, 363–380.

Geller, D., Biederman, J., Griffin, S., Jones, J. *et al.* (1990) 'Co-morbidity of obsessive compulsive disorders with disruptive behaviour disorders.' *Journal of the American Academy of Child and Adolescent Psychiatry 35*, 1637–1646.

Geller, D., Biederman, J., Jones, J., Park, K. *et al.* (1998) 'Is juvenile OCD a developmental subtype of the disorder? A review of the paediatric literature.' *Journal of the American Academy of Child and Adolescent Psychiatry 37*, 420–427.

Goodman, W.K., Price, L.H., Rasmussen, S.A., Mazure, C. *et al.* (1989) 'The Yale-Brown Obsessive Compulsive Scale.' *Archives of General Psychiatry 46*, 1006–1011.

Heyman, I., Fombonne, E., Simmons, H., Meltzer, H. *et al.* (2001) 'Prevalence of obsessive compulsive disorder in the British nationwide survey of child mental health.' *British Journal of Psychiatry 179*, 324–329.

Hollander, E. (1997) 'Obsessive compulsive disorder: The hidden epidemic.' *Journal of Clinical Psychiatry 58* (Supplement 12), 3–6.

March, J.S. and Mulle, K. (1998) *OCD in Children and Adolescents: A Cognitive-Behavioural Treatment Manual.* New York: Guildford Press.

Rapoport, J.L. and Inoff-Germain, G. (2000) 'Practitioner review: Treatment of obsessive compulsive disorder in children and adolescents.' *Journal of Child Psychology and Psychiatry 41*, 419–431.

Rosenberg, D.R. and Hanna, G.L. (2000) 'Genetic and Imaging strategies in obsessive-compulsive disorder: Potential implications for treatment development.' *Biological Psychiatry 48*, 1210–1222.

Scahill, L., Riddle, M.A., McSwiggin-Hardin, M., Ort, S.I. *et al.* (1997) 'Children's Yale–Brown Obsessive Compulsive Scale: Reliability and validity.' *Journal of the American Academy of Child and Adolescent Psychiatry 36*, 844–852.

Waters, T.L., Barrett, P.M. and Marsh, J.S. (2001) 'Cognitive-behavioural family treatment of childhood obsessive-compulsive disorder.' *American Journal of Psychotherapy 55*, 372–387.

Chapter 15

Obstetric complications and neuro-developmental problems

Alison Mantell

INTRODUCTION

Most pregnancies are completed uneventfully, producing a healthy infant at around 40 weeks of gestation. This process is strongly canalized and pre-determined, and there are clear genetic instructions according to which the fertilized egg differentiates first into an embryo and then into a foetus. The way in which this pattern unfolds is broadly similar for every developing human being.

Problems may arise at any stage of a pregnancy (which is classically divided into three equal trimesters) or during labour. These difficulties may be due to acute or chronic illness in the mother, due to a predisposition to problems within the developing foetus or due to external causes such as infection. Environmental hazards, particularly teratogens (which may include prescription medication, illicit drugs, exposure to chemicals or radiation) are especially harmful during the embryonic period. However, the foetal brain is vulnerable to many different forms of insult at different stages of development.

This chapter will outline some common obstetric complications and the impact which these problems may have on the developing foetus. Possible neurological sequelae will also be discussed, with consideration of the clinical problems that may later develop in childhood. Neuro-developmental problems associated with genetic causes will not be considered as these have already been discussed in Chapter 8. However, it is important to keep in mind that such congenital problems may predispose the foetus to a difficult third trimester and complications during labour.

WHY IS OBSTETRIC HISTORY SO IMPORTANT?

Thorough examination of an infant or child should always include some form of enquiry into their pregnancy and delivery, as well as the birth of any siblings. This may offer clues as to the presence, and perhaps even the nature, of possible neuro-developmental problems. The information may prove equally important in simply excluding difficulties which would otherwise need to be seriously considered. Parents may not offer these details spontaneously, and may inadvertently omit details. For example, the changes of behaviour observed in children following minor head injuries are more often due to parental perceptions than due to acquired minimal brain damage. There may also be significant variation in the amount of information and detail elicited or provided depending upon the age of the child and the difficulties with which he or she is presenting.

An account of conception, and any difficulties experienced, may provide essential information. The presence of acute or long-standing maternal illness, substance misuse, prescribed medication and dietary habits during pregnancy should be elicited. It is important to explore these details in terms of both the period of pregnancy and length of time. Other relevant information will include exposure to radiation, contact with toxins and vaginal bleeding during pregnancy.

It is always significant to note any concerns regarding the foetus, such as reduced or excess amniotic fluid, intra-uterine growth retardation or proving 'small-for-dates'. The details of labour may provide essential information, including the infant's presentation, foetal distress or premature rupture of membranes. The mode of delivery (especially if induced, assisted or caesarean) may be relevant, as may size and APGAR scores. APGAR is a clinical form of scoring applied to newborn infants at one minute post-delivery, and again at five minutes. The lower the total score, the greater the potential need for resuscitative measures. A score of 7 to 10 is normal whereas, with a score below 3, a newborn infant requires immediate resuscitation. The state of the infant following birth, such as respiratory problems, infections, seizures, floppiness and time spent in intensive care units also needs to be explored.

From a psychological perspective, it is essential to understand the parental response to pregnancy and impending delivery. It is also important to consider any incidents which may have influenced attachment and bonding (Chapter 5), such as protracted periods in an incubator or a special care baby unit. Parents may experience a wide array of significant thoughts and feelings, which may affect their future relationship with or attitude towards the child.

OBSTETRIC COMPLICATIONS AND BEHAVIOURAL DISORDERS

While there are many potential complications that may endanger the foetus and impede foetal brain development, the link between brain pathology and behavioural disorders remains poorly understood. Even severe perinatal complications may prove relatively harmless, and it is unlikely that complications during pregnancy and delivery will result in a severely disordered infant. For example, a study investigating cerebral palsy showed that even infants with an APGAR of 3 or less at five minutes (which would indicate serious neonatal distress) were significantly more likely to have achieved normal development at the age of 7 than to suffer from cerebral palsy. Other studies into obstetric complications and neuro-developmental problems have also shown that around half of the developmentally normal group suffered from similar prenatal or perinatal complications to the children with overt pathology but without any adverse neuro-developmental effects.

A history of obstetric or perinatal difficulties therefore does not automatically imply that brain damage has potentially occurred, and severe prenatal or perinatal complications appear to account for only a few cases of abnormal postnatal development. Even where there are associated neurological problems, the obstetric difficulties may prove secondary to underlying genetic or developmental abnormalities of the foetus. An abnormal foetus is likely to have a greater predisposition to a potentially difficult pregnancy and delivery and, in these cases, perinatal complications may serve to compound rather than cause prenatal damage.

Many children with cerebral palsy and concomitant birth asphyxia have additional features suggestive of abnormalities present prior to labour, such as congenital malformations. Similarly, with regard to mental retardation, adverse perinatal events are likely to be markers which reflect pre-existing causes of reduced IQ. Research has shown that only 10 per cent of cases with moderate or severe mental retardation are actually due to prenatal and perinatal causes, with problems being predominantly genetic or chromosomal in aetiology. For example, the association of motor coordination problems in a child with obstetric complications may be due to abnormal intra-uterine development but not necessarily evidence of brain damage.

These findings would suggest that obstetric complications are not a likely cause of major neurological difficulty, and that such complications are unlikely to result in behavioural problems or learning difficulties. These children have previously been described as having minimal brain damage (Chapter 13). However, the term 'damage' suggests that the brain developed normally and then suffered an insult which actively contributed to the resulting clinical picture. The term 'disorder', with suggestion of permanence of the problem, may be a more appropriate description, where the underlying cause is either delayed or precocious neuronal maturation. Even the presence of 'soft' neurological signs should reflect immature motor development rather than proving that something 'is wrong' with the child's brain.

MEDICAL COMPLICATIONS

- *Cardiovascular:* Some maternal cardiac conditions are severe enough to be considered as a contra-indication to pregnancy due to the risk posed to both the mother and the foetus. The most common cause of such cardiac problems is congenital heart disease in the mother. This will place physical limitations on the pregnant woman, and the severity of her heart condition will determine the potential difficulties likely to be experienced during pregnancy and delivery. Other potential risks are anaemia, placental insufficiency and a difficult labour. Prescribed cardiac medication, particularly warfarin for replaced heart valves, may also adversely influence foetal development and heighten risk to the foetus during labour.

- *Respiratory:* Pregnancy probably has little effect on well-controlled asthma, but severe and uncontrolled asthma may result in low-birthweight infants and an increased infant mortality. Problems may also occur with prescribed respiratory medications, such as steroids.

- *Gastrointestinal:* Chronic bowel conditions, such as Crohn's disease, may worsen during pregnancy. This deterioration may require medication, such as steroids, or even surgical procedures.

- *Haematological:* Anaemia is common during pregnancy and may affect both mother and foetus. It may inhibit foetal growth, and render the mother vulnerable to loss of blood during delivery. Clotting mechanisms are impeded in thrombocytopenia (reduced platelets), with an increased risk of intra-cranial haemorrhage in the foetus. Haemolytic disease of the newborn is caused by the presence of maternal antibodies to foetal red blood cells. The most severe form is due to Rhesus incompatibility in which the foetal blood is Rhesus positive (Rh+) and the maternal blood is Rhesus negative (Rh-). Antibodies generated by the mother cross the placenta to the foetus and destroy its red blood cells as the mother's immune system does not recognize the foetus as being an integral part of herself. In severe cases, the foetus may die. Infants who are born alive may present with jaundice, an enlarged liver and spleen and low birthweight. Jaundice, due to bilirubin from broken-down blood cells, is highly toxic to foetal nerve cells and may cause brain damage (kernicterus) with spasticity, paralysis, sensory deficits and mental retardation.

- *Cancer*: Treatment of maternal cancer may seriously affect the growing foetus. Chemotherapy is especially teratogenic during the first trimester of pregnancy and radiation treatment, especially in the area of the foetal head, may result in cerebral defects.

- *Endocrine*: The severity of diabetes mellitus during pregnancy will influence perinatal outcome for the foetus. A high rate of foetal anomalies may occur, including neurological problems, especially with poor glucose control early in the pregnancy. Maternal diabetes may also contribute to placental abruption, foetal distress and premature birth, which is invariably associated with foetal lung immaturity. Infants born to mothers with diabetes are often large with an excessive birthweight (macrosomia). Gestational diabetes, which develops during the pregnancy but resolves afterwards, may also represent a potential risk to both the mother and the infant during development and delivery.

- *Trauma to the pregnant abdomen*: This is the leading non-obstetric cause of foetal death during pregnancy. The severity of the injury to the mother will determine the outcome for both herself and the foetus. Apart from direct injury to the foetus, trauma to the mother can also lead to premature labour, premature rupture of membranes, anoxic damage and placental abruption.

COMMON INFECTIONS

There are a number of serious maternal infections which may infect the foetus across the placenta or directly during delivery. The outcome and severity of these maternal infections on the foetus, newborn or child will vary according to the period of pregnancy. However, they may all potentially complicate pregnancies to a greater or lesser extent. The impact of these infections may include structural brain abnormalities, deafness, blindness, physical abnormalities, hydrocephaly, microcephaly, intra-uterine growth retardation, mental retardation and pre-term delivery with neurological sequelae.

- *Toxoplasmosis* is caused by a parasite which infects both animals and man. In humans, infection is typically through eating infected raw meat, via cat excrement or from contaminated soil. While toxoplasmosis is common in the UK, with 50 per cent of people aged 70 being infected, the majority of infections are not recognized and do no harm. Women who contract toxoplasmosis during pregnancy develop a flu-like illness, but only 30 to 40 per cent of foetuses will become infected. However, the later that the mother becomes infected, the greater the possible impact on the child. Women who have been previously infected present no risk to the foetus during pregnancy, and new infections are easily avoided by basic hygiene and properly prepared food.

- *Varicella* is the virus that causes chicken pox, and maternal infection may cross the placenta and infect the foetus in 1 per cent of cases. The virus may lead to foetal deformity during early trimesters or shortly before delivery. Shingles, a reactivation of the virus in a person who was previously infected with chicken pox, has not been found to cause infection or damage to the foetus.

- *Cytomegalovirus* is a common herpes-like virus which passes easily from person to person. It causes a flu-like infection with swollen glands, and can be passed to the foetus either via the placenta or after birth. It is the commonest congenital viral infection in humans, affecting 1 per cent of live births in the USA, and 25 per cent of women infected for the first time during their pregnancy will deliver affected infants. While infection prior to pregnancy will not prevent maternal transmission, it may lessen the severity of the outcome. Infection during pregnancy may be prevented by simple hygiene.

- *Rubella* is the virus which causes 'German measles', a generally mild illness of childhood. However, it may cause congenital malformations in up to 50 per cent of infants whose mothers become infected during the first trimester of pregnancy. The likelihood of problems falls to 6 per cent in infants with maternal infection in the second trimester. The severity of congenital rubella is such that tests for previous exposure are carried out on most women early in their pregnancy so that they may avoid any risk of infection.

- *Parvovirus* may be mistaken for rubella with fever, malaise, joint pains and both facial and body rash. It is relatively common in the general population, and the highest risk to pregnant women who have not previously been exposed to this virus is through infected children living in the same household.

- *Herpes simplex virus (type II)*, or genital herpes, is a sexually transmitted infection occurring in up to 10 per cent of the adult population in the UK. However, only one-third of people are aware of their infection. The primary presentation is flu-like, associated with clusters of painful superficial genital ulcers. Trans-placental transmission, although rare, may cause serious problems. Infection during the first trimester, especially a first infection, may lead to spontaneous abortion, and the risk of foetal damage increases significantly if infection occurs after 28 weeks. A reoccurrence during pregnancy poses a lesser risk, but there is a very high risk of meningitis in the newborn if active and acute infection is present in the birth canal during delivery.

- *Listeria* is a bacterium commonly found in water and soil. Infection occurs via contaminated foodstuffs such as unwashed vegetables, unprocessed meat or dairy products and food contaminated after processing. It causes fever and malaise, often with nausea and diarrhoea. Pregnant women, newborns and adults with lowered immunity are 20 times more likely to become infected and one-third of cases occur during pregnancy. The infected newborn will suffer more serious effects than the infected mother herself.

- *Gonorrhoea* results from a sexually transmitted bacterium that causes infection of the genital tract in both males and females. If untreated, it can spread upwards to the womb and fallopian tubes, causing pelvic inflammatory disease and possible infertility. Foetal infection occurs via the placenta or, more commonly, during delivery via an infected birth canal. Gonorrhoea is now relatively rare in the UK with 1 per 1000 females infected.

- *Syphilis* is caused by a bacterium and can be clinically divided into four phases. It is increasing following a decrease at the end of the last century. In primary and secondary syphilis, which can last for one to two years, an infected but untreated mother will pass the infection on to her foetus in up to 70 per cent of cases. The latent and tertiary phases are not contagious but will cause severe damage to many organ systems in the untreated person. Also, infection with syphilis will increase the risk of transmitting or contracting HIV by three to five times.

- *Streptococcal infections*, also caused by bacteria, are very common but generally not harmful to healthy children or adults. They are often the organisms that cause injuries to produce pus. However, group B streptococci may be pathogenic to the newborn during delivery. This bacterium is found in the lower genital tract of 10 to 35 per cent of healthy females on a temporary basis without causing any problems. In some pregnant women, it may cause urinary tract infections or even complicate late-stage pregnancies through infection of the amniotic fluid, premature rupture of membranes, premature delivery and neonatal sepsis. Of every 100 pregnant women who carry this infection, 1 to 2 per cent will deliver a compromised baby who will become unwell soon after birth and require treatment. Infection may cause neonatal pneumonia, blood infections or meningitis within the first week post-partum, contributing markedly to chronic conditions such as mental retardation and neurological disabilities.

- *Human immunodeficiency virus (HIV)* is the cause of AIDS (acquired immunodeficiency syndrome), a sexually transmitted disease that may also be spread through blood and blood products. HIV may be transmitted from an infected mother to her foetus via the placenta or, more commonly, via secretions during vaginal delivery. HIV may also be transmitted to the infant via breast milk. Being pregnant will not impair the health of an HIV-infected woman or increase the likelihood of developing HIV-related illnesses. Most babies born to HIV-infected women will not contract the virus. Infants who were infected during pregnancy will show signs of infection at a far earlier stage of life than those infected during delivery. These infants make slow developmental progress or fail to advance having reached a certain developmental plateau. They may also develop HIV dementia and lose skills acquired earlier. The risk of transfer from an infected mother to her child is 1 in 4, although this risk is significantly reduced if the mother receives antiviral medication throughout the pregnancy. This risk may fall to 1 per cent or lower if the infant is delivered by caesarian section.

IATROGENIC DISORDERS

The term 'iatrogenic' is applied to any illness or disorder which can be directly attributed to medical interventions or surgical procedures. It has also been expanded to include medication prescribed to pregnant mothers, and illicit substances misused during pregnancy. The possible causes of iatrogenic disorders are extensive, and many include complicating factors that may contribute to neurological deficits during foetal development or later childhood. While some iatrogenic factors represent risks, others are direct insults and the outcome from any given cause cannot be predicted with certainty.

The first two weeks following conception are considered an 'all or none' period in that, following any insult, the embryo will either survive or perish. During the next period, from two to eight weeks post-conception, the embryo or developing foetus is highly susceptible to the influence of teratogens. These are any agents that may cause a permanent defect in foetal function or structure, reaching the foetus across the placenta from the maternal blood, and acting upon the foetus during a susceptible period. The critical time frame for brain growth and development is from 3 to 16 weeks. Unfortunately, this covers the period when, for many, the pregnancy has not yet been recognized and thus potentially toxic substances may be unknowingly administered to or taken by the mother-to-be.

Potentially toxic agents taken by pregnant women, even when aware of their pregnancy, include tobacco, alcohol and illicit drugs. Tobacco use by pregnant mothers frequently results in low birthweight babies, and similar effects may arise from intense passive smoking. Alcohol ingestion may cause complications with regard to both foetal development and obstetric processes. While there is no clearly defined 'safe' level of alcohol use during pregnancy, even two alcoholic drinks per day by pregnant mothers may prove toxic to the foetus, leading to possible congenital abnormalities and mental retardation. At six or more drinks (units of alcohol) per day, foetal alcohol syndrome may develop. This is a leading non-genetic cause of mental retardation, which also contributes to intra-uterine growth retardation, central nervous system deficits and classic facial abnormalities or phenotype. Serious alcohol misuse may also lead to a seven-fold increase in perinatal mortality, with increased stillbirth rates and a greater likelihood of premature labour.

Cocaine use during pregnancy may contribute to low birthweight infants, premature labour, intra-uterine growth retardation, placental abruption and stillbirths. These complications may be compounded by other vulnerability factors among substance misusers such as maternal malnutrition, poor antenatal care and low socioeconomic status. Infants of mothers who misuse cocaine during pregnancy are often irritable and poor feeders, with an increased incidence of learning difficulties and behavioural problems later in childhood. Foetal anomalies due to ischaemic events during pregnancy may also occur, affecting the child's limbs and central nervous system. The use of narcotics such as heroin and methadone during pregnancy may similarly increase the rate of obstetric complications. The newborn neonate may also experience narcotic withdrawal symptoms, with central nervous system and respiratory complications. Marijuana misuse during pregnancy may cause intra-uterine growth retardation and slight mental retardation.

Small, premature babies have a heightened risk of complications in the neonatal period including infections, hypothermia and cerebral haemorrhage. Birth injuries due to malpresentation, foetal distress, assisted and rapid deliveries are other potential causes of intra-cranial haemorrhage. The most severe forms of cerebral bleeding, especially with respect to subsequent brain function, cause bleeding into the substance of the brain, leading to permanent damage. Obstetric complications such as abnormal presentations, cephalo-pelvic disproportion and multiple births are factors that may predispose the foetus to a lack of oxygen and birth asphyxia. This is often caused by a delay in spontaneous respiration after delivery and, unless neonatal breathing commences within a few minutes, there is an increased risk of permanent brain damage. During the birth process, foetal distress is a significant indicator that the infant is becoming hypoxic either prior to, or in the course of, delivery. These postnatal problems may lead to intellectual impairment, visual defects, hearing deficits, mental retardation and cerebral palsy.

Iatrogenic problems may also be psychological in nature, for example, the seriously ill infant who is removed from his or her mother for prolonged medical treatment in an incubator. This separation may affect early bonding behaviour, as well as disrupting the establishment of feeding and sleeping patterns. It may also lead to later over-protection of the child and other forms of maladaptive parenting behaviour. Even when obstetric complications have not contributed to overt neurological damage, the sense of blame felt by parents may impact negatively on both the child and the family, distorting the normal course of childhood social development and contributing to parental discord.

PSYCHO-PATHOLOGICAL SEQUELAE

In 1976, a study to determine the rates of emotional and psychiatric problems in children and adolescents was carried out on the Isle of Wight (Rutter, Taylor and Hersov 1994). It highlighted how children with a proven neurological disability, such as cerebral palsy, were at far greater risk of developing psychiatric problems than children with epilepsy, physical disabilities or no problems at all. Since then, many studies have investigated this potential association with regard to other neurological and developmental conditions.

Particular interest has been shown in children with intellectual and developmental delay due to genetic or congenital causes, with up to 40 per cent of affected individuals being found to suffer from some form of psycho-pathology including severe mental illnesses such as psychosis and mood disorders, disruptive behaviour and Attention Deficit Hyperactivity Disorder (ADHD), anxiety traits and autistic spectrum disorders. These difficulties may be further influenced by genetic inheritance, neurological deficits, personality factors and social stigma. However, in children and adolescents with intellectual or developmental delay, psycho-pathological symptoms may manifest more simplistically, be masked by these impairments or prove more diverse than within a normal population.

Reduced cognitive ability may impact negatively on the problem-solving skills needed by the child to cope with the demands of everyday life. This may result in distress, anxiety, aberrant behaviour and a limited sense of self. Poor self-image may follow with low expectations of both oneself and others, together with unrealistic self-appraisal, experiences of failure, uncertainty and learned helplessness. The child or adolescent with intellectual impairment may therefore present with reduced enjoyment of any success, low self-esteem, sadness, withdrawal and potentially depression. Within the social environment, these children and adolescents are therefore at risk of abuse and exploitation, with social stigma further reducing their opportunities and contributing to peer rejection and ostracization.

While these difficulties may be ameliorated by positive support and social inclusion, family stress may contribute to poor adjustment. The capacity of a family to cope with the challenges of a developmentally delayed child may depend on age, gender, IQ and the aetiology of the problem. Other factors that may influence the level of support provided by a family include coping styles, parental perceptions of the child and disciplinary practices. It is this interplay between the risk and protective factors for psycho-pathology that will contribute to possible outcomes within this group of children and adolescents.

SUMMARY

There are many factors which may cause complications during pregnancy and labour, although the outcome of these difficulties remains unpredictable and problems will not automatically produce an infant with neuro-developmental damage. The potential causes of many neuro-developmental problems therefore remain elusive, although multi-factorial influences are likely to combine both genetic predisposition and the environmental determinants which act upon the developing individual before birth and into childhood.

REFERENCES AND FURTHER READING

Brown, J.S. and Crombleholme, W.R. (1993) *Handbook of Gynaecology and Obstetrics*, 1st edn. Norwalk, CT: Appleton and Lange.

Dykens, E.M. (2000) 'Annotation: Psychopathology in children with intellectual disability.' *Journal of Child Psychology and Psychiatry 41*, 407–417.

Emerson, E. (2003) 'Prevalence of psychiatric disorders in children and adolescents with and without intellectual disability.' *Journal of Intellectual Disability Research 47*, 51–58.

Moore, K.L. (1988) *The Developing Human*, 4th edn. London: Saunders.

Rutter, M., Taylor, E. and Hersov, L. (1994) *Child and Adolescent Psychiatry*, 3rd edn. Oxford: Blackwell Science.

Smith, P.K., Cowie, H. and Blades, M. (2003) *Understanding Children's Development*, 4th edn. Oxford: Blackwell Publishing.

Chapter 16

Semantic pragmatic deficit syndrome

Deba Choudhury and Uttom Chowdhury

The term Semantic Pragmatic Deficit Syndrome has been used to describe a condition in which children have subtle developmental speech and language difficulties. This includes a significant impairment of both the semantics and the pragmatics of language. Although initially used to described children who did not meet the diagnostic criteria for autism, controversy still exists as to whether this is a separate condition or simply a variation of an autistic spectrum disorder. Unfortunately, little evidence-based research has been undertaken with regard to this condition. The following chapter is a brief summary of the main features of semantic pragmatic deficit syndrome.

WHAT IS SEMANTIC PRAGMATIC DEFICIT SYNDROME?

Semantic pragmatic deficit syndrome (SPDS) has been identified as a communication disorder. The name was coined by Rapin and Allen in 1983, and the condition involves impairment of two salient features – semantics and pragmatics. Semantics refers to difficulties in identifying the relationship between words and sentences, which impacts on the meanings of language. Pragmatics refers to the appropriate use of language in context. Pragmatic language functions would include general greetings, starting of conversations, commenting, requesting and changing a topic. Children and adolescents with semantic and pragmatic difficulties will therefore experience problems in both understanding the meaning of what other people say and in understanding how to use speech appropriately.

There are two main descriptive classifications relating to developmental language disorders: Rapin and Allen (1983), and Bishop and Rosenbloom (1987). Both classifications include a sub-type of language impairment in which phonology and grammar are normal, but in which the use of language is abnormal. Rapin and Allen (1983) describe this sub-type as Semantic Pragmatic Deficit Syndrome, while Bishop and Rosenbloom (1987) describe this sub-type as Semantic Pragmatic Disorder. However, there are many similarities between the two classifications. The main difference is that semantic pragmatic deficit syndrome describes communication problems which may arise from any cause. Thus the term SPDS may be applied to children who have organic brain illnesses such as hydrocephalus, and it can equally be applied to those with autism. In contrast, semantic pragmatic disorder implies that intelligence (IQ) is normal, that there is no known organic cause and that the child does not meet the diagnostic criteria for autism.

WHAT ARE THE SYMPTOMS OF SPDS?

Children with SPDS have difficulty in listening to and then processing the meaning of language. They thus find it difficult to follow conversations. Also, their language may appear grammatically complex yet fluent, which is similar to patients with acquired right hemisphere lesions (Shields 1991). Parents of children with SPDS often describe how they have not responded to their names being called in their early years but have obviously heard the doorbell or telephone ring. These children also display deficits in comprehension. For example, they have difficulty in following instructions that act in contrast to their normal routine. Such comprehension problems often improved with speech therapy interventions. Anecdotally, children with SPDS seem to fare better academically in more linear subjects such as mathematics and science.

Children with SPDS may experience problems when playing with their peers, especially with regard to sharing and turn taking. They can appear as selfish, domineering, aggressive, over-confident, shy and withdrawn. Unfortunately, these difficulties often result in their being subject to behavioural treatments without significant success. SPDS children struggle to process information, and they cannot easily extract core meaning or salience from academic exercises or life events. They have difficulty in grasping the meaning of new situations or contexts, and cope by trying to retain a semblance of sameness and predictability. They therefore prefer routines, tend to eat only certain foods and may develop obsessional interests. When faced with more stimulating situations, the child with SPDS may find it even more challenging to obtain and understand information from the environment, both aurally and visually.

As some of the features of semantic pragmatic deficit syndrome are very subtle, the condition should only be diagnosed by a speech and language therapist or a clinician with expertise in language disorders and autistic spectrum disorders. The features with which children and adolescents may present include difficulty with listening to language, difficulty in understanding language, difficulty in talking, difficulty with theory of mind and difficulty with creative and imaginative play.

Box 16.1 Symptoms of semantic pragmatic deficit syndrome

- Delayed language development
- Difficulties understanding questions
- Getting confused between 'I' and 'you'
- Difficulty following conversations
- Often repeating phrases out of context
- Learning to talk by memorizing phrases
- Poor comprehension which may lead to behavioural problems
- Possibly appearing rude or arrogant
- Problems with abstract concepts
- Word-finding deficits
- Comprehension deficits
- Atypical word choices
- Poor conversational skills
- Poor maintenance of topic
- Speaking aloud to no one in particular
- Answering besides the point of a question

Listening to and understanding language

Children with SPDS are easily distracted by visual and aural stimuli in their environment. They find it very difficult to focus their listening appropriately, and individuals with SPDS may therefore struggle to respond to questions that require them to listen efficiently. As a result, their behaviours have been often viewed as impulsive or inattentive. In addition, they struggle to understand words, time concepts and non-literal expressions. These children and adolescents also find it difficult to determine what the speaker is thinking and proposing. For example, a child with SPDS would struggle with questions such as, 'what have you done today?' However, they will be more able to follow instructions like, 'please pass me the red pen on top of the blue book' because the latter question is literal and involves a here-and-now time concept.

Talking

Children with SPDS demonstrate specific pragmatic difficulties in the way they make use of language (Bishop 1989). When learning a language, they memorize words and sentences rather than grasping the inherent patterns and meanings. As a result, they are less able to use language as freely as other children. Their language also fails to differentiate between different people and different conversations. In other words, adults, parents and children are all approached in the same way. This is consistent with their desire to maintain a degree of similarity within their environment. SPDS language also includes limited emotional information in terms of how people are feeling or what they are thinking.

Individuals with SPDS have limited insight into what their conversational partner may be thinking, feeling or intending. They are therefore likely to believe that their partner is interested in their obsessions, and willing to listen to these details in great depth. As a result, children with SPDS may ignore or dismiss the fact that the listener is bored or disinterested. Since they have little awareness of their conversational partner's intentions, they may also respond vaguely to questions or turn the conversation around to focus on something that they understand and feel comfortable talking about.

Theory of mind

Some clinicians argue that children with SPDS do not have a theory of mind (Chapter 4). They are therefore unable to appreciate that other people may think differently to them. Theory of mind in children has traditionally been tested by the use of false belief tasks and deception tasks (Baron-Cohen, Leslie and Frith 1985). However, an individual who falls within the autistic spectrum (Chapter 7) may experience similar problems in understanding other people's thoughts and intentions. In contrast to an autistic child lacking in theory of mind, the SPDS child is able to develop an improved theory of mind later. This simply happens slower and later than other comparable developmental skills.

Creative and imaginative play

From the age of about 18 months, children are able to engage in imaginative and creative play by thinking abstractly (Chapter 1). They may already pretend that a banana is a telephone, but they also come to appreciate that it is a banana too. However, abstract thinking is a difficult concept for SPDS children to grasp. They therefore find it difficult to participate in imaginative and creative play, which may lead to social and communication problems with their peers.

More able children with SPDS may attempt to master pretend play by imitating people's actions. They copy, rather than understand, behaviours and responses which they may have seen in a cartoon, on a film or in real life. These actions are usually highly elaborate in detail, as is the case when they copy someone's speech. To maintain consistency and sameness, an individual with SPDS is highly likely to draw the same picture story on each and every occasion. Likewise, they may often limit creative pursuits such as drawing to something within their obsessional interests.

SUPPORTING CHILDREN WITH SPDS

Research has suggested that there are three key areas which require specific attention in helping children who have SPDS to achieve their natural potential. These areas are social development, language and academic performance.

Social development

If a child with SPDS attends a mainstream school, then his or her peers should be given an explanation about the condition. This may reduce any initial anxieties being experienced by the child, and also helped to nurture relationships with peers. It is equally important to maintain a high degree of predictability as this will help to reduce anxiety-provoking issues further. The child should also be encouraged to work in small groups as this will help to foster interactions with his or her peers. Unambiguous rules on appropriate behaviour should be given, but the teacher or parent should be careful not to criticize the child or express any negative judgements. Sharing strategies should be conveyed to SPDS children to assist them in better managing their peer relationships, while not losing sight of their specific needs and deficits. They will also respond more effectively to practical hands-on tasks, and simple rule-based games like hide and seek should be introduced. Wherever possible, the child with SPDS should receive constant positive feedback.

Language

Children with SPDS should be able to socialize with appropriate conversational partners, who operate on the same level of understanding as themselves or who are less conversationally advanced. They are more likely to benefit from similar children who will interact with them, rather than from more able children who may ignore them. It is also important to talk at a slow pace, and not to overwhelm the individual with questions. Patience is required in waiting for the child or adolescent to respond to questions. Rather than saying 'tidy up' to the child with SPDS, saying 'please could you put all the toys away in the blue box?' would be of more help in allowing the individual to understand the instruction. When new topics are introduced, it is recommended that gestures and visual stimuli are used to encourage the child with SPD to understand better and to attach some form of meaning to the topic. Sarcasm should be avoided or, if it is used, then it should be accompanied by an explanation. In addition, if metaphors are used, then they should be explained as well. Idiomatic expressions should also be used with the child, and appropriate playground language should be incorporated. Instructions are best written down to avoid confusion and to maintain clarity, such as structured timetables. Finally, in order to confirm if a child with SPDS has understood an instruction, the optimal route is simply to ask what he or she believes is being expected of him or her.

Academic performance

Visual cues should be used as much as possible to enhance understanding. If the child with SPDS has obsessional interests, then these could be used to enhance understanding and knowledge. To improve comprehension skills, adults should read a story out loud and then discusses the plot with the child. This can be accompanied by questions and discussions to stimulate the child, and to help him or her to capture the salience of the story. To increase their self-esteem, children with SPDS should be encouraged to read some books that are above their comprehension level. If they are hyperlexic, then this opportunity may assist them in feeling that they are as capable as other children in the class. Another method for increasing self-esteem in children with SPDS is to identify something that they excel at in comparison to their peers.

Early interventions are highly recommended. The objective is to enhance communication skills, and to reduce the secondary behavioural repercussions of inappropriate communication (Rapin 1996). It is also important to keep parents actively involved, and to keep them informed about both effective and ineffective therapeutic interventions. Speech therapy interventions are essential as the aim is not only to teach language to the child with SPDS but to also encourage the appropriate use of language for communication. Each discipline, whether psychology, psychiatry, neurology or speech therapy, has interventions available which may be of use to the child with SPDS. The overall goal is therefore to achieve a better quality of life for the child with SPDS through a multidisciplinary approach moulded to help this specific client group.

Other supportive approaches and strategies

- Visual cues for learning
- Small group work
- Simple instructions, spoken slowly

- Social skills training
- Clear rules and boundaries
- Written instructions
- Avoiding sarcasm or metaphors
- Responding to the child's intentions and not to what he or she is saying
- Improving self-esteem though encouragement, praise and responsibility.

REFERENCES

Baron-Cohen, S., Leslie, A. and Frith, U. (1985) 'Does the autistic child have a "theory of mind"?' *Cognition 21*, 37–46.

Bishop, D.V.M. (1989) 'Autism, Asperger's syndrome and semantic pragmatic disorder: Where are the boundaries?' *British Journal of Disorders of Communication 24*, 107–121.

Bishop, D.V.M. and Rosenbloom, L. (1987) 'Classification of childhood language disorders.' In W. Yule and M. Rutter (eds) *Language Development and Disorders: Clinics in Developmental Medicine.* London: MacKeith Press.

Rapin, I. (1996) 'Practitioner review: Developmental language disorders: A clinical update.' *Journal of Child Psychology and Psychiatry 37*, 643–655.

Rapin, I. and Allen, D. (1983) 'Developmental language disorders: Nosologic considerations.' In U. Kirk (ed) *Neuropsychology of Language, Reading, and Spelling.* New York: Academic Press, pp.155–184.

Shields, J. (1991) 'Semantic-pragmatic disorder: A right hemisphere syndrome?' *British Journal of Disorders of Communication 26*, 383–392.

Chapter 17

Schizophrenia in childhood and adolescence

Paramala J. Santosh, M. Tanveer Alam and Iris Carcani-Rathwell

INTRODUCTION

Schizophrenia is a serious mental illness defined by fundamental and characteristic distortions of thinking and perception. It is also accompanied by inappropriate or blunted affect, hallucinations, mood disturbance and several other symptoms (World Health Organization 1992). Clear consciousness and intellectual capacity are usually maintained, although certain cognitive deficits may evolve during the course of the illness. Although most cases of schizophrenia have their onset in late adolescence and early adulthood, the disorder has also been identified in children.

'Childhood schizophrenia' is often referred to as 'pre-pubertal' schizophrenia, although current definitions are based on chronological age and not physical development. The term 'early-onset schizophrenia' (EOS) is now being used interchangeably with 'childhood-onset schizophrenia' (COS) to mean schizophrenia that has an onset in childhood or adolescence. This is defined as an onset of illness before the age of 18 years. Within these parameters, 'very early-onset schizophrenia' (VEO) is defined as onset before 13 years, with 'adolescent-onset schizophrenia' being those with an onset between 13 and 17 years.

DIAGNOSIS

No specific diagnostic criteria are available for childhood-onset schizophrenia in the recognized mental health classificatory systems. In DSM-IV (American Psychiatric Association 1994), schizophrenia is characterized as a disturbance that lasts for at least six months and includes at least one month of active symptoms.

Two or more of the following symptoms would need to be present: delusions, hallucinations, disorganized speech, grossly disorganized or catatonic behaviour, and negative symptoms. In ICD-10, the above symptoms must be clearly present for most of the time during a period of one month or more. In cases of less than one month duration, the diagnosis is limited to an acute schizophrenia-like disorder. The phenomenology of schizophrenia can be grouped into positive and negative symptoms. The positive (or active) symptoms include delusions, hallucinations, thought disorder, excitement and suspiciousness. Negative symptoms (or deficit) usually comprise flattening of affect, alogia (poverty of speech), apathy, anhedonia (loss of capacity to experience pleasure) and asociality (few social contacts).

PREVALENCE

Childhood schizophrenia with a very early onset is extremely rare but, when it occurs, it has significant clinical and research importance (Nicolson and Rapoport 1999). The prevalence of childhood-onset schizophrenia is estimated to be 1.6–1.9 per 100,000. However, studies that have been able to differentiate between autistic spectrum disorders and childhood schizophrenia estimate an even lower prevalence of the latter.

In younger children, the onset tends to be insidious and the sex ratio is in favour of males. Schizophrenia with an onset in adolescence is a much more common disorder. It affects 0.23 per cent of the general population of adolescents, and 1.34 per cent of those with mental retardation. The onset is very acute in adolescence, and there are no gender differences.

Early onset of schizophrenia is thought to be associated with poorer outcome. However, the meaning of this association remains unclear since the psychotic illness usually has a profound impact on other aspects of the child's development (Remschmidt 2001).

DEVELOPMENTAL ASPECTS

Childhood development has a unique impact on the expression of various clinical features of early-onset schizophrenia. These effects can be observed with regard to the form and content of delusions, the nature of hallucinations and the disturbance of thought processes. It is therefore generally difficult to demonstrate psychotic processes in young children due to developmental limitations in their cognitive and linguistic abilities. In addition, there is a significant age-dependant variation in schizophrenic symptoms as children grow older.

Well-formed delusions are very rare in young children, while hallucinations and disorganized thinking only become more common after the age of 6 and particularly in those over 8 to 9 years of age. In younger pre-school children, sleep-related and developmental phenomena, including beliefs in fantasy figures and imaginary friends, may be mistaken for possible signs of psychosis. Transient symptoms, such as hallucinations, may also be observed in younger children in relation to stress and anxiety. However, the presence of thought disorder and delusional thinking is very difficult to establish within this age group.

The complexity of psychotic phenomena increases with age and developmental level. Although psychotic phenomena are generally uncommon in middle childhood, if symptoms occur they tend to prove more ominous, more persistent and more frequently associated with serious disorders of mental health, such as schizophrenia, in later life. At this age, the content of hallucinations and delusions tends to revolve around developmental issues. Symptoms often relate to familiar figures or aspects of identity, and are seldom as complex or as systemized as symptom formation in adults. In adolescence, the clinical features of psychosis gradually become more similar to those in adulthood. However substance misuse, as well as the increased frequency of brief psychotic episodes associated with other conditions such as borderline personality disorder, often complicates the task of differential diagnosis.

Although the overall intelligence of children and adolescents with early-onset schizophrenia is suggested to be lower than that of the general population, with 10–20 per cent having an IQ under 70, the small number of cases reported so far within these very young age groups makes it difficult to draw definite conclusions. However, children and adolescents with early-onset schizophrenia may have high rates of pre-morbid impairment (Nicholson *et al.* 2000a) and early developmental abnormalities, such as language (Hollis 1995). They may also present with motor delay, hypotonia (abnormal muscle tone) and unusual responses to the environment. In addition, a lack of responsiveness in infancy has been found to be present more frequently in schizophrenia with a very early onset. Research has shown that children with greater disruptions in their pre-morbid development tend to have greater familial vulnerability for schizophrenia and more obstetrical complications (Matsumoto *et al.* 2001), although this is not always the case (Nicholson *et al.* 2000b).

AETIOLOGY

Childhood-onset schizophrenia is regarded as a heterogeneous illness, not only from a phenomenological perspective but also with regards to aetiology. Both genetic and environmental factors may contribute to the early age of onset. Twin, adoption and family studies strongly suggest that schizophrenia aggregates in families (Asarnow *et al.* 2001) and, compared to adults with schizophrenia, children with early-onset schizophrenia appear to have more severe pre-morbid neuro-developmental abnormalities and more cytogenetic anomalies. Together with potentially greater family histories of schizophrenia and related disorders, this all suggests a greater genetic vulnerability (Nicholson *et al.* 2000).

Many of the neuro-cognitive, linguistic and psycho-physiological abnormalities observed in adult-onset schizophrenia, as well as the changes in brain structure observed in adult-onset schizophrenia, are present in childhood-onset schizophrenia. This suggests that childhood-onset schizophrenia and adult-onset schizophrenia may have a common neurobiological basis (Asarnow *et al.* 2001) and there is increasing evidence suggestive of schizophrenia being a progressive neuro-developmental disorder. However, data from monozygotic twins discordant for schizophrenia indicate a possible non-genetic neuro-degenerative process that may worsen or trigger the illness.

Various structural brain abnormalities have been reported in early-onset schizophrenia including decreased brain volumes, progressive grey matter loss, reduced size of the left hippocampus, thalamic abnormality, relative increase in ventricular volume, decrease in temporal lobe structures and cerebello-striato-frontal circuitry impairment (Kumra *et al.* 2001; Rapoport and Inoff-Germain 2000). The lack of white matter abnormalities, and the probability that genes involved in early neuro-development also contribute to later brain development, lend further support to the neuro-developmental model of schizophrenia (Rapoport and Inoff-Germain 2000).

The diagnosis of schizophrenia carries uncertainty at all ages, but this is even greater in childhood. The diagnosis of childhood schizophrenia is difficult and requires time-consuming evaluation processes. It is important for clinicians and researchers to understand the degree of uncertainty inherent in the diagnostic process, and the need for diagnostic validation. This may require further refinement of diagnostic cut-offs, possibly using symptom rating scales to improve accuracy of early diagnosis (Remschmidt 2001).

The stability of the diagnosis of early-onset schizophrenia is relatively good although not perfect. There appears to be a particular risk of misdiagnosing schizophrenia in bipolar disorders with very early onset, and in some autistic spectrum disorders due to a significant symptom overlap. The classification is easier to apply in adolescents as their presentation becomes increasingly similar to adult patients. There are, however, ongoing diagnostic difficulties with regard to some psychotic children who appear to fall outside of current syndrome boundaries. It is therefore still unclear as to whether the available diagnostic approaches are appropriate for use in younger children, especially those younger than 12 years old, as the criteria are based mainly on work with adolescents and adults, and do not take into appropriate consideration the potential impact of developmental issues.

DIFFERENTIAL DIAGNOSIS

Affective psychosis (psychotic depression and bipolar disorder)

Psychotic symptoms are common in other paediatric neuro-psychiatric disorders and in various medical illnesses. Positive symptoms may occur in bipolar disorders and affective distinctions, such as mood congruency, can be difficult to apply. Although negative symptoms occur in depression, it is possible to distinguish between the affective flatness associated with despair and depression and the 'blunted' or incongruous emotional expression commonly seen in schizophrenia. Onset patterns and pre-morbid functioning may also be helpful with differentiation. It is therefore important to carefully rule out other psychotic illness before making a diagnosis of schizophrenia since psychotic mood disorders may respond well to mood-stabilizing and/or anti-depressant medication.

Schizo-affective disorder

The diagnosis requires a period of illness in which the patient has both a significant mood disorder (major depression, mania or mixed) and psychotic symptoms. There must also be a period of at least two weeks during which hallucinations and delusions persist in the absence of predominant mood symptoms, although mood symptoms must be present for a substantial portion of the overall illness. Schizo-affective disorder has not been well-defined in youth, and remains unreliable, with this diagnosis only being made infrequently and only when associated with the most severe impairment.

Asperger syndrome and the autistic spectrum

DSM-IV does not exclude a diagnosis of schizophrenia in cases with autistic spectrum disorders if prominent delusions or hallucinations are present for at least one month. In Asperger syndrome and milder forms of autistic disorders, social and cognitive impairments are more long-standing with less marked progressive deterioration of pre-morbid functioning when compared to the rate and severity of social and scholastic deterioration in childhood and adolescent schizophrenia. This distinction becomes increasingly difficult in childhood schizophrenia with a very early onset. The question remains whether schizophrenic presentations are best viewed as autistic 'phenocopies' or as distinct co-morbid conditions.

Childhood disintegrative psychosis

This is a disorder characterized by developmental regression and marked behavioural changes following a normal development over the first two years of life. There is a loss of acquired receptive and expressive language skills, as well as of coordination and bowel or bladder function (Volkmar and Rutter 1995). Children with disintegrative psychosis become socially withdrawn and develop ritualistic behaviours, unusual sensory interests and mannerisms that are similar to those in autism. The main difference between disintegrative psychosis and autism is that the regression is more severe and occurs across development and does not just impact on language skills. In a typical disintegrative disorder the regression extends over several months although, in some cases, deterioration continues with increased motor difficulties, development of seizures and localized neurological signs (Corbett *et al.* 1997). In most cases, no cause can be identified. However, investigations should be repeated, particularly if there is progressive deterioration, as they can initially be negative even when a neurological disorder is later eventually identified.

Neuro-degenerative disorders

These include juvenile metachromatic leukodystrophy, adrenoleukodystrophy, Wilson's disease and Huntington's chorea. They are all associated with movement disorders, particularly gait disturbance. A full neurological examination is mandatory in the assessment of all psychotic patients, and must attempt to distinguish between primary and anti-psychotic induced movement disorders. Also, the progressive loss of cognitive skills in these disorders is in contrast to the relative decline seen in schizophrenia whereby loss of previously learned skill is also unusual.

Drug-induced psychosis

Substances that cause drug-induced psychoses include cocaine, amphetamines and hallucinogens. Withdrawal from alcohol, sedatives, hypnotics and anxiolytics may also cause psychotic symptoms. Substance misuse history, the presence of drug metabolites in the urine and persistence of psychotic symptoms for at least a month following drug withdrawal may help in distinguishing drug-induced psychoses from schizophrenia.

Temporal lobe epilepsy

Seizures from the left temporal lobe, which is the most common origin of epileptic psychotic phenomenon, is differentiated on the basis of clouding of consciousness, the brief and episodic nature of the presentation and partial amnesia for the episode. Twenty-four-hour EEG recording with event monitoring may establish the association between temporal lobe discharge and psychotic or behavioural symptoms.

MANAGEMENT
Psycho-social interventions

Adolescents suffering from schizophrenia show early social impairments which may often lead to rejection by peers, difficulties in school and stress on family members. Promising approaches to the psycho-social treatment of adult schizophrenia that merit evaluation for adolescents include family interventions which emphasize psycho-education and coping skills, individual and group interventions designed to build life skills and competencies, and early intervention strategies. At present, there is insufficient available data on this subject to be definitive and prescriptive about its use. However, it is generally accepted that psycho-social interventions should be part of the care package in schizophrenia, especially in the form of psycho-education, compliance therapy, risk management and prevention of relapse. Cognitive behavioural strategies may also be useful in decreasing non-responsiveness to medication and in reducing psychotic phenomena such as hallucinations.

Pharmacotherapy

Despite the severity of their illness, children with childhood-onset schizophrenia often show dramatic responses to atypical anti-psychotics. These anti-psychotic drugs have better proven efficacy in schizophrenia, particularly in managing negative symptoms and refractory forms of illness. They have a lower incidence of some serious side-effects, although rigorous treatment trials of anti-psychotic medication in childhood psychosis are needed to document safety and efficacy better (Rapoport and Inoff-Germain 2000).

Despite limited research being available in early-onset schizophrenia, risperidone (1–6 mg/day) or olanzapine (2.5–20 mg/day) are commonly used (Sholevar, Baron and Hardie 2000) although baseline liver function studies prior to the initiation of these medications are recommended. Risperidone is generally well tolerated, although there is a risk of extrapyramidal symptoms (EPS) and hyperprolactinaemia. Bodyweight gain is a common adverse effect, although somewhat less than that reported with olanzapine. Overall, there tends to be a dramatic and sustained weight gain in patients maintained on atypical anti-psychotic drugs for two or more years. Treatment trials with agents that appear to be weight neutral (such as aripiprazole or ziprazidone) or agents that may permit the use of lower doses of concurrent anti-psychotics (such as glycine augmentation) are needed with regard to this group patients. Aripiprazole, another atypical neuroleptic, may also reveal beneficial cognitive effects of particular importance to this paediatric population.

Clozapine has been shown to be effective in childhood and adolescent schizophrenia with therapeutic superiority in the treatment both of the acute phases of the illness and chronic negative symptoms. It has fewer adverse extra-pyramidal effects and, therefore, fairly good tolerability (Remschmidt *et al.* 2000). However, because of clozapine's possible adverse haematological effects (such as decreased white cell count), it should not be used as a first-line anti-psychotic medication. Other adverse effects relate to the cardiovascular system, the central nervous system, fever, liver function and weight gain. The latter may present a particular problem in adolescents and young adults. Careful monitoring of haematological parameters and other adverse effects are therefore preconditions for a successful treatment programme (Remschmidt *et al.* 2000).

Post-psychotic depression

Post-psychotic depression in schizophrenia has been described since the beginning of the last century and, in clinical practice, represents a real challenge. Its prevalence has been estimated to be 25 per cent, although a wider prevalence range (7–70%) has also been reported due to diagnostic difficulties. The clinical picture resembles that of major depression although it is difficult to distinguish these features from the negative symptoms and extra-pyramidal symptoms associated with schizophrenia and anti-psychotic treatment. Post-psychotic depression impacts on quality of life and increases suicide risk, thus worsening the prognosis of acute schizophrenia. In clinical practice, post-psychotic depression can be successfully treated with the addition of an anti-depressant to the anti-psychotic regime.

Case example: Nathan

Nathan, a 14-year-old boy, had presented to various Child and Adolescent Mental Health Services over several years with vague behavioural symptoms, including separation anxiety and possible attention deficit hyperactivity disorder. No definite diagnosis was ever reached, but family therapy had been recommended given stresses within the family. Nathan had also experienced some difficulties with social skills. Most recently, Nathan had been frightened to go to bed as he was convinced that there were 'horrible things' in the dark. His mother had tried to reassure him, and had interpreted his concerns as normal childhood fears. However, Nathan's anxiety gradually increased until he could no longer go to bed on his own and insisted on sleeping in his mother's bed.

He was again seen by a child psychiatrist, who took a brief history once he had established good rapport with Nathan. At interview, it emerged that Nathan was experiencing both auditory and visual hallucinations. The auditory hallucinations included a voice calling Nathan's name, which also told him to do simple things. He was extremely frightened by this experience, hence his reluctance to talk about it. At the same time, he became extremely worried about going to school due to a persistent sense that both teachers and pupils were watching him. Because of these hallucinations and paranoid ideas, it was decided that a trial of medication should be commenced and Nathan started on risperidone 0.5 mg twice a day, increasing to 1 mg twice a day.

Over the next six weeks, his acute symptoms gradually faded and he became more relaxed. Although Nathan's mental state improved, he still needed regular follow-up and review of his medication. His school work had also deteriorated during the acute phase of his illness and a significant level of liaison with local schools was required in order for them to support Nathan, both academically and therapeutically. He was subsequently diagnosed as having experienced an acute psychotic episode, and it is hoped that the early introduction of medication, together with psychological and emotional support, will help prevent potential relapse and ultimately improve the long-term outcome and prognosis.

CONCLUSIONS

Although early-onset psychosis is rare, it can present Child and Adolescent Mental Health Services with difficulties in identification and management, especially in the very young. It is often difficult to differentiate from affective disorders, and requires the use of both atypical anti-psychotics and psycho-social interventions. Early-onset schizophrenia is, to a large extent, similar to adult-onset schizophrenia but has significant developmental difficulties associated with it and probably a poorer prognosis. Research into developmental differences between adult-onset schizophrenia and early-onset schizophrenia, and treatment trials in childhood-onset schizophrenia, are essential in order to personalize and optimize outcomes.

REFERENCES

American Psychiatric Association (1994) *Diagnostic and Statistical Manual of Mental Disorders*, 4th edn (DSM-IV). Washington, DC: American Psychiatric Association.

Asarnow, R.F., Nuechterlein, K.H., Fogelson, D., Subotnik, K.L. *et al.* (2001) 'Schizophrenia and schizophrenia-spectrum personality disorders in the first-degree relatives of children with schizophrenia.' *Archives of General Psychiatry 58*, 581–588.

Corbett, J., Harris, R., Taylor, E. and Trimble, M. (1997) 'Progressive disintegrative psychosis of childhood.' *Journal of Child Psychology and Psychiatry 18*, 211–219.

Hollis, C. (1995) 'Child and adolescent (juvenile onset) schizophrenia. A case control study of premorbid developmental impairments.' *British Journal of Psychiatry 166*, 489–495.

Kumra, S., Shaw, M., Merka, P., Nagayama, E. *et al.* (2001) 'Childhood-onset schizophrenia: research update.' *Canadian Journal of Psychiatry 46*, 923–930.

Matsumoto, H., Takei, N., Saito, F., Kachi, K. *et al.* (2001) 'The association between obstetric complications and childhood-onset schizophrenia: A replication study.' *Psychological Medicine 31*, 907–914.

Nicholson, R., Lenane, M., Singaracharlu, S., Malaspina, D. *et al.* (2000a) 'Premorbid speech and language impairments in childhood-onset schizophrenia: Association with risk factors.' *American Journal of Psychiatry 157*, 794–800.

Nicholson, R., Lenane, M., Hamburger, S.D., Fernández, T. *et al.* (2000b) 'Lessons from childhood-onset schizophrenia.' *Brain Research: Brain Research Reviews 31*, 147–156.

Nicholson, R. and Rapoport, J.L. (1999) 'Childhood-onset schizophrenia: Rare but worth studying.' *Biological Psychiatry 46*, 1418–1428.

Rapoport, J.L. and Inoff-Germain, G. (2000) 'Update on childhood-onset schizophrenia.' *Current Psychiatry Reports 2*, 410–415.

Remschmidt, H., Fleischhaker, C., Henninghausen, K. and Schulz, E. (2000) 'Management of schizophrenia in children and adolescents. The role of clozapine.' *Paediatric Drugs 2*, 253–262.

Remschmidt, H. (2001) *Schizophrenia in Children and Adolescents.* Cambridge: Cambridge University Press.

Sholevar, E.H., Baron, D.A. and Hardie, T.L. (2000) 'Treatment of childhood-onset schizophrenia with olanzapine.' *Journal of Child and Adolescent Psychopharmacology 10*, 69–78.

Volkmar, F.R. and Rutter, M. (1995) 'Childhood disintegrative disorder: Results of the DSM-IV autism field trial.' *Journal of the American Academy of Child and Adolescent Psychiatry 34*, 1092–1095.

World Health Organization (1992) *International Statistical Classification of Diseases and Related Health Problems*, 10th revision (ICD-10). Geneva: World Health Organization.

Chapter 18

Tics and Tourette syndrome

Uttom Chowdhury

INTRODUCTION
Tics

Tics are involuntary, recurrent and non-rhythmic motor or vocal actions, which are also sudden, rapid and purposeless. For descriptive purposes, they can be divided into simple or complex tics. Simple motor tics are fast and meaningless and include eye blinking, grimacing and shoulder shrugging. Complex motor tics tend to be slower and may appear more purposeful such as hopping, kissing, touching objects, echopraxia (imitating movements of other people) or copropraxia (obscene gestures). Simple vocal tics include coughing, clearing one's throat and whistling, while complex vocal tics include repeating certain words or phrases, such as 'oh boy', or repeating a phrase until it sounds 'just right'. Other complex vocal tics include differences in articulation of speech (such as variation in rhythm, tone and rate) and coprolalia, the repetitive use of obscene or socially unacceptable words or phrases.

Transient tic disorders

These tics last only a few weeks or months and, although the affected area of the body may vary, they are usually confined to the face and neck. Motor tics are more common but sometimes vocal tics can occur too. The age of onset is usually 3 to 10 years, with more boys being affected than girls. While transient tics, by definition, do not persist for more than a year, it is not uncommon for a child to have series of transient tics over the course of several years.

Chronic motor or vocal tics

These tics are present for more than one year and, unlike transient tics, tend to remain the same (such as blinking or neck movements). Community surveys indicate that between 1 and 12 per cent of children will manifest some form of transient or chronic motor tic.

TOURETTE SYNDROME (COMBINED MULTIPLE MOTOR AND VOCAL TICS)

According to ICD-10 (World Health Organization 1992), the following symptoms constitute the diagnostic criteria for Tourette syndrome:

- Multiple motor tics and one or more vocal tics have been present at some time during the disorder, but not necessarily concurrently.

- The frequency of tics must be many times a day, nearly every day, for more than 1 year, with no period of remission during that year lasting longer than 2 months.

- Onset is before the age of 18 years.

The onset of tics is usually mild and infrequent, and occurs between the ages of 2 and 21. The mean age of onset is around 7 years (Robertson 1994), and boys are affected four times more than girls. The clinical history in Tourette syndrome is that tic symptoms will usually fluctuate in severity and frequency during the day as well as between days. This is often referred to as 'waxing and waning' of the tic symptoms. Patients also often describe a premonitory feeling or sensation prior to the tics, which is separate to the actual tic itself. Tics often increase in severity up to and during puberty, but then reach a relatively stable plateau during early adulthood. The patient with Tourette syndrome is likely to have a number of different motor and vocal tics, but head and neck tics are the commonest. Coprolalia (repetitive use of obscene or socially unacceptable words or phrases) rarely occurs in young children, and only occurs in 10 to 30 per cent of clinic populations. It is therefore not diagnostic of Tourette syndrome (Robertson 1994).

HISTORY

The first description of a patient with actual Tourette syndrome in the medical literature was by Itard in 1825, who wrote about a woman, the Marquise de Dampierre, who was severely affected by motor and vocal tics. In 1885, the French physician, Georges Gilles de La Tourette, described nine patients with childhood-onset tics, accompanied by uncontrollable noises and utterances. Although Tourette considered the disorder he described to be hereditary, it was ascribed to psychogenic causes for nearly a century after the original report. The perception of Tourette syndrome as a rare, psychological disorder began to change in the 1960s with recognition of the beneficial effects of neuroleptic drugs on the tic symptoms. This led to significant research into the condition, which is now recognized as a biological, genetic disorder with a spectrum of neuro-behavioural symptoms.

EPIDEMIOLOGY

Studies of school-aged children estimate the prevalence of Tourette syndrome to be between 0.4 and 1.85 per cent (Hornsey *et al.* 2001). However estimates vary markedly, with some estimates as high as 4.2 per cent when all types of tic disorders are included. There are many reasons for this wide variation including different methods of identifying cases, different study populations and different clinical criteria.

AETIOLOGY

Although the precise aetiology is not known, several studies support the fact that Tourette syndrome is an inherited, developmental disorder of synaptic neuro-transmission resulting in the disinhibition of the cortico-striatal-thalamic-cortical circuitry in the brain. Postmortem studies have not revealed any specific changes but other studies show that the pathogenesis of Tourette syndrome is likely to involve an imbalance in the dopaminergic system in the brain most likely involving the basal ganglia (Leckman *et al.* 1997). There is also likely to be a genetic component linking Tourette syndrome, chronic motor tics and obsessive compulsive disorder (Eapen, Pauls and Robertson 1993).

ASSESSMENT

The history of clinical symptoms should determine whether a child has transient tics, chronic tics or Tourette syndrome. The site, severity and frequency of tics, as well as precipitating and relieving factors, should be recorded. Co-morbid symptoms, such as those of Attention Deficit Hyperactivity Disorder (Chapter 6) and Obsessive Compulsive Disorder (Chapter 14), should also be noted. Other associated symptoms include self-harm and secondary depression.

It is important to enquire how the child is affected by the tics in relation to daily functioning at home and at school, and also ask about the child's self-esteem. How the family copes with and responds to the child's tics is imperative too as this may determine prognosis. A family history of tics or obsessive compulsive disorder (OCD) should be recorded. A good drug history is also important, especially as some children with attention deficit hyperactivity disorder (ADHD) may have been prescribed stimulant medication which can, in turn, precipitate or exacerbate tics in children who are predisposed to Tourette syndrome and tic disorders. School-related issues worth asking about include whether there is any bullying and teasing taking place and also about the child's academic abilities. The assessment is completed with a mental state examination and neurological examination of the child.

CO-MORBID SYMPTOMS
Obsessive compulsive disorder (OCD)

OCD, as described in Chapter 14, is characterized by recurrent upsetting thoughts or images that intrude on the patient's mind (obsessions) and also by an inner feeling or need to perform certain acts or rituals (compulsions). There is often a marked degree of distress in response to these thoughts and feelings, and rituals are performed to relieve the sense of subjective discomfort.

Examples of obsessions include excessive concern with contamination, persistent anxieties about illness or fear of losing things. Examples of compulsions include excessive handwashing, repeated checking, repeated counting and hoarding. There is increasing evidence that the OCD symptoms in children with tics are different from those symptoms in OCD patients without tics. Children with tics tend to have marked OCD symptoms such as the need to 'even things up', to touch things a certain number of times or to perform tasks until they 'feel right' (Rapoport and Inoff-Germain 2000).

Attention deficit hyperactivity disorder (ADHD)

ADHD, as described in Chapter 6, is a developmental condition usually present from early childhood. The core features include hyperactivity, inattention and impulsivity (Academy of Child and Adolescent Psychiatry 1997). The condition is pervasive, and symptoms thus occur both at home and at nursery/school. In children with Tourette syndrome, ADHD symptoms will invariably predate the onset of tics.

DIFFERENTIAL DIAGNOSIS

A good history is usually sufficient to differentiate the diagnosis of tics from other movement disorders such as chorea, myoclonus and stereotypies. Neuropsychiatric disorders that may be associated with tics include autism, Asperger syndrome, ADHD, OCD, schizophrenia and mental retardation. Other disorders with a genetic basis, such as Huntington's chorea and Wilson's disease, should be considered as should acquired motor tics associated with trauma or encephalitis. Sydenham's chorea should also be considered. As mentioned above, some medications can induce or worsen tics including stimulants, anti-psychotics, anti-depressants and some anti-epileptics such as cabamezipine (Kumar and Lang 1997).

Paediatric autoimmune neuro-psychiatric disorders associated with streptococcal infection (PANDAS)

There have been several recent studies, over the last few years, linking the sudden onset of obsessive compulsive symptoms and/or tics with Group A haemolytic streptococcal infection (GABHS). The evidence is based on a number of clinical and neuro-immunological findings, including volumetric MRI analysis of children with PANDAS which showed that basal ganglia structures were significantly larger than in a healthy control group (Giedd *et al.* 2000). It has been proposed that an immune-mediated mechanism, similar to the process in Sydenham's chorea, occurs in which antibodies produced against GABHS cross-react with neuronal tissue in the basal ganglia (Singer, Giuliano and Hansen 1999).

However, despite these studies, there have been no prospective epidemiological studies linking tic disorders or OCD directly with streptococcal infections and further research is therefore needed in this area. However, PANDAS remains worth keeping in mind when the onset or worsening of tics coincide with throat infections or related illnesses. The diagnostic criteria include: (1) the presence of OCD and/or tics; (2) pre-pubertal age at onset; (3) sudden onset and remission of symptoms; (4) a temporal relationship between symptoms and GABHS; and (5) the presence of neurological abnormalities including hyperactivity and choreiform movements (Swedo *et al.* 1998).

MANAGEMENT

Reassurance and psycho-education

Once a diagnosis of Tourette syndrome has been made, it is important to explain the natural history of the condition, and the related clinical symptoms, to the family. In particular, family members and teachers need to be reminded that tics should not be regarded as wilful behaviours. A useful analogy to present to parents is that of eye blinking: 'we all have the ability to temporarily suppress eye blinking but eventually and inevitably we do give in to the need to blink' (Peterson and Cohen 1998). An explanation of the biological basis of Tourette syndrome is also important to reinforce the fact that the child does not have full control of the tics, thus avoiding blame.

Families often find it useful to hear that Tourette syndrome is by no means a rare condition, and that it is simply at one end of a spectrum of tic disorders which are prevalent in the community. It is also helpful to explain to families that prognosis does not necessarily depend on severity of the tics but on other important factors too. These include the degree of understanding of the condition at home and school, the child's self-esteem, the child's general coping abilities and his or her attitude to and outlook on life. In mild cases, diagnosis and reassurance may be all that is required since the child and family may already be coping reasonably well without the need for further intervention or treatment. However, if treatment is warranted, then a range of behavioural and medical treatments are available.

Psychological interventions

A number of studies have demonstrated that psychological therapies can be effective in reducing tics (O'Conner *et al.* 2001), and may prove to be all that is needed in children with mild symptoms. As stress can precipitate and worsen tics, any reduction of stress will be beneficial and relaxation combined with concentration on enjoyable tasks may help to reduce tic symptom severity. This could include playing computer games or watching television. The use of relaxation tapes which involve guided imagery may also prove beneficial, and a basic knowledge of some simple psychological techniques may prove a helpful complement to medication.

Some children find it helpful to 'practise' their tics prior to going to school or during the school break. This may help the child be tic-free for a short period of time, and may prove especially helpful prior to stressful situations such as exams or performing on stage. Some children also may benefit from doing exercise and releasing 'pent up' energy. This can be done during time-out breaks at school, by letting the child run out in the local playing fields or by using a punch-bag.

Prognosis depends on a number of factors, including self-esteem and the child's outlook on life. Thus general support and encouragement should be emphasized within the family. Parents should also be encouraged to develop calm and competent parenting skills with clear reasonable achievable boundaries and targets.

Medication

It is unlikely that medication will result in tics stopping altogether, and it should therefore be stressed to parents that the aim of using medication is to allow the child to function at school and at home at an acceptable level. The lowest effective dosage of medication should be used, with the dose being titrated to achieve positive therapeutic effects while watching out for possible side-effects. Parents and children should be reminded of the nature of tics, that the condition will 'wax and wane', and that it may therefore be necessary to increase the drug during waxing of tic symptoms.

Dopamine antagonists (such as haloperidol) and atypical neuroleptics (such as risperidone and sulpiride) are often effective in reducing tics. However possible side-effects, including sedation, weight gain and tardive dyskinesia, may render parents and children reluctant to take the medication. Selective serotonin re-uptake inhibitors (such as fluoxetine or paroxetine) may be used to target specific OCD symptoms in patients with Tourette syndrome and co-morbid OCD.

Clonidine, an alpha-adrenergic pre-synaptic agonist, is a useful drug particularly if there are associated ADHD symptoms. Possible side-effects may include hypotension and sedation. It is important to note that stimulant medications used for children with ADHD, such as methylphenidate, may precipitate or worsen tics in some patients. However, this may not necessarily prove a contra-indication for its use in Tourette syndrome with co-morbid ADHD as the patient may benefit enormously if his or her ADHD symptoms can be reduced. However, a full explanation should be given to the family and child, with medication being stopped if tics worsen.

School

It is often helpful for parents to discuss their child's condition with teachers at school. This creates a more understanding environment for the child, and may prevent the child being unduly punished for behaviours related to Tourette syndrome. The child may also have problems with learning (Erenberg, Pauls and Roberson 1986), or problems associated with ADHD (Abwender *et al.* 1996). A Statement of Special Educational Needs may be warranted, and involvement of educational psychologists may help to identify the child's specific strengths and weaknesses.

Case example: Josh

Josh, a 10-year-old boy, was referred by his general practitioner to the local child psychiatrist for 'behaviour problems'. He had been aggressive to several pupils and his school teachers were concerned that he may have ADHD. At his first appointment, Josh said very little but his mother spoke about Josh being the victim of bullying for several years. She felt that Josh was taking out his anger on other children. She also felt he was struggling to keep up with his peers. On more detailed questioning, it appeared that Josh was called names such as 'noddy' or 'twitch' by his peers when he started developing a motor tic affecting the head and neck shortly after his eighth birthday. Josh had always struggled at school and, in particular, had extremely poor handwriting. His school reports often commented on his lack of concentration in lessons.

Further detailed questioning and use of questionnaires revealed that Josh was displaying symptoms of ADHD and motor tics. There were no vocal tics. His father had also experienced motor tics when he was the same age. After careful explanation to the family, it was decided that a trial of clonidine should be started. Josh immediately started to feel more relaxed in class as the motor tics were less prominent. Although he continued to struggle with some lessons, his overall school work and behaviour started to improve over the following term. It was also commented on by his parents that his self-esteem had improved. Josh felt so confident that he even gave a talk about Tourette syndrome to his classmates at a recent assembly. Josh is now doing well, and he and his family have joined the national Tourette Syndrome Association which they feel has been really beneficial and supportive.

REFERENCES

Abwender, D.A., Como, P.G., Kurlan, R., Parry, K. *et al.* (1996) 'School problems in Tourette syndrome.' *Archives of Neurology 53*, 509–511.

American Academy of Child and Adolescent Psychiatry (1997) 'Practice parameters for the assessment and treatment of children, adolescents and adults with attention-deficit/hyperactivity disorder.' *Journal of the American Academy of Child and Adolescent Psychiatry 36* (Supplement), 85S–121S.

Eapen, V., Pauls, D.L. and Robertson, M.M. (1993) 'Evidence for autosomal dominant transmission in Tourette syndrome. United Kingdom cohort study.' *British Journal of Psychiatry 162*, 593–596.

Erenberg, G., Cruse, P.R. and Rothner, A.D. (1986) 'Tourette syndrome.' *Cleveland Clinical Quarterly 53*, 127–131.

Giedd, J.N., Rapoport, J.L., Garvey, M.A., Perlmutter, S. *et al.* (2000) 'MRI assessment of children with obsessive compulsive disorder or tics associated with streptococcal infections.' *Biological Psychiatry 45*, 1564–1571.

Hornsey, H., Banerjee, S., Zeitlin, H. and Robertson, M.M. (2001) 'The prevalence of Tourette syndrome in 13–14-year-olds in mainstream schools.' *Journal of Child Psychology and Psychiatry 42*, 1035–1039.

Kumar, R. and Lang, A.E. (1997) 'Tourette syndrome. Secondary tic disorders [review].' *Neurology Clinics 15*, 309–331.

Leckman, J.F., Peterson, B.S., Anderson, G.M., Arnsten, A.F.T. *et al.* (1997) 'Pathogenesis of Tourette syndrome.' *Journal of Child Psychology and Psychiatry 38*, 119–142.

O'Conner, K.P., Brault, M., Robillard, S., Loiselle, J. *et al.* (2001) 'Evaluation of a cognitive-behavioural program for the management of chronic tic and habit disorders.' *Behaviour Research and Therapy 39*, 667–681.

Peterson, B.S. and Cohen, D.J. (1998) 'The treatment of Tourette syndrome: Multimodal, developmental intervention.' *Journal of Clinical Psychiatry 59*, 62–72.

Rapoport, J.L. and Inoff-Germain, G. (2000) 'Practitioner review: Treatment of obsessive compulsive disorder in children and adolescents.' *Journal of Child Psychology and Psychiatry 41*, 419–431.

Robertson, M.M. (1994) 'Annotation: Gilles de la Tourette's syndrome – an update [review].' *Journal of Child Psychology and Psychiatry 35*, 597–611.

Singer, H.S., Giuliano, J.D. and Hansen, B.H. (1999) 'Antibodies against a neuron-like (HTB-10 neuroblastoma) cell in children with Tourette syndrome.' *Biological Psychiatry 46*, 775–780.

Swedo, S.E., Leonard, H.L., Mittleman, B.B., Allen, A.J. *et al.* (1998) 'Pediatric autoimmune neuropsychiatric disorders associated with streptococcal infections: Clinical description of the first 50 cases.' *American Journal of Psychiatry 155*, 264–271.

World Health Organization (1992) *International Statistical Classification of Diseases and Related Health Problems*, 10th revision (ICD-10). Geneva: World Health Organization.

FURTHER READING

Carroll, A. and Robertson, M.M. (2000) *Tourette Syndrome. A Practical Guide for Teachers, Parents and Carers.* London: David Fulton Publishers.

Chowdhury, U. (2004) *Tics and Tourette Syndrome: A Handbook for Parents and Professionals.* London: Jessica Kingsley Publishers.

Robertson, M.M. (2000) 'Invited review: Tourette syndrome, associated conditions and the complexities of treatment.' *Brain 123*, 425–462.

Part 3
Disorganized Children

Chapter 19

The disorganized child

Samuel M. Stein and Uttom Chowdhury

INTRODUCTION

The clinical concept of 'disorganized children' has been generated over the past decade by the growing number of young people who are experiencing mild but debilitating emotional and behavioural problems either at home or at school. These children are often referred on to Child and Adolescent Mental Health Services (CAMHS), and present with an almost identical array of complaints and features. Many have also previously been assessed by educationists, social workers, health visitors, general practitioners and paediatricians without a specific diagnosis being reached, and without any significant response to the treatment options being implemented. Unfortunately, due to the lack of definitive diagnosis and the minimal impact of treatment regimens, the child's presentation is then deemed to be within his or her conscious control. The emotional and behavioural problems for which he or she was initially assessed are subsequently attributed by parents, teachers and health care professionals to defiance, disobedience, oppositional attitudes, difficulties with authority or deliberate attempts to be anti-social and naughty.

However, on detailed questioning, the parents of these disorganized children soon describe how they were aware of 'problems' from almost the moment that their child was born. They often raise early infantile difficulties relating to sleeping and feeding, as well as their struggles with persistent crying, restlessness and the child's need for constant attention. Parents also tend to highlight early worries about delayed developmental milestones, features of poor motor coordination, restricted social abilities, decreased cognitive function, behavioural problems, a need for sameness and difficulties in processing information. Sadly, many parents talk of not being able to convince teachers or health care professionals of their growing concerns, with the most common response being described as 'they will soon grow out of it'.

While these early clinical features would be consistent with potential neuro-developmental problems evident from infancy, disorganized children often only come to the attention of educational, social care, medical and mental health professionals later on when the increasing demands of their chronological development start to exceed their restricted coping strategies. Except for isolated and particularly stressful occasions, their underlying neurological deficits may have been of insufficient severity to generate overt problems at home or at school before then. However, as social and academic pressures increase with age, these inherent neuro-developmental processing limitations increasingly come to the fore and present as either emotional or behavioural difficulties, often within both the classroom and the family setting.

As the clinical features with which disorganized children present are often mild and relatively vague, they invariably fail to meet the diagnostic specificity of any formally defined mental health or paediatrics disorders. Unfortunately, the perceived absence of an identifiable medical problem then shifts the emphasis almost exclusively onto potential family difficulties, emotional issues, conduct problems and other psychological explanations. Yet careful assessment of these children and adolescents will quickly identify overt traits and symptoms of well-established childhood presentations such as attention deficit hyperactivity disorder, Asperger syndrome or Tourette syndrome whose neurological origins are extremely well documented in the available research literature.

Disorganized children therefore cannot be truly understood, or managed effectively, if considered only within current social models of illness which are based largely on diagnosable conditions being either fully present or totally absent. Instead, an essential shift in thinking, which has already altered the understanding of and approach to autism, needs to take place with regard to other neuro-developmental problems. Prevalent 'all or none' diagnostic models need to be superseded by a more flexible understanding of neurologically based signs and symptoms, which are instead recognized as occurring along a continuous spectrum that extends from almost normal to overtly pathological. This will bring to light the wide range of previously invisible children and adolescents who exist along this spectrum, and whose presenting problems fall somewhere between the extreme poles of normality and diagnosable illness.

While they may not warrant a definitive medical diagnosis, or prove amenable to specific treatment modalities, these disorganized children are nonetheless seriously hampered by a wide range of sub-clinical neuro-developmental symptoms and difficulties (Figure 19.1) which are of sufficient severity to impair their daily function at home and at school. Unless recognized early, and actively addressed, these hidden neurologically based deficits may impact subtly but significantly on personal, social and educational development, leading to the subsequent emotional and behavioural problems with which these children and adolescents ultimately present.

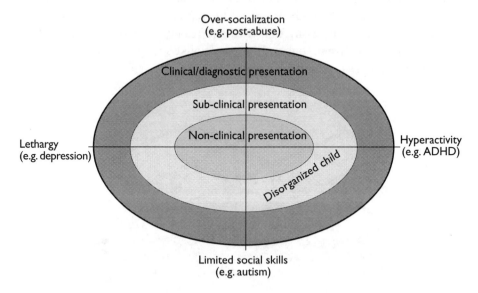

Figure 19.1

NEUROLOGICAL DEVELOPMENT

Given the mild and vague features with which disorganized children often present, it is essential to understand something about their potential neurological and developmental deficits. It is otherwise very difficult to comprehend clearly the particular emotional and behavioural problems with which they struggle, or to set appropriate treatment strategies in motion. Unfortunately, these subtle neuro-developmental deficits cannot be overtly demonstrated using available clinical options such as blood tests, brain scans or intelligence quotients. Instead, the likely patterns of neuro-developmental function which characterize disorganized children need to be inferred from the recent literature on brain injuries, cerebral infections, anatomical studies, physiological research and mental health developments. Using this information, we have been able to develop a theoretical working model to explain schematically the subtle differences in neurological development and function that may contribute to the overt difficulties experienced by disorganized children.

The starting point is an understanding that the human brain is made up of more than 10 billion neurons, which are the basic cellular building blocks of neurological development. Each of these nerve cells can have several thousand synapses or connections with other brain neurons, creating an immense web of communicating cerebral tissue. It is through this sophisticated network of neurological fibres that the brain then communicates with both itself and with other organs within the body. However, the representation of these complex neural structures can be easily simplified and readily visualized as a straight-forward grid of interconnecting pathways not unlike a telephone switchboard, a road map or a railway junction (Figure 19.2).

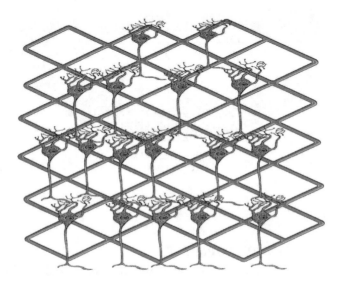

Figure 19.2

When the individual's brain is working effectively within its residual capacity, then signals pass quickly and efficiently along the communicating network (Figure 19.3). Feelings, thoughts or planned movements are readily communicated within the body, allowing appropriate responses to be generated. For most people, the number of different signals being processed simultaneously is incalculable, and the communications take place almost instantaneously.

In children and adolescents with neuro-developmental difficulties, this network and communication system may be marginally impaired. Instead of unimpeded pathways capable of instantaneously processing complex information, their network can be schematically characterized by potential breaks in and obstacles to smooth signal transmission (Figure 19.4) in keeping with the clinically evident processing problems experienced by disorganized children.

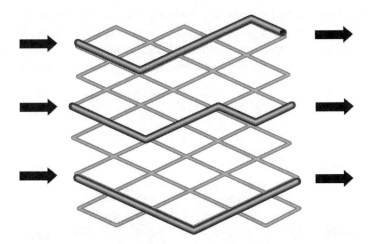

Figure 19.3

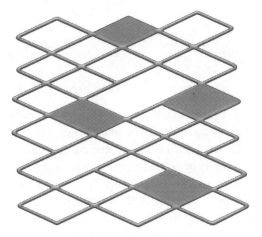

Figure 19.4

Even with these potential neuro-developmental and structural problems, disorganized children are still able to process complex information appropriately (Figure 19.5). However, the signals being communicated are likely to encounter breaks and obstacles within the network, which then need to be circumnavigated. Given the sophistication of neurological development and brain function, these detours are simply set in motion without any evident problems being generated by the minimal delays which result. For most day-to-day tasks, especially those free from stress and time pressures, children and adolescents with mild neuro-developmental difficulties will therefore not demonstrate any overt differences to more neurologically efficient peers.

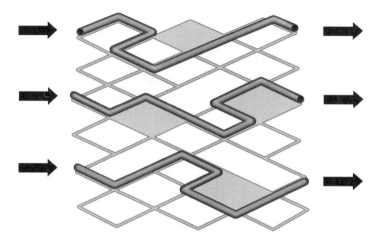

Figure 19.5

As long as the activity required of the network remains within manageable levels, then no overt deficit appears as the brain simply takes the delay and detour of signals in its stride. However, difficulties become increasingly apparent when the number, volume or intensity of communications within the neural network start to escalate. As the number of signals which need processing increases, it becomes more and more difficult to orchestrate these alternative routings effectively. A level of activity is then reached in which the neural network can no longer cope with the flow of communications and, above a given threshold, signals increasingly encounter obstacles which cannot be overcome. As a result, only a fixed proportion of the ongoing communications can be processed by the brain, with the remainder of signals failing to reach their destination (Figure 19.6). Due to these disruptions, as can be seen with overloaded telephone switchboards or gridlocked motorways, neurological processing becomes increasingly inefficient. Unfortunately, the impact of these subtle neuro-developmental deficits in disorganized children are difficult to detect due to their fluctuating and erratic presentation, and the very individual levels of activity manageable by each child or adolescent.

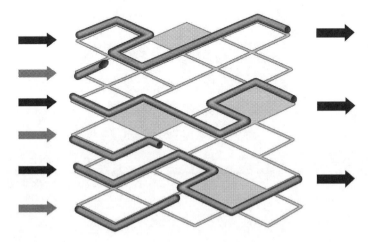

Figure 19.6

Disorganized children therefore do not present with discrete or defined neuropathology, and their neuro-developmental deficits do not appear as a clear-cut or constant loss of function. Instead, they present with subtle processing problems which are almost invisible at lower levels of network activity and yet which become clinically significant when the intensity and volume of communication and signals increases. This network overload has the potential to disrupt the internal neurological feedback loop between the basal ganglia, the cortex and structures in the limbic system such as the hypothalamus (represented very simply in Figure 19.7) with resultant emotional and behavioural problems. These arise when disorganized children are no longer able to ensure efficient and active pathways of communication between their thinking, their feelings and their intentions. Depending on which components of neuro-developmental function are most affected, and depending on which feedback loops are most disrupted, children and adolescents may therefore present with intermittent and sub-clinical features of diagnoses such as attention deficit hyperactivity disorder (ADHD), autistic spectrum disorder, Tourette syndrome, dyslexia and dyspraxia (see Figure 1 in the Introduction).

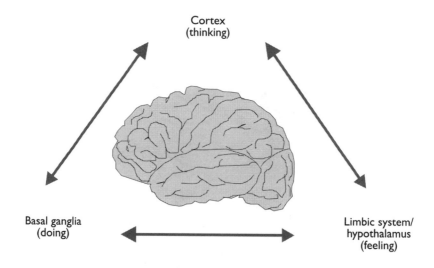

Figure 19.7

CLINICAL PRESENTATION

Many disorganized children are not readily identified as having subtle neuro-developmental problems in spite of presenting with overt difficulty in coordinating their thinking, their feelings and their actions. As their symptoms are erratic, and do not persist across a wide range of settings, disorganized children often do not meet sufficient diagnostic specifications to warrant definitive neuro-developmental diagnosis (Figure 19.1). Instead, their presenting features are attributed to non-neurological causes such as emotional difficulties, behavioural problems, anxiety, defiance, oppositional attitudes, laziness, parenting issues or family dynamics. While these mental health components may well be present, and contribute actively to the problems being experienced by disorganized children, they may be the consequence of underlying neuro-developmental deficits rather than the cause of the difficulties.

Box 19.1 Presenting features of disorganized children

- Restricted coping strategies
- Not learning from experience
- Patchy cognitive function
- Preference for structured activities
- Lack of organization
- Impaired short-term memory
- Overloaded by complex stimuli
- Restlessness and poor attention span
- Fear of failure
- Reduced comprehension
- Inability to sequence data
- Limited sense of other people
- Social and communication difficulties
- Cannot use symbolic concepts
- Unable to generalize data
- Lack of time management
- Poor motivation
- Preference for routine
- Obsessions and rituals
- Poor motor skills and coordination
- Restricted personality
- Low esteem and confidence

The way in which disorganized children think, feel and act therefore differs significantly, although only subtly, from the emotions and behaviour of their peers. These differences are evident in their cognitive function, in their organizational abilities, in their language use, in their relationships, in their self-esteem, in their motivation, in their capacity for symbolic thought, in their patterns of behaviour, in their impulsivity and in their coping strategies (Box 19.1). However, rather than being a reflection of intelligence or overall ability, these difficulties instead reflect the problems experienced by disorganized children in processing more

complex and intense sequences of information. This deficit in processing efficiency and speed, together with the resultant frustration which arises, can effectively and appropriately explain all of the presenting features characteristic of
disorganized children, and help to clarify the significant impact of their neuro-
developmental problems on day-to-day life at home and at school.

Restricted coping strategies

Many disorganized children present to CAMHS due to concerns about aggressive
and violent behaviour. These referrals from schools and health care professionals
often describe unpredictable and unprecipitated outbursts of verbal and physical
abuse. However, on detailed questioning, it soon becomes apparent that these
children and adolescents lash out impulsively, in an undirected manner that is free
from any premeditation or malicious intent. Their outbursts are not directed at
specific targets, and they inevitably feel remorse afterwards. As such, these
episodes are more likely to represent an inappropriate response to escalating and
uncontrollable frustration rather than constituting directed and intentional
aggression.

This process can be readily visualized by looking at patterns of stress over
time (Figure 19.8). All children and adolescents have a stress-related threshold,
above which they cease to function effectively. Day to day, individuals levels of
stress may fluctuate, often quite significantly, depending on experiences at home
and at school. However, few children tend to reach or exceed their upper limit of
stress tolerance (which has been randomly demarcated as 10 on the graph) unless
exposed to serious events such as the death of a parent or a major accident or
illness.

In contrast, children with ADHD exposed to the same daily life events would
find that their basic threshold for coping with stress was exceeded frequently
throughout any given day (Figure 19.9). If this restricted coping capacity is
designated as 3 on the graph, compared to an average of 10, then disorganized
children can be categorized as having a threshold for coping with stress of about
7. This marked limitation in their coping capacity, and their significantly reduced
ability to generate appropriate alternative strategies under stress, is almost
certainly a direct consequence of their neuro-developmental deficits. As a result,
when overloaded by either internal or external stimulation (or any stress which
exceeds their threshold of 7), the links between thinking, feeling and action
become increasingly impeded and disrupted. These disorganized children will
then tend to react impulsively to their growing sense of frustration and their sense
of being overwhelmed by the world around them. However, because their
underlying neuro-pathology is often very mild and very subtle, the isolated and
intermittent outbursts which occur when their stress-related threshold is
exceeded are quickly attributed to deliberate and controllable behaviour.

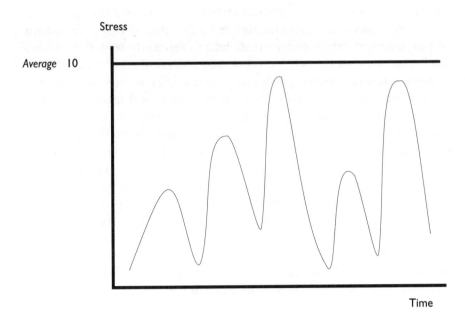

Figure 19.8

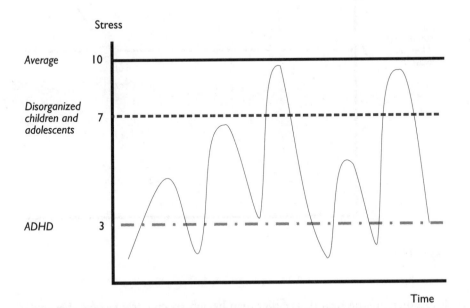

Figure 19.9

Parents, teachers and health care professionals tend to reach this conclusion as they cannot easily identify specific triggers for the outbursts or specific patterns of behaviour with which disorganized children present. Instead, they observe sudden and unprovoked episodes without apparent justification or cause. Yet, if observed carefully, often using daily diary sheets, a different pattern emerges. For most disorganized children, the build-up of pressure and tension is gradual (Figure 19.10). As the day progresses, they move gradually towards their coping threshold, with each life event adding to the escalation, irrespective of its intensity or magnitude. For example, a troubled night may start the day on a stress level of 1, with the unavailability of a favourite shirt pushing the stress factor up to 2. Friction over cereal choice with a sibling at breakfast may move the stress level up to 3, with some teasing on the school bus escalating the level up to 5. A forgotten assignment or request to stop talking in class may add further stress up to level 6. At this critical point, almost any interaction, whether positive or negative, is likely to precipitate a seemingly unprovoked and unpredictable outburst when the disorganized child suddenly finds his or her coping strategy ceiling of 7 overwhelmed and exceeded by events around him or her.

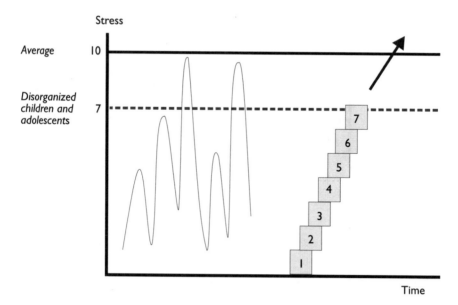

Figure 19.10

It can therefore be seen that, rather than having specific triggers for their outbursts, disorganized children instead respond to an escalating pattern of stressful experiences which carry them over their inherent coping threshold. Because of this neuro-developmental deficit, they are readily overwhelmed by multiple stimuli, large groups of people, anxiety, noise or interpersonal conflict. As the pressure builds, they quickly reach their personal cut-off point, after which the slightest increase in stress will precipitate a reaction. Having passed their threshold, they suddenly lose almost total control of their emotions and behaviour. It is then very difficult for either the disorganized child, or the adults at home and at school, to manage these episodes. To date, no specific interventions have been described for dealing with these outbursts other than gradually allowing them to dissipate over time.

Unfortunately, as their inherent susceptibility to stress forms an irrevocable component of their neuro-developmental deficit, the basic coping threshold of disorganized children cannot be directly altered or improved. The only viable approach to reducing the outbursts, and limiting their impact, is therefore to focus on prevention and on finding ways to enhance basic coping strategies. Ideally, an 'early warning line' needs to be identified just below their individual coping threshold, for example at a stress level of 6.5 (Figure 19.11). As the disorganized child moves slowly towards his or her stress ceiling, parents and teachers need to watch for the tell-tale signs of this escalation, which are usually self-evident and obvious. Examples of possible warning features may include restlessness, fidgeting, irritability, distraction or moving off task.

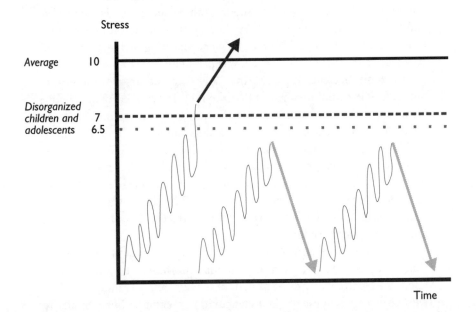

Figure 19.11

Once a gradual progression towards the crisis point or level is identified, steps can be taken to reverse the trend and to find ways of reducing or dissipating the child or adolescent's experience of rapidly escalating pressure and tension. If implemented well before the stress threshold, this approach should prove effective for most disorganized children as the trigger, which is any stress-inducing action close to their cut-off point, can then be effectively avoided. However, as these children may move quickly towards their maximum threshold level several times each day, ongoing vigilance by parents and teachers is essential, with repeated efforts being needed to bring them back onto an even keel each time their sense of stress begins to escalate.

Case example: Henry

Henry is an 8-year-old boy who was referred for assessment because of frequent unpredictable and unprovoked attacks on other children at school. His teachers said, having watched him before and during these episodes, that no triggers were evident for his behaviour. It was therefore decided to monitor Henry, both at home and in the classroom, using a detailed diary (Figure 19.12) to track his behaviour from waking up until going to bed. This exercise classified Henry's behaviour as (1) on task; (2) off task but in his seat; (3) off task and wandering around but not interfering with others; (4) interrupting others and becoming intrusive; and (5) becoming disruptive. Diary sheets were collected for nearly four weeks, and then reviewed by a multi-agency meeting including CAMHS pro- fessionals, school teachers and his parents.

It soon became apparent that Henry's outbursts were not as unpredictable or unprovoked as first thought. In terms of predictability, Henry started to move off task, with wandering around and then intrusion on almost every occasion before a major outburst. The diary sheets highlighted this escalating pattern, as well as occasions on which the escalation had been prevented by vigilant action by either his parents or his teachers. A set of early warning signals, such as restlessness and loss of attention, were subsequently identified to allow the adults involved in Henry's care to predict potential outbursts effectively, and then to take appropriate evasive action.

The diary sheets also helped to identify the sources of provocation for Henry's behaviour. For example, Monday mornings and Friday after- noons were particularly difficult periods for him, and any minor conflicts with peers during these fragile times could trigger an outburst. Similarly, breaks and lunchtime could prove stressful and this was resolved by providing Henry with esteem-enhancing tasks during these periods in order to reduce both time spent in the playground and the level of over-stimulation that was taking place. It was also possible to identify certain teachers and certain subjects which were more likely to escalate Henry's behaviour, as well as highlighting events and people at home who would potentially contribute to pending outbursts. In this way, it was possible to structure Henry's days according to his neuro-developmental needs with a significant reduction in his seemingly unprovoked and unpredictable outbursts.

Note: The tick at the top of Figure 19.12 indicates that you may photocopy this figure for your own use.

Learning from experience

Disorganized children struggle to learn from their past experiences. One of the most common concerns described by parents is the need to repeat basic safety instructions again and again, without their child learning to implement these strategies independently. They therefore repeat potentially dangerous behaviours, either through forgetting to implement the appropriate process or through having forgotten the consequences of a previous attempt of the same action. These difficulties are linked to their limited short-term memory, and a failure to link cause and effect effectively. The latter stems from their reduced capacity to process and store information in appropriate sequences. Their ability to learn from experience is therefore reduced by their inability to internalize these experiences as memories, and to draw on them later for guidance and decision-making. As a result, they tend to act or speak before thinking, which is further enhanced by the reduced impulse control characteristic of almost all disorganized children. In spite of their chronological age, this often makes it unsafe to leave these children alone, in home or classroom settings, as they tend to be oblivious to dangers. Disorganized children therefore need higher levels of supervision, and a significant level of repetition before they learn to associate past or dangerous actions with future consequences. This recurring inability to process overt links between cause and effect often leaves parents feeling frustrated, with a tendency to then see the inappropriate behaviour as lazy, naughty or disobedient.

Name:.. Observer:.. Date: ....

TIME	MON	TUE	WED	THU	FRI	SAT	SUN	COMMENTS
Before 8.00								
8.00								
8.15								
8.30								
8.45								
9.00								
9.15								
9.30								
9.45								
10.00								
10.15								
10.30								
10.45								
11.00								
11.15								
11.30								
11.45								
12.00								
12.15								
12.30								
12.45								
13.00								
13.15								
13.30								
13.45								
14.00								
14.15								
14.30								
14.45								
15.00								
15.15								
15.30								
15.45								
16.00								
16.15								
16.30								
16.45								
17.00								
17.15								
17.30								
17.45								
18.00								
18.15								
18.30								
18.45								
19.00								
19.15								
19.30								
19.45								
After 20.00								
	On task	Off task (in seat)	Off task (out of seat)	Interrupts/ intrudes	Disruptive	Not observed		
	~	#	X	/	O			

Figure 19.12

Case example: John

John was a 10-year-old boy, who presented to CAMHS via Casualty. He had been hit by a slow-moving car, having run out into the road near his home. His mother was very concerned about his apparently 'suicidal' behaviour as John, who was extremely unhappy at both home and school, had nearly been involved in a similar accident only days previously. She also described how she had been teaching John appropriate road safety strategies since he was very young. In spite of this, he still tended to cross the road without looking properly at an age when he really should have known better. This was particularly evident as his younger sister was far more safety conscious than John. At interview, it soon became apparent that John did not often remember his mother's instructions, and he also did not remember clearly the previous road traffic incident although it had only just happened. He remained confused about left/right directions, and showed a tendency towards impulsivity and inattention. His behaviour, while unsafe, therefore did not represent a deliberate attempt at self-harm but instead reflected his poor short-term memory, his poor coordination and his weak information processing abilities.

Patchy cognitive function

Disorganized children tend to confuse and frustrate both parents and teachers due to the apparently erratic and inconsistent nature of their intellectual abilities. They seem to manage some complex tasks extremely well, only then to fail in adhering to very simple instructions. This differential often leads to accusations of being lazy or oppositional, especially where adults consider the child's highest attainment to be indicative of his or her general ability. This may prove an appropriate assumption in most children, whose performance and verbal skills (which can be formally assessed by IQ testing) tend to show a relatively constant attainment. In contrast, disorganized children tend to demonstrate a significant discrepancy between their verbal skills (which are often very good) and their performance skills (which do not match their higher verbal ability). They therefore present as having marked areas of strength and marked areas of weakness, which is termed patchy cognitive function (Figure 19.13). As a result, these children and adolescents often struggle to convert sophisticated thoughts into actions, or to convert their thinking into comparable written work.

It is therefore essential for children to be assessed in a holistic manner, to ensure that their overall levels of function, as well as specific strengths and weaknesses, are appropriately catered for both at home and at school. Because of this inherent spiky or patchy presentation, which is often indicative of

neuro-developmental problems, disorganized children cannot use their strengths
to compensate for their weaknesses. This pattern does not reflect their overall
intelligence, which may be high, but rather their inability to use different aspects
of their thinking, feeling and acting in a coherent and coordinated manner
(Figure 19.7). As a result, they tend to focus on particular topics or behaviours
(which represent their strengths) while avoiding other activities or approaches
(which represent their weaknesses). These 'patchy' peaks and troughs of ability
will further impede already compromised cognitive processing skills, meaning
that almost everything will take longer than expected in a child of corresponding
age. Parents and teachers therefore struggle to understand how an obviously
intelligent child can attain high levels of function one minute and significantly
reduced levels of function a moment later.

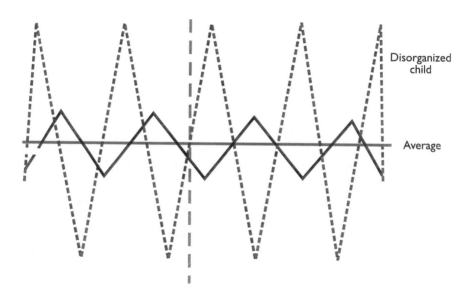

Figure 19.13

Case example: Sally

Sally's parents were becoming increasingly angry and frustrated with her
behaviour at home and at school. She presented as a very capable
8-year-old girl, who could express herself verbally far better than her
older brother. However, when asked to commit these thoughts into
writing or action, she performed at a level more appropriate to her

younger sister. While able to undertake complex mathematical problems and understand sophisticated computer programmes, she still proved unable to hold her knife and fork properly or to eat without mess. Her parents therefore attributed her reluctance for written work as laziness, and saw her inability to learn table manners as defiance, including her deliberate slowness in carrying out routine tasks. Having received appropriate help, they were soon able to recognize her verbal/performance mismatch, and deal with different aspects of home and school life according to Sally's individual abilities. With clear instructions, longer time allocations, appropriate special needs input in class and patient parental support, she was soon able to enhance some of her weaknesses and build on her strengths.

Structured activities

Disorganized children respond poorly to change, especially if it is unexpected. They prefer structured activities, and a clear pattern to their days and weeks. As a result, they tend to be most comfortable with familiarity and routine, with a preference for timetables and sameness. This probably reflects the increased psychological stress and effort inherent in managing unfamiliar or unpredictable situations, and the anxiety which this then generates. While this response is common to many children and adolescents, their effective neuro-developmental processing will allow them to take new patterns on board and to make the necessary adaptive changes to new scenarios. However, for disorganized children, much of their day-to-day functioning often feels marginal, achieved only by immensely hard work and effort. They therefore describe a sense of impending doom and catastrophic decompensation when confronted with unexpected changes in their routine.

This fear of sudden change is intensified by their inability to link cause and effect, their inability to generalize information from one situation to another, their tendency towards concrete responses to perceived threats, their rigid interpretation of available information and their lack of adaptability and ad hoc reasoning. As a result, these children may not understand the innovative and creative solutions or actions required when faced with unexpected or altered situations. Instead, they are most content and manage best within established boundaries and within set routines which require little active choice, enhanced thought or novel action. This reliance on structure allows them to maximize their strengths, while also avoiding weaknesses linked to their neurologically reduced cognitive and coping strategies.

Case example: Harry

Harry, a 14-year-old boy, was finding the transition from junior school to senior school very difficult. He had enjoyed the more protected environment of his first school, where the weekly timetable was straightforward and where the teachers often reminded him of his commitments. He was aware of the various rules, which had been clearly spelled out over time. In contrast, the senior school operated according to a two-weekly timetable, which Harry found difficult to remember. He became quickly confused as to the week within which he was meant to be operating. He was also struggling with the more covert rules that governed senior education, with an emphasis on individual responsibility and increased autonomy rather than on clearly stated routines and deadlines. The boundaries were more vague, with greater scope for choice, which suited the chronological development of his peers. They were also finding the introduction of new subjects, such as modern languages, and rotating teachers more interesting than the restricted academic remit of junior school. However, these changes to Harry's established routine were escalating his anxiety and reducing his coping capacity. As a result, his school work began to suffer and he presented to CAMHS with a reluctance to attend school. Once appropriate strategies has been agreed with the school to increase Harry's ability to master the new timetable, new rules, new subjects and new teachers, he soon settled well into the more stimulating environment.

Lack of organization

Children and adolescents with mild neuro-developmental difficulties are often very disorganized. They struggle to coordinate their feelings, thoughts and actions in a coherent way. As a result, the holistic and combined approaches used by other people to generate forward planning, decision-making and organization are less efficient in these disorganized children. This process, also known as 'executive function', includes activities such as self-monitoring, initiation of actions and behavioural flexibility. It also links closely with other organization skills like time management, sequencing of information and multi-tasking.

The decreased executive function experienced by disorganized children, while ever-present, is less visible under contained and familiar conditions. However, it becomes more and more apparent as the novelty of the instructions, the unfamiliarity of the environment or the time pressures being applied increase. This can be seen most easily when creative thinking, rapid responses or prioritization are demanded of the child or adolescent. For example, a disorganized child who is given a large amount of money to spend within a limited period of time is most likely to emerge from the shop without anything as the task of coordinating the money available, the products on sale, their individual value and the time factors involved will have seriously exceeded his or her organizational ability.

Unfortunately, from the perspective of parents and teachers, the organizational skills of these disorganized children seem to fluctuate from day to day. They often mistake a marked tendency towards sameness or routine as strong organizational ability, and fail to understand why this approach alters from situation to situation. As a result, inherent neuro-developmental disorganization is often misinterpreted as disobedience or laziness. What seems apparent is a child or adolescent who is capable of organizing him- or herself for one activity yet unable to do likewise for another similar or related activity. However, by understanding the processing problems experienced by disorganized children, it becomes increasingly clear that they are only able to organize themselves within specific settings or situations, and only when their thoughts, feelings and actions work in harmony. They therefore need high levels of guidance and support in tasks of daily living, especially when they are young. These tasks may already be in keeping with their chronological age but not yet within reach of their mild neuro-developmental processing problems. Parents and teachers, in order to assist these children and adolescents, may need to find alternative ways of enhancing their impaired organizational skills through explaining requests differently, using frequent repetition, providing aide-memoires, devising information flowcharts, reducing time pressures and restricting choices (Figure 19.14).

Case example: Jonathan

Jonathan is a 17-year-old boy who was planning on leaving home after finishing school. He had always struggled with organizing himself, ever since he was young. When he first started school, his mother needed to lay out all of his clothing each morning to ensure that he dressed correctly. For several years, she laid out his clothes in order of underpants, socks, shirt, trousers, tie and jumper to help him memorize and understand the organizational sequence for getting dressed. She also drew up a flowchart to help him organize his personal hygiene, such as washing his face, brushing his teeth, doing his hair and using deodorant. She was now trying to teach him to wash his own clothing at the local launderette. Whenever his clothes needed cleaning, they sorted out the colours, measured out the washing powder, filled the identified machine, inserted the correct coins and then tumble-dried the clean clothes. This was done in slow stages, with Jonathan doing more and more of the actions on each occasion, as he came to understand the sequence. Finally, his mother suggested that he undertake the task on his own, having mastered it in her presence. On the day, he returned home shortly afterwards to say that the machine which they had always used was busy and he therefore wasn't sure how to proceed. Jonathan, due to his lack of organization skills, was not able to recognize that all of the machines in the launderette were identical, and that he could apply the sequence which he had learned to any of them with the same effect.

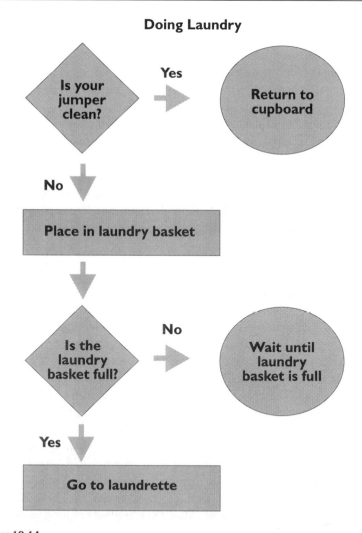

Doing Laundry

Figure 19.14

Impaired short-term memory

Many disorganized children experience memory problems. The majority struggle more with recent recollection, while retaining an ability to recall incidents from many years before. They present most frequently with an inability to remember immediate and recent events or information. Yet, at the same time, they astound teachers and parents by remembering items from their distant past. This discrepancy between short-term and long-term memory is very much in keeping with significant neuro-developmental processing problems. Also, while short-term memory deficits may present as the most overt symptom, the problem is actively related to comprehension and retention of data as well as to its simple recall. Disorganized children tend to struggle with understanding, especially in relation to complex sequences of information, which means that they are even less likely to remember these details. However, once they have understood a topic, and recognized its meaning, they seldom forget the facts, which they are then able to recall with little difficulty.

Unfortunately, as with many other symptoms, this differential in memory function may be interpreted by parents and teachers as laziness or disobedience when faced with children or adolescents who fail to complete simple short-term memory-linked tasks while also demonstrating remarkable long-term recollection. While this may frustrate parents and teachers, it also needs to be recognized as a significant source of frustration for the disorganized children themselves as they are often left feeling stupid, slow and incompetent due their poor retention of short-term information. It is then very common, having forgotten recent details, for these children, consciously or unconsciously, to confabulate or make up information to fill the gap in order to avoid embarrassment, ridicule or punishment. As these naïvely revised memories are easily disproved, this adaptive and defensive strategy simply adds to the negative behavioural reputation of disorganized children who increasingly come to be perceived as dishonest and manipulative.

Facilitating an improvement in the immediate retention and recall of information by these children and adolescents requires a great deal of patience on behalf of parents and teachers. It first requires a significant change in perception, and recognition of the presenting problem as indicative of neuro-developmental processing problems. It also requires modification of teaching and training approaches, to help disorganized children to understand better the sequence of information which they are being asked to remember. Once they have understood the concept in a meaningful way, significant repetition is still needed to help embed these details in their memory for later recall. As can be seen from Figure 19.15, they need to be taught in smaller and more manageable steps. Figure 19.16 serves to highlight the need to explain concepts until they are fully comprehended, and the need to then repeat these explanations until the ideas are firmly memorized by the disorganized child. Unfortunately, these inherent memory problems will be intensified by their distractibility, their susceptibility to become quickly overloaded by information and their tendency to move off task. However, as their neuro-developmental difficulties are not indicative of their intelligence, they may well achieve the same degree of learning as their peers, provided that they are helped to understand and retain the information in a piecemeal fashion.

Case example: Judith

Judith is a 14-year-old girl who was causing concern at school due to her poor academic performance. Her teachers were worried about the increasing difference between Judith and her peers, especially as she was falling further and further behind. At the same time, attempts to help her were met with a bored stare, lack of homework, missed coursework deadlines and non-attendance at additional lessons which were set up for her. Judith's response to any requests for clarification were simply met with 'I forgot', which was then interpreted as an unwillingness to learn and poor academic motivation. In contrast, Judith was struggling to understand the growing hostility which she was experiencing from her teachers and their decreasing willingness to help her.

In spite of being embarrassed by her slow responses to questions, and upset about her poor memory for facts and activities, Judith was hoping to do well at school and undertake higher education. She did her best to remember learned information and her school timetable, but found both difficult especially when given large amounts of new facts all at once or when faced with sudden changes to her routine. The extra lessons being set up intermittently by the teachers to help her were proving very difficult to remember, as were the increased volume of information and the additional homework which was being prescribed. Judith often felt so overwhelmed that she could only sit in the classroom and stare in front of her. Both Judith and her teachers were becoming increasingly disillusioned with one another, and an adolescent who was once keen to succeed academically was failing to meet her intellectual potential due to an unrecognized learning difficulty.

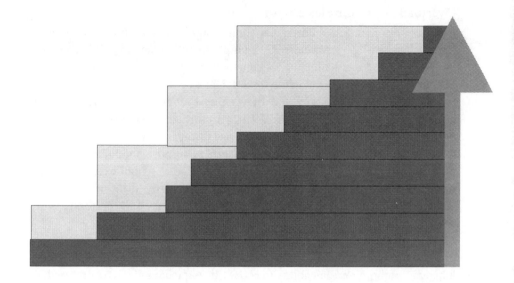

Figure 19.15

Figure 19.16

Overloaded by complex stimuli

Parents of disorganized children may soon recognize that their child or adolescent becomes easily overwhelmed by multiple stimuli or messages. It is as if they can only respond to a set number of signals at any one time before overloading. Should they receive more incoming signals than they can manage or process, they rapidly reach their threshold and they either become unresponsive or their behaviour deteriorates (see Figure 19.10). Unfortunately, positive stimuli can prove as overwhelming as negative stimuli, and disorganized children are as likely to react adversely to good experiences (such as surprise shopping trips or a birthday party) as to less desirable experiences (such as school exams or being punished). Parents often find this response particularly difficult as, having arranged a special trip or bought a special present, they are still confronted with temper outbursts or social withdrawal.

Disorganized children therefore function best when the level of stimulation (positive or negative) to which they are exposed is carefully balanced within their inherent threshold. As their ability to cope with extraneous messages or stimuli is actually much lower than expected for their chronological age, this would explain why children with neuro-developmental processing problems react badly to busy shopping centres, school assemblies, group activities, surprise parties and high levels of noise. Not surprisingly, they manage better in one-to-one interactions, and in quiet situations with few distractions. They also cope more appropriately if given single instructions which are focused on a single task. Any attempt to manage multiple communications or to multi-task are likely to prove overwhelming.

Not only do disorganized children find it difficult to tolerate high levels of stimulation, but they also struggle to filter out important from irrelevant signals. This is exacerbated by their slower mental processing and heightened anxiety. At times of stress or pressure, they often become increasingly aware of trivial signals, from within their own body and from the external environment, which adds to the sense of information overload. In contrast, children and adolescents with more effective processing are able to respond to overwhelming stimuli by filtering out the least relevant information and focusing on the most important communications. Only in extreme cases do people with unimpaired sensory monitoring become overwhelmed by stimuli in the way that disorganized children experience these problems on a daily basis (Figure 19.17).

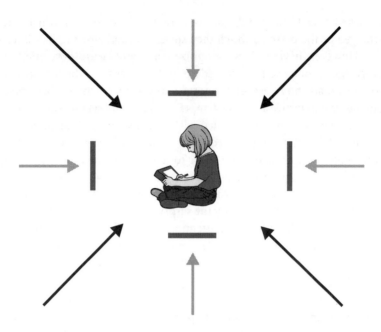

Figure 19.17

Case example: Callum

Callum is a 9-year-old boy who had apparently been reacting increasingly badly to Christmas each year. He seemed unable to join in with the general sense of family excitement, and also seemed reluctant to participate in enjoyable activities such as choosing and decorating the Christmas tree. Instead, he was becoming more and more withdrawn each December in the build-up to Christmas. Callum also found it difficult to choose presents for his parents or siblings, and he found the shopping malls particularly stressful due to the noise and crowds. As Christmas Day itself approached, he become more overtly excited but this soon led to very agitated behaviour and temper outbursts.

Callum often showed no interest in his presents once they had been opened, and he interfered with gifts given to his siblings. Christmas dinner always proved a very difficult event, with Callum often disrupting the extended family meal with adverse behaviour and an inability to settle down. His parents found this response very difficult as they enjoyed fond memories of their own childhood Christmas celebrations, and were saddened that Callum did not seem to enjoy the events which they arranged or the presents which they spent time and effort to buy him.

However, having since recognized his mild neuro-developmental processing problems, they started to look at ways in which Christmas could be made more user-friendly for a disorganized child. They spread out the various festive activities across December, and set up a timetable on the kitchen wall which detailed all Christmas-related plans well in advance. Callum was given added warning of any potentially over-whelming activities, and given scope to remain at home or do something else instead. He was assisted in choosing presents for family members, and given clear indications as to what his own present might be to reduce the level of excitement generated by the surprise and expectation. He was also given specific tasks to focus his attention during Christmas dinner, which was reduced to a more manageable number of people. As a result, not only Callum, but the entire family, enjoyed a happier Christmas each year.

Restlessness and poor attention span

While most disorganized children do not meet the diagnostic criteria for ADHD, they are nonetheless often very restless and fidgety children who are incessantly on the move. They also tend to be impulsive, with a need to touch nearby items and to climb on any high objects. They struggle to remain seated and find it diffi-cult to focus on tasks, either at home or in the classroom. This is accompanied by poor concentration and a tendency to distractibility.

Similar to ADHD, disorganized children find it difficult to complete tasks and to focus on prolonged exercises. Instead, they often look out of the window or daydream. As they cannot recognize their own processing problems, these children will instead describe the work as boring or irrelevant in preference to admitting that they are finding it difficult or cannot do it. This persistent restlessness and failure to settle down serves as a significant source of concern and frustration for both parents and teachers. Peers at school also find disorganized children difficult as they interfere with their work or belongings and prove disruptive. These children are equally problematic in the playground where they are often overactive, intrusive and boundary-less.

However, in contrast to children or adolescents with ADHD, disorganized children are capable of sustained periods of pro-social and on-task behaviour at a level which rules out a hyperactivity diagnosis. Diary-keeping exercises (Figure 19.12) readily highlight these extended periods of focused behaviour and a capacity to remain engaged. What becomes increasingly evident with careful assessment is just how sensitive disorganized children are to the way in which they are managed, both within home and school. They invariably tend to revert to adverse behaviours in relation to specific people, specific places or specific activities. These intermittent episodes of restlessness and inattention may therefore be triggered by losing track of what is happening in a lesson, by being obliged to engage in a sport at which they are no good or by the way in which they are treated by their grandparents.

Some of these children and adolescents may receive a trial of stimulant medication (such as methylphenidate) given their poor attention span and restless behaviour. However, the results in disorganized children are invariably equivocal and seldom achieve the benefits seen in children who clearly meet ADHD diagnostic specifications.

Case example: Lucy

Lucy is a 10-year-old girl. She raised shared concerns between her parents and her teachers at a school meeting when they had the opportunity to compare her restlessness and inattention in both home and school settings. Lucy's parents and teachers all felt that she was persistently hyperactive and impulsive with a poor attention span. A referral to the local paediatricians followed, and Lucy was placed on a low dose of stimulant medication. As this had little impact, the dose was progressively increased over the next 12 months. Having been on high doses of medication with uncertain results for some time, Lucy was subsequently referred to the local CAMHS to consider whether psychological or family issues were impinging on her behaviour.

Assessment highlighted her mild neuro-developmental deficits, which were confirmed by psychometric testing. The results indicated a severe discrepancy between Lucy's verbal and performance scores, as well as highlighting her good intellectual ability. What became increasingly apparent was Lucy's difficulty in understanding complex concepts, problems with reading and writing, poor fine motor control and an inability to put thoughts into action. Diary keeping further demonstrated that Lucy was only off task and restless intermittently during the day, irrespective of her medication regime. A decision was therefore made to reduce her stimulant treatment in parallel with special education provision designed to tackle her academic weakness and to build on her academic strengths. This was achieved without problems, making active use of both diary keeping and repeated educational testing. Lucy has since been able to achieve her full academic potential, while behaving in a pro-social way, without the use of medication.

Fear of failure

One of the frustrating features of disorganized children described by both parents and teachers is that they are immensely reluctant to tackle any tasks, academic or practical, at which they may prove unsuccessful. This means that they are seldom willing to take on novel challenges or to try new things. If activities are unfamiliar, these children and adolescents would rather not participate than risk being made to look stupid or to find that they do not understand or cannot cope. This pattern has often been established through a long history of perceived failure, both at home and at school. As a result, they lack the self-esteem and self-confidence necessary to meet potentially challenging situations. For some disorganized children, frequent punishment and negative reactions to their previous lack of success has exacerbated their underlying anxiety. They therefore come to see the outside world as very persecutory, and fail to develop an internal sense of themselves as a competent and effective person.

Children and adolescents with mild neuro-developmental processing problems need to be gently encouraged to undertake new tasks or activities. They require significant levels of praise and reward, especially as they are often lacking

Figure 19.18

in internal motivation. The approach to any novel situations needs to be explained slowly, in bite-size pieces, with frequent repetition, until they are sufficiently confident about their role to move forward. Explanations also need to be very concrete and exact, in keeping with the way in which disorganized children see the world around them. Otherwise, when faced with daunting and unfamiliar tasks, these children and adolescents cannot be persuaded to act. If anything, this added pressure simply makes them more likely to resist the new activity or situation as their anxiety escalates.

Schematically, many parents and teachers view children who are facing new experiences as standing at the bottom of a mild learning gradient, up which they could be actively pulled or pushed (Figure 19.18). In contrast, it is essential to see disorganized children, in similar situations, as standing either at the top or the bottom of a high cliff. No amount of pulling or pushing is likely to create any movement as the child or adolescent already feels both trapped and anxious. Their response to these novel tasks or roles is then either to shut down completely and freeze, or to react with fear and aggression. Only by understanding their anxieties and poor self-esteem, together with creative approaches to problems and new activities, can disorganized children be encouraged to learn and grow in keeping with their neuro-developmental limitations.

Case example: Sarah

Sarah's mother became increasingly worried about her 9-year-old daughter given a sudden increase in the number of detentions which she was receiving at school. This surprised Sarah's mother, as Sarah had always been an enthusiastic student who enjoyed school. Up until recently, she had never been given a detention or punished in any way. Sarah's mother therefore arranged a meeting with the teacher, who had only just joined the school on a temporary basis. It emerged that Sarah was being disobedient and stubborn in class. She was also refusing to follow instructions given by the teacher, and would not complete work according to the class approach.

Sarah's mother was then able to explain to the new teacher that Sarah experienced difficulty with novel tasks due to her mild processing problems. She also described how Sarah needed gentle encouragement and creative but concrete explanations in order to take on unfamiliar tasks or activities in smaller and slower steps. Provided that she could be approached in this esteem-enhancing manner, rather than being confronted with anxiety-provoking punishment, Sarah was likely to take novel concepts and expectations on board without seeming disobedient or unresponsive. The teacher subsequently applied the strategies being recommended by Sarah's mother and was surprised to see how able and friendly a student Sarah was if managed in accordance with her educational needs.

Reduced comprehension

Disorganized children struggle to understand much of the world around them. They tend to think concretely, in very straight lines, and become easily confused by complexity and inconsistency. This is primarily because their neuro-developmental processing problems prevent them from linking separate items of information together in a meaningful way. As a result, disorganized children find it difficult to carry knowledge or understanding over from one context or subject to another. Instead, they tend to learn each set of facts in isolation, and use it only for the purpose for which it was learned. Every educational topic therefore exists as a stand-alone piece of information, to which no cross-referencing takes place later in the learning process. This can be conceptualized visually as in Figure 19.19 which compares disorganized thought processes, and the lack of linking involved, to a ship's wheel or a wagon wheel in which all spokes radiate out from a central hub without being connected to one another. In contrast, children who do not suffer from neuro-developmental deficits have thinking which can be

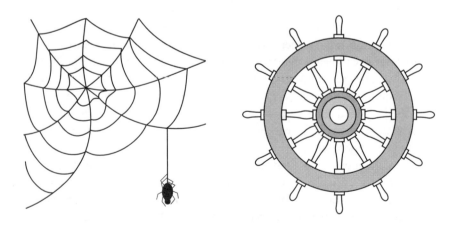

Figure 19.19

compared to a spider's web in that each strand of information is inherently linked to the whole structure.

Given this inability to connect separate pieces of information effectively, disorganized children find it difficult to think flexibly, to make correlations or to apply principles of cause and effect. Instead of being able to extrapolate or draw on existing knowledge, they prefer to return to first principles and work things out from the beginning. This reduces their reliance on memory and bypasses their inability to learn from experience. As can be seen from Figure 19.20, disorganized children therefore prefer linear subjects which have a defined starting point, a clear structure and an inherent logic. Given their processing difficulties, these subjects provide cues to guide disorganized children, enabling them to rely on their more rigid scientific strengths while avoiding their creative weaknesses.

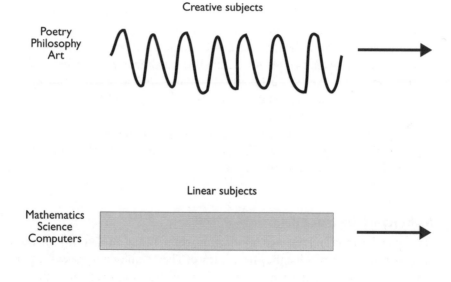

Figure 19.20

Case example: Darren

Darren is an 11-year-old boy, who wanted to become a little more independent. He therefore asked his mother if she could show him how to make himself a cup of tea. Being aware of his learning difficulties, his mother explained the process slowly and simply, using a flowchart tacked to the inside of a nearby kitchen cupboard. Darren soon became proficient at making tea, and often did this for his mother. However, on one occasion, she decided that a cup of coffee would be nice. Hoping that Darren would simply apply his tea-making skills to a jar of instant coffee, she asked for this instead. In contrast to his normal efficiency, Darren then seemed to be taking a great deal of time. His mother could also hear an increasing amount of noise from the kitchen, followed by a loud crash and swearing. As a result, she went to see what had become of her drink.

In the kitchen, she found Darren surrounded by several cups of half-made coffee, all undrinkable. Some were too weak, some were too strong and some had the consistency of gravy. The jar of coffee lay shattered against the far wall where Darren had thrown it in a moment of frustration. It soon became apparent that he had not been able to extrapolate his understanding of tea-making to a cup of instant coffee. Instead, he had approached the task as something completely novel without learning from his related past experiences. This left him unable to decide on how much coffee to use, in what sequence to mix the ingredients or how it should taste. Darren became increasingly concerned that his family would laugh at his stupidity, which increased his sense of stress and led to the eventual physical outburst. His mother, recognizing that an angry or undermining response would be very unhelpful, offered to help Darren clean up the mess. She then sat down with him, and produced a second set of instructions on how to make instant coffee. Over time, this was followed by similarly typed instructions for making instant soup, hot chocolate and other drinks.

Inability to sequence data

Having understood and retained information, children and adolescents still need to make some sense of what they have learned. These thinking processes require not only the linking of different pieces of data but also an ability to place the collected information into some sort of appropriate order. This task requires a very high level of executive function and organization as the individual pieces have to be identified, labelled, prioritized and arranged in a sequence that lends itself to effective use. This sequencing process, which usually happens extremely rapidly and even unconsciously, is needed for both immediate use and long-term planning. These memory sequences or connected pieces of information are built up through growth and development, and come to form a library of easy access responses which have been learned from experience.

As daily life becomes more complicated, with more and more quick choices and effective decisions needed each day, this capacity become increasingly important. At the same time, it is a major processing deficit experienced by disorganized children. Given that they have impaired attention, comprehension, memory, linking and coping skills, it is easy to see how these children and adolescents struggle to understand, organize and then use information efficiently within daily life as they get older. As a result, many day-to-day tasks which would not trouble their peers in any way prove difficult, anxiety-provoking and ultimately unsuccessful. This is not reflective of their intellectual ability but instead reflects an inability to organize information into useful sequences for rapid use. Disorganized children therefore need time to slowly arrange their scattered and random thoughts into some sort of workable sequence which can be applied to a problem of daily living. This difficulty can be compared to a railway shunting yard, and the number of carriages which a train can effectively and quickly move around as needed (Figure 19.21).

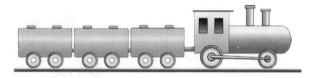

Effificient sequencing and processing

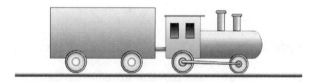

Disorganized child

Figure 19.21

This inability to sequence information often proves very frustrating for parents and teachers who see obviously bright children and adolescents having to work basic tasks out from the very beginning, as if they had never been taught to undertake a similar task before. Also, while the final response is likely to seem extremely logical within the linear thinking approach of a disorganized child, the sequencing may prove very confusing or inefficient to other people. The time which these tasks then take may prove another source of frustration to parents and teachers who are expecting an immediate and effective response. However, disorganized children are able to take thoughts and actions forward effectively and quickly if the instructions which they receive fall well within their ability to understand and sequence information (Figure 19.22).

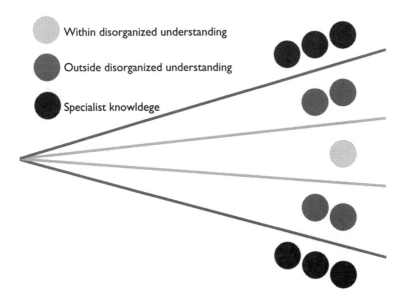

Within disorganized understanding

Outside disorganized understanding

Specialist knowldege

Figure 19.22

Case example: Carol

Carol, a 15-year-old girl, was proving an immense frustration to her stepmother. On each occasion that she came to visit, family life slowed to an intolerable and unmanageable pace with Carol seeming unwilling to follow instructions or make decisions. This was developing into a source of growing friction between Carol and her stepmother, as she was being viewed as oppositional and lazy. The situation was not helped by Carol using up all the hot water each time she bathed. As things were only getting worse, the family was referred on for professional help. At interview, it soon emerged that Carol often did not understand what she was being asked by her stepmother, who was also expecting very quick responses to a number of different things at once. For example, she would ask Carol to go upstairs to quickly undertake several minor tasks and then be frustrated when Carol failed to complete all of the requests, as well as taking an excessive amount of time to undertake the tasks which she did complete.

The therapist, recognizing that Carol was presenting with neuro-developmental processing problems, explained to the stepmother how Carol struggled with sequencing of information, especially under time pressure. She helped Carol and her stepmother to recognize the need to give Carol only one instruction at a time, and to explain clearly the short sequence of actions needed to complete the task. If given too many different instructions at once, or instructions that involved too many different components, Carol was unable to sort out and prioritize her actions, leading to confusion and an inability to complete the tasks. As for the bath, it turned out that Carol had not recognized the need to mix hot and cold water to achieve a comfortable temperature. As a result, she was simply running the hot tap until the water cooled to a manageable level before filling her bath. Once a more appropriate way to organize her task had been explained to Carol, together with only being given one instruction at a time, the situation improved dramatically.

Limited sense of other people

As children grow and develop, they come to understand more about their own thoughts and actions. Over time, they also develop a capacity to understand how and why other people think and act. The end result is a simultaneous ability to understand both their own perspective, and that of another person. This 'theory of mind' allows children and adolescents to increasingly understand the potential impact of their thoughts and actions on others, with a growing sensitivity towards other people's feelings and emotions. This mutual capacity to understand and respond to family members, peers and strangers is essential to successful human relationships.

The absence of empathy is most often associated with autistic spectrum disorders. While they may not meet the diagnostic criteria for autism or Asperger syndrome (Figure 19.1), disorganized children often present with autistic traits. As a result, their ability to understand 'theory of mind' and the impact which they may have on other people is reduced. Many parents describe how these features present early in disorganized children who tend to be very independent while also demanding high levels of attention. They are also often described as distant, cold, remote or aloof. Disorganized children therefore struggle to understand both their own thoughts and emotions, and the thoughts and emotions of others. This often presents as a lack of empathy through failing to recognize the other person's needs or views. They may even appear lacking in conscience and morality as these concepts, in addition to being very complicated and abstract, are also dependent on a working understanding of other people.

Causing offence and upset, which are frequent complaints about disorganized children, then happens without intention as they are unlikely to recognize the impact which their honesty may have on other people. Parents frequently describe insensitive comments made in public about strangers' height, weight, facial features or clothing. Taking turns, sharing and being considerate are likewise very difficult concepts for these children and adolescents to grasp and implement, and group activities may therefore prove extremely anxiety-provoking. As a result of the frequently hostile responses which they receive from parents, teachers, peers and even strangers, they may develop anxieties about social interactions with a tendency to avoid other people and a preference for activities which can be enjoyed alone. Because of this lack of understanding, and their inability to predict the thoughts and actions of people around them, disorganized children often come to see the world as illogical, persecutory and unkind.

Adults involved with disorganized children, either at home or at school, frequently complain about their manipulative behaviour. However, this does not correlate with their inability to understand other people effectively. The very nature of manipulation requires a sound 'theory of mind' as the basis on which to predict how others will react to certain situations. It also requires an ability to hold complex sequences of thought in mind, together with a capacity for symbolic and abstract thought. As disorganized children lack these facets of thinking and feeling, it is highly unlikely that they can manipulate people or situations in the deliberate and premeditated manner often described by parents and teachers. It is therefore essential, before seeing the actions of these children and adolescents in a complex and negative light, for adults to consider carefully the limited interpersonal understanding of disorganized children and the often simplistic goals which they are trying to achieve.

Case example: Liam

Liam's mother was very embarrassed about her 10-year-old son. She had taken him into town for the Remembrance Day service, having lost her own grandfather in World War II. On the way there, Liam had talked incessantly, hardly allowing her to get a word in at all. On the few occasions when she had spoken, Liam simply dismissed her point of view. He seemed interested only in his own perspective on the topic, and did not realize that his mother wanted to share in the discussion. This left her feeling that Liam was being both selfish and rude, and quite insensitive to her thoughts and emotions.

The situation was not helped when they arrived at the church service. Liam promptly began talking openly and honestly about people's appearance. A large lady and a bald man some rows ahead clearly overheard his loud pronouncements and seemed quite upset by the comments. To make matters worse, mothers from the local school were all talking about a forthcoming party being held by one of Liam's peers. It was taking place on the following day, and Liam had evidently not been invited due to his inability to relate easily with other children. Finally, Liam then talked right through the minute of silence held to honour the dead.

Although his mother had explained the need to be quiet during this period on the way to church, he had forgotten her explanation and could not understand why she did not want to hear his latest thoughts. When a soldier reacted angrily to his intrusion, and told him to be quiet or face punishment, Liam could not understand what he had done wrong. He was unable to predict that such a response would be forthcoming, or the impact which his talking may have had on others. Instead, he was left feeling unfairly treated and his thoughts turned to going fishing alone after he returned home.

Social and communication difficulties

The limited sense of other people experienced by disorganized children is further complicated by their poor social and communication skills. These children and adolescents, because they cannot predict states of mind or reactions, struggle in social situations as they are unable to interpret social cues and signals effectively and appropriately. As a result, they tend to misinterpret the intentions or expectations of other people. Subtlety and nuances are especially difficult for them to understand.

One of the primary difficulties with which disorganized children struggle is an understanding of personal space and boundaries. They either come across as cold and distant, or they tend to be over-familiar with people. These children and adolescents react in an 'all or nothing' manner and find it difficult to moderate their boundaries according to social situations. For example, they find it hard to understand why it is acceptable to stand right next to someone in a lift or on the subway whereas this would be seen as rude or intrusive at a party. As their approach to social situations differs from their peers, they are readily teased and bullied because of their poor communication skills.

These problems come to the fore especially in adolescence. Disorganized children find it difficult to cope with the fluid nature of adolescent groups, and the focus on being rather than doing. They fail to monitor fashion or trends, and are therefore easily identifiable as being outside of the group. This again opens them up to being picked on, and creates a preference for younger peers who will overlook their shortcomings or older adults who will be more accepting. Few of the disorganized children find it easy to manage within their own peer group, which tends to prove both most complex and most intolerant. Also, the larger the group, the more they are likely to struggle.

The situation is not helped by their linear sense of humour. Disorganized children often fail to catch jokes, especially if the punchline is somewhat abstract or involves a play on words. They instead prefer cartoon-like or slapstick humour, which they often find very funny regardless of their chronological age. In contrast, sarcasm and witticisms are lost on these children and adolescents. However, because they are prone to making naïve or inappropriate comments, other children find them very amusing. As this may prove their only access to peer acceptance, disorganized children may take on the role of class clown. They do not realize that their peers are laughing at them rather than with them, and that they are being taken advantage of to disrupt lessons or create entertainment. Frequently, they also bear the brunt of any subsequent punishments, further escalating their sense of social persecution and the desire for solitary activities.

Some disorganized children, due to wider neuro-developmental deficits, may also struggle with language. They tend to forget names easily, and struggle with word-finding during conversations. They also find it difficult to arrange their written or spoken language in the correct sequence, and the resultant order then seems strange and inappropriate to others. Their vocabulary may also be limited, with repetition of certain favourite words or phrases. Disorganized children often cope with this problem by practising sentences out loud before they speak, or by repeating things softly to themselves. This again opens them up to bullying and ridicule, especially if associated with nervous tics or unusual stress-related movements.

Case example: Jason

Jason, who was approaching 16, was invited to a party. It was the first event to which he had been invited, although he was aware that his peers had been gathering in large social groups for some time. They often met at the local shops or sat around the cricket pavilion, but Jason had never felt confident enough to join them. Although they occasionally laughed at things which he inadvertently said or did, this seldom lasted long and he was usually left on his own when they became bored or distracted. Sometimes he was also unpleasantly teased or even bullied by a group of older boys.

At the party, he found himself next to Trisha, whom he particularly liked although he had never spoken to her. She would occasionally smile at him in the corridor at school, which Jason had interpreted as the wish for a boyfriend. He therefore decided to move closer to her, and to tell her about his alphabetized CD collection in great detail. Unfortunately, given that it was important to him, he did not realize that she soon became bored with the topic. Jason also found himself having to move forward every few minutes as Trisha moved away from him, which made the already unnerving eye contact with her even more difficult. When he finally recognized her lack of interest in his CD collection, Jason opted to try humour. However, even though he had been told the joke in the boys' locker-room, he did not anticipate that Trisha may be offended. He was therefore extremely surprised by her angry and disgusted reaction to something which he had found very funny.

Abstract thinking and symbol formation

When young, children depend on very concrete forms of thinking. Thoughts and feelings are translated very literally, and the child tends to store information as an exact image of what can be seen or felt. With growth and development, children's thinking becomes more sophisticated and they learn to use abstract and symbolic thought. This allows them to develop a mental shorthand for storing, retaining and understanding information, given the vast amount of data which needs to be both remembered and comprehended on a daily basis. Symbolization occurs when thoughts and feelings are linked together in sequences and then stored as a combined but condensed concept in the mind. These symbolic images can then be easily recovered by the individual, when faced with certain emotional or physical experiences, to enhance efficient thinking and decision-making. Very specific data may also be used to understand and represent more general situations in a process known as abstraction.

Disorganized children struggle to convert simple concrete signs into complex abstract symbols as they grow older. Their problems with linking and sequencing of information make it very difficult for them to organize and condense experiences and understanding into coherent concepts, with wider applications for use in a variety of different situations. Instead, they tend to see each piece of information or each emotion as something separate, as a stand-alone entity. As a result, their thinking is very fragmented, very literal and

very linear. They therefore struggle to understand more complex communications such as sarcasm, humour, idiom and metaphor as these processes are all
dependent on the ability to develop abstract symbols in the mind. For example,
understanding justice as an abstract concept is very different from taking on
board the details of a specific court case. Similarly, children and adolescents with
neuro-developmental processing problems will return after 60 seconds if you ask
them to 'wait a minute', or take off their footwear if asked to 'put themselves in
someone else's shoes'. Likewise, if asked to write an essay on where they went on
holiday, disorganized children may simply respond with 'I went to London'.
They have technically answered exactly what they were asked, without realizing
that the homework embraced a much wider question about where they went,
who they went with, why they went there and what they enjoyed most.

As disorganized children cannot abstract or symbolize, they often appear as
lacking in imagination or fantasy. They tend to prefer working with information
which they can concretely see, hear or feel. This often proves easier for them than
trying to understand abstract theoretical concepts which exist only as ideas in the
mind (Figure 19.20). Even where some creativity and fantasy may be evident, it
often falls within the more linear parameters of computers or science fiction and,
on careful analysis, may prove very repetitive with only minor changes from
situation to situation. It is also not unusual for disorganized children to confuse
their thoughts with reality. If a thought or feeling is emotionally intense or
otherwise very meaningful, it may be interpreted as being real even though it is
only in the child's mind. They therefore become easily confused between what
they wanted to do or thought of doing as compared to having actually done it.
They similarly talk out loud or sing, under the impression that they are quietly
thinking, as the boundaries between what goes on outside of them is blurred with
what goes on inside of their mind. This is often confused with psychotic
symptoms or hearing voices whereas it is simply a very concrete representation of
otherwise complex internal thoughts and feelings.

Case example: Thomas

Thomas was a 12-year-old boy whose grandmother had recently died,
and he was struggling to come to terms with the situation. He had
repeatedly asked his mother what death meant, and where his grandmother had gone. However, he found her answers about Heaven very
difficult to understand as he did not know where Heaven was or how one
reached it. He also did not know anyone who had been to Heaven, and he
had never seen a picture of it. Although his slightly younger sister had
grasped the concept without difficulty, Thomas was struggling to make

sense of these abstract and symbolic ideas. His mother then remembered how she had explained lightning and thunder to Thomas as God moving his furniture around, even at an age when he should have been able to understand the scientific concept. This had proved a more satisfying answer to Thomas than any talk of clouds and electricity, until his thought processes matured. Having recognized the problem, she obtained an art encyclopaedia which included many depictions of God and Heaven. She showed these to Thomas and discussed them in relation to his grandmother. This explanation made more sense to Thomas now that he was able to see and feel something about Heaven, and he asked for a photocopy of one particular painting. He kept this pinned up in his room while he came to terms with his grandmother's death in a more concrete manner which better suited his understanding and thinking.

Time keeping and motivation

Given that it is a product of symbolic thinking, disorganized children find time keeping very difficult. This is often in spite of their high intellect, and their apparent success with a range of more complex activities. Not only do they struggle to concretely tell the time, but they also struggle with the more abstract concept of time itself. In contrast to their peers, they seem to lack an internal clock against which the passing of time can be measured. This is further complicated by forgetfulness and difficulty in prioritizing. As a result, they are often late or miss scheduled events in spite of frequent reminders.

Disorganized children also struggle to make sense of longitudinal time in terms of weeks and months. While they may remember the date of their birthday or Christmas Day, they can seldom place these events within the context of a calendar year. Activities are either deemed to be happening on the day or seen as taking place some time in the future, be that the next day, the next week or the next year. All future happenings are therefore interpreted as equidistant from the present, due to the lack of a symbolic internal calendar. Similarly, these children and adolescents find it difficult to conceptualize the past or to describe accurately when certain events took place. They also struggle to conceptualize the length of time that any given activity may require, either leaving far too little opportunity to complete the task or else setting aside far too much time.

The inability to measure and conceptualize time has a direct impact on levels of self-motivation. This lack of internal motivation is often characteristic of disorganized children which, together with a reduced understanding of the need to please others occasionally, frequently proves a major source of frustration for parents and teachers. However motivation, together with related concepts such as ambition and achievement, requires forward planning along a perceived time line. Unfortunately, as disorganized children live very much in and for the present, they are unable to engage a process of creating opportunities within a vague and uncertain future. They therefore lack any sense of long-term perspective, and cannot comprehend that their actions in the present may influence situations which they encounter in the distant future. This is not helped by their frequent sense of inevitable failure, and the fact that even activities in the present feel burdensome enough. In addition, as they lack a 'theory of mind', disorganized children can seldom be encouraged to undertake these future-oriented tasks just to please other people.

Case example: Ellie

Ellie, who is 13, found herself in trouble again. She had asked her mother if she could go out after dinner to spend time with her friends. Her mother agreed, provided that she was back no later than 8 o'clock to finish her homework. Ellie happily agreed, and went off to meet the others. Engrossed with the activities, she did not see that other girls were gradually drifting off home. Soon she was left alone with only one other peer. As the light faded, Ellie suddenly thought of the time and looked at her watch. It was just after eight. She was thinking of rushing off home when her remaining friend suggested one last game. When she returned home at 8.30 that evening, Ellie was surprised by her mother's response.

Ellie could not understand why her mother had been so worried about her or the significance of coming home after dark. She also could not understand why her mother was placing so much emphasis on homework as she had already been at school all day. Ellie said that she was finding it difficult enough to keep up with the work in class without having to ruin her evenings doing homework. She also could not see the relevance of the work to her future life, nor the benefits which might accrue from working hard in the present. In her experience, the teacher invariably found fault with her work, and she was better off staying out with her friends. When instructed to complete her homework, Ellie did the minimum that was required of her, as quickly as she could, and then went off to watch her favourite television show.

Routines, rituals and obsessions

While all children benefit from established routines and a sense of familiarity, this trait is more noticeable in disorganized children. Given their inability to sequence and symbolize information, they are more dependent than their peers on the external environment. Whereas most children gradually internalize their world, allowing them to separate from their parents or to tolerate change, these children and adolescents find such abstract life tasks very difficult. They are instead guided by their immediate reality and environment, which they strive to keep the same, as this helps to avoid anxiety and to sustain their limited coping abilities. Many disorganized children therefore function best in unchanging situations, where there are defined structures and timetables. They also cope best if they are given advance warning of any changes, and are actively prepared for new situations. As adults, these children and adolescents often manage best in jobs which promote sameness and high levels of routine and structure.

Many children also present with mild obsessions and compulsions, but these seldom persist over time. Disorganized children, given their overall neuro-developmental deficits, tend to present with more of these ongoing symptoms although they seldom reach diagnostic proportions for conditions such as OCD. They therefore often complain of repetitive thoughts or images that intrude into their thinking, which contribute to their already heightened levels of anxiety. These obsessions can spill over into compulsions when the child or adolescent feels compelled to carry out specific actions such as handwashing, touching things in a certain order or repeating an action over and over. These strategies are set up to combat anxiety, and many people use similar approaches to cope with day-to-day life, by tending to take the same route to work each day or sitting mainly in certain chairs at home. However, the rigidity with which disorganized children may pursue this sameness and structure can lead to friction within families.

Disorganized children opt for these routines and rituals as the anxiety generated by change and uncertainty may otherwise prove overwhelming. The routines bypass the need for planning and organization, with which they struggle, as the coping process is identical on each occasion. Similarly, they avoid having to make choices or having to react to novel situations in new ways. The effect is to reduce their inherently high levels of anxiety, which then leads to a growing sense of safety. This pattern may present across all aspects of their life, such as fussy eating habits or strict bedtime routines. For children and adolescents who manage in this way, their approach is impervious to logic. If anything, as the behaviour inevitably results in them feeling better, the routines and rituals may take on a magical quality. For example, a young boy's concerns about an absent father while on a business trip abroad may be alleviated by touching his shoes three times each morning on the way out of the door as, each time this took place, his father returned safely.

These routines and rituals are often a source of frustration for parents, siblings, peers and teachers. The disorganized child is frequently very dependent on them, and will not embrace any threatened change to their daily structure or timetable. As a result, the arrival of a temporary teacher, unexpected school closure, a field trip or a prolonged assembly may prove sufficient to derail their coping ability. In a child or adolescent who is otherwise thought to be managing well, this need may come across as immature and infantile. Attempts are therefore made to actively prevent the repetitive response and, as a result, the disorganized child becomes increasingly anxious and even more likely to be rapidly over-whelmed by minor life events. A balance therefore needs to be found which allows the child or adolescent sufficient familiarity and sameness for the maintenance of tolerable levels of anxiety while also introducing them to well-planned and actively managed change.

Case example: Ryan

Ryan, who is 7, was barely managing to cope with primary school. However, he soon became acclimatized to his teacher, her way of teaching, the structure of the classroom and the school timetable. His reports showed him to be doing well, until the arrival of a new headmistress half-way through the year. In order to improve the school, she introduced a range of new educational measures. This unexpected change took Ryan by surprise, especially as his teacher was also moved to another class. The sameness and structure which Ryan had created around him to manage his anxiety and coping was therefore inadvertently destroyed.

His new teacher soon complained that he was touching her desk repeatedly, and saying phrases over and over to himself. Ryan became increasingly reluctant to go to school and, when there, he was very irritable. He could not concentrate and his academic work deteriorated. The teacher also noted that Ryan was increasingly frustrated, especially when she stopped him from carrying out his behaviour patterns, which culminated in him hitting out at another pupil. Following a parent/teacher meeting, it was decided to place Ryan back with his original teacher. He quickly settled into his familiar routine, and both his work and behaviour returned to their previously satisfactory levels.

Poor motor skills

Parents of disorganized children often describe their child as 'walking awk-wardly' or 'standing funny'. This is invariably due to mild neuro-developmental problems with motor function and coordination. These neurological 'soft signs', which cannot be localized to one area of the brain, tend to present as clumsiness and problems with fine motor control. They may also present as illegible handwriting, frequently spilled drinks or an inability to tie shoelaces. As a result, disorganized children often struggle to use a knife and fork, and will instead use their fingers to eat far beyond the expected chronological age. Yet parents and teachers find it very frustrating when otherwise capable children still cannot differentiate their left from their right, or put basic table manners into practice.

Children and adolescents with motor control problems tend to struggle both at school and within their peer group. They are often chosen last for games, given their poor hand/eye coordination and limited ball skills. They are also frequently teased for their ungainly posture or strange running action. When bullied physically, they often lack the necessary motor skills to fight back effectively. Disorganized children also lack the ability to organize their actions into appropriate sequences, making the motor deficit seem even worse.

Other physical difficulties which these children and adolescents may experience include tics, restlessness and poor temperature regulation. Given their motor function deficits, disorganized children may be prone to irregular involuntary movements or tics. These are sudden and uncontrollable twitches of the head, face, arms or legs. If the child is under stress, these movements are likely to escalate. In particular, trying to suppress the movements may increase stress levels and therefore inadvertently make the problem worse. They also struggle to maintain an appropriate body temperature, often wearing heavy coats all summer and running around in shirt-sleeves all winter. This is particularly noticeable when asleep, with a tendency to cast off all covers even when the room is quite cold. Disorganized children can be frustrating to live with as they are often very restless. As a result, watching television or sitting at the dinner table can be accompanied by finger tapping or foot movements which prove very irritating to other family members.

Children with mild neuro-developmental problems tend to sleep badly. This is something which parents notice from infancy, and which continues throughout adolescence. Disorganized children struggle to create organized bedtime routines which, together with their poor concept of time, often leads to late nights. They are then tired at school on the following day, which exacerbates their already compromised attention and motivation. They are also prone to nightmares and sleep-walking, especially when under pressure or anxious.

Case example: Kieren

Kieren, who had just turned 14, was upset when his older sister refused to take him along to the school disco. Although he believed himself to be a good dancer, his sister said that he had embarrassed her on the dance floor with his awkward movements and funny gestures. She also said that he had embarrassed and upset the girls with his poor social skills and insensitive comments. His sister added that he had spilled drinks on two of her friends when pouring himself a glass, and that he had eaten crudely with his mouth open. This was made worse by remaining in his coat throughout the evening in spite of the hall being extremely warm. Kieren had not been aware of this, having enjoyed both dancing and feeling that he had received a positive response from some of the girls at the last school event.

Restricted personality

The purpose of childhood development is to allow the child and adolescent to move into adulthood, having developed a balanced and robust personality. This process is dependent on good infant attachment, positive parenting, experiences of childhood success, appropriate peer relationships, self-esteem and self-confidence. Given that many disorganized children struggle to attain these essential milestones, they often move into adulthood without having developed an appropriate level of maturity.

Children with neuro-developmental problems can prove quite difficult during childhood, often preferring independence and distance to close interpersonal relationships. This may impact negatively on long-term parental bonding and attachment. Disorganized children may also, throughout childhood, experience high levels of adverse and negative experiences, often being seen as oppositional, defiant, lazy, rude, cold and unfriendly. This predisposes them to friction with parents and teachers, as well as estranging them from their peer group.

Already struggling with intimate relationships, these children and adolescents are then further isolated and alienated by bullying and victimization. Unfortunately, as they can be very controlling and rigid, it proves difficult for these disorganized children to make and maintain the kind of friendships that help peers to overcome similar adversities. Their inability to relate is labelled as odd or awkward, and they soon internalize the external perception which people have of them. This inevitably leads to very poor self-esteem and self-confidence, with few of the positive and self-confirming experiences which help to define a desirable self-image.

This poor sense of who they are, and what they are capable of, crosses over into their adult lives. Many find it difficult to maintain balanced and healthy adult relationships as they remain disinhibited, restless and self-focused as they get older. They may prove insensitive to the needs of partners or spouses, and may struggle with the stress of bringing up children of their own. They tend to expect continued compliance with their structure and routine, in spite of major life changes. These expectations also carry over into employment settings, where again they can prove abrasive, opinionated and lacking in a sense of other people.

Given their restricted personality development, disorganized children often fail to achieve their academic or employment potential. They also struggle with interpersonal relationships and social situations, with a preference for solitary activities and a boundaried lifestyle. This does not necessarily equate with failure or unhappiness, as many of these children and adolescents find a niche for themselves in higher education or employment situations, as well as meeting like-minded peers with whom they have successful relationships. However, the need for early identification of problematic symptoms in childhood, and appropriate action, can do much to alleviate distress, shape personality and provide the disorganized child with life skills that can be successfully carried over into adulthood.

Case example: Adam

Adam's wife recently suggested that they seek marital counselling. She had met Adam when they were both 22, and he was a shy and introverted young student. Even at that time, she realized that Adam was 'odd' and that he often struggled to understand or acknowledge her point of view. However, at other times, she found him loving, caring, responsible and protective. After knowing each other for some five months, they decided to get married. Although Adam was very much in favour of this, it clearly made him anxious. Once married, he gradually implemented a range of rituals and routines at home, and often reacted to adult situations in quite an adolescent manner.

After five years, Adam's wife became increasingly aware of how restricted their lifestyle had become. Adam would only eat certain meals, which needed to be served at specific times. He was reluctant to go out in the evenings or over weekends, and her friends no longer invited them over. Adam would not consider applying for promotion, even though he had been encouraged to at work and was deemed able to undertake the new role. Any pressure from his wife regarding the need to be more ambitious and successful was met with an outburst of temper, after which he would storm out of the house. This also happened if his wife tried to correct his table manners or suggest more appropriate ways of managing social situations. His only interest was fishing, which he did alone on Sundays.

When their daughter was born, Adam found meeting her needs very difficult. The baby would not fit in with his routines, and he was instead having to operate in unplanned and unstructured ways. This led to a resurgence of old rituals and routines, which left most of the child care to his wife. She found this added responsibility difficult, especially as Adam was proving more emotionally distant as well. Discussions with Adam's mother showed that these coping strategies had been evident even when he was young, particularly under stress. She therefore decided to seek external help for both herself and Adam to help manage their family life more effectively while acknowledging his long-standing social and emotional difficulties.

CONCLUSION

Disorganized children form an invisible and often overlooked group of young people. The symptoms with which they present are often misinterpreted as defiance and disobedience, rather than being correctly seen as the unavoidable consequences of mild neuro-developmental processing problems. Some of these children and adolescents are then referred on for specialist help, where their emotional and behaviour problems are correctly attributed to underlying neurological difficulties. When the cause of the problems is appropriately explained to parents and teachers, with innovative and creative strategies being put in place, these disorganized children often flourish. They come to recognize their own limitations, and manage them in ways which are self-enhancing. This is preferable to being treated in ways which are perceived as punitive or unfair, with a resulting loss of self-esteem and self-confidence. Otherwise, their primarily negative life experiences may impact adversely on their later personality development, maintaining an unfortunate cycle of rejection and disadvantage.

These approaches need to be set in motion both at home and at school, and will soon lead to improved function within the family and within the classroom. Having said this, it needs to be recognized that even problems with a defined neuro-developmental basis do not exist in isolation. Social and family issues need to be taken into account, as do school issues, so that the disorganized child is approached in a holistic and multi-faceted way. This may require the input of various different professionals, working closely with the child or adolescent and his or her parents.

By highlighting neuro-developmental disorganization rather than mental health diagnoses, the aim has been to avoid labelling and inappropriate medicalization of problems which can be equally, if not more effectively, managed through psychological and educational principles. The following section will therefore explore multi-disciplinary and multi-agency approaches to disorganized children which address their biological limitations, their psychological issues and their social problems.

Part 4
Principles of Management

Chapter 20

A child psychiatry approach

Uttom Chowdhury and Samuel M. Stein

INTRODUCTION

Child and adolescent psychiatrists are medically qualified doctors who specialize in understanding and working with the mental health problems of children and young people (Royal College of Psychiatrists 1999). Evaluation by a child and adolescent psychiatrist is appropriate for any child or adolescent with emotional and/or behavioural problems (American Academy of Child and Adolescent Psychiatry 1997). A large part of the child and adolescent psychiatrist's work is therefore to identify the problem, understand the causes and advise about what may help. Occasionally child psychiatrists may prescribe medication, and they may also play a major role in advising and assisting other professionals in schools and social services to plan how best to help the child and his or her family (Royal College of Psychiatrists 1999).

The main role for child and adolescent psychiatrists is therefore to intervene when medical input is needed. They are best placed to provide assessments and treatments that require specialist medical and psychiatry training. This input may include diagnostic assessment, treatment of children, the use of pharmaco-therapy, consultation to other professionals and preventative work. Psychiatrists should also identify co-existing problems and carry out mental state examinations where and when appropriate. As qualified doctors, child and adolescent psychiatrists are also trained to explore possible medical causes of mental health symptoms, to undertake neurological examinations and to identify the contribution of subtle neuro-developmental processing difficulties to the child's presentation.

ASSESSMENT

A comprehensive psychiatric evaluation may require several hours, over one or more visits. It is essential for mental health professionals to gather as much information as possible on the child, both prior to assessment and during the evaluation process. As many of the children and young people who are referred to child and adolescent psychiatrists may previously have come into contact with various professionals in the past, there may already be valuable assessment reports, test results or other documents available, such as speech and language reports, medical investigations or psychometric testing.

However, as these children and adolescents are seldom the person actively asking for help, except perhaps with regard to bullying or depression, both the child psychiatrist and the parents need to be sensitive to the child's needs and thoughts during the interviews. The assessment should initially include the whole family as this will allow analysis of family dynamics, provide an opportunity for siblings to contribute and also bring to light any differences between the child and his or her brothers and sisters. In addition to the child and immediate family, the assessment may also need to include other significant people such as grandparents, teachers, social workers and general practitioners.

CLINICAL HISTORY

Comprehensive evaluation should start with a description of the presenting problems and symptoms. The aim is to obtain an overview of the various issues, as well as gaining as much information as possible about each of the presenting difficulties. It is important to build up an understanding of when the problem started, what the possible triggers are, whether it is continuous, who notices it, how others respond to it and if any help has been sought. By following this approach for each of the presenting difficulties, a comprehensive and holistic picture can be developed regarding both the patient and the family situation. Other important areas for exploration include past medical history, family history, developmental history, educational history, general functioning and potential neuro-developmental problems.

Developmental history

As described in Part 1, which focuses on child development and growth, a developmental approach is essential to understanding children and adolescents. Psychiatrists therefore need to be familiar with the processes that underlie both normal and abnormal development. They then build up a picture of the child's early years and long-term growth by accumulating information and details from conception all the way through to the date of interview (Barker 1988). This includes information about the course of the pregnancy, any perinatal complications, the child's birth and possible neonatal conditions. Child and adolescent psychiatrists also want to know about the progress of development over time including motor function, speech, feeding patterns, sleep, toilet training, social behaviour, adjustment to change and competencies at school. Descriptions of a child's behaviour as a baby, as a toddler and at the present time can therefore serve as an important guide to motor, social and psychological development.

Unfortunately, unless children present with striking developmental problems, most parents will have difficulty in accurately recalling when they first noticed the emergence of any symptoms. This is particularly prevalent in disorganized children as their presenting problems are often subtle and irregular. Parents may therefore find it helpful, in trying to recall both information and the timing of events, to bring along health visitor records, diaries relating to early development, childhood photographs, pictures and paintings that were saved, school reports or any other documents that may prompt their memory and recollection. This process may be further aided by helping parents to focus on specific activities such as birthdays, moving house, the first day of school and other key events. It is often difficult for parents to recall developmental milestones, and it may prove helpful to compare their child's growth and advancement with siblings, peers, other children in the neighbourhood or even their own experience of growing up. These separate items of information all contribute, like the pieces of a jigsaw puzzle, to building up a comprehensive and holistic picture of the child who has now been referred with emotional or behavioural problems.

Neurological history

It is important, when assessing young people, to obtain a comprehensive insight into any potential neuro-developmental difficulties. This serves not only to exclude one of the more serious conditions described in Part 2, but it also helps to collate evidence of the subtle but medically evident neurological and processing problems that characterize disorganized children. Questions should therefore be asked about possible problems with concentration, hyperactivity, social skills, peer relationships, fine motor function and gross motor coordination.

As highlighted in Part 3, the defining neuro-developmental features which are found in disorganized children include:

- restricted coping strategies
- not learning from experience
- patchy cognitive function
- preference for structured activities
- lack of organization
- impaired short-term memory

- overload by complex stimuli
- restlessness and poor attention span
- reduced comprehension
- inability to sequence data
- limited sense of other people
- social and communication difficulties
- inability to use symbolic concepts
- inability to generalize data
- lack of time management
- preference for routine
- obsessions and rituals
- poor motor skills and coordination.

Educational history

An understanding of how children and adolescents are coping within the school and classroom setting is essential in working with disorganized children as many of the problems which they experience, and with which they present, are school-related. These issues are therefore discussed in greater detail in Chapter 23. However, as a general guide, the child psychiatrist is likely to ask about any concerns that were evident at pre-school, and any subsequent problems evident in junior school. Questions about the child's educational history would probably also include topics such as:

- What exactly were the teachers concerned about?
- What was the child's behaviour like in class or in the playground?
- Did he or she progress as expected academically?
- What were the subjects which he or she was particularly good or poor at?
- What about school friends and social skills?
- How did the child cope in group situations?
- What about completing homework or projects?
- What is his or her coordination like in sports such as football or gymnastics?
- Is he or she the last person to get picked for teams?

- What do teachers or peers say about the child?
- Does he or she get extra support at school?
- Does he or she need additional help in class?

Family history and interview

Children and adolescents do not exist in isolation, and the ways in which families function, and how this may impact on the disorganized child, are the focus of Chapter 24. However, it is essential for all professionals who work with young people to learn something about the family with whom they are hoping to engage. In addition to the child and immediate family, the assessment may also need to include other significant people such as grandparents, teachers, social workers and general practitioners.

It is often useful first to collect basic details about the family background such as family composition, the educational level of parents and grandparents, occupational status, social stressors, financial circumstances, location of relevant family members and extended family support. This can be followed by questions which explore relationships within the family, and the personal experiences of different members within the same family setting. The assessment should initially include the whole family as this will allow analysis of family dynamics, provide an opportunity for siblings to contribute and also bring to light any differences between the child and his or her brothers and sisters. It is also important to consider parenting trends within the family, and parental approaches to discipline and boundary setting.

The child psychiatrist, as part of the family assessment, should enquire about other members of the family who may have experienced similar difficulties. This should include questions about physical illness within the family, any history of psychiatric illness within the family, a background of substance misuse, relatives with developmental delay and any other experiences of abuse.

Interviewing the identified patient alone

The first step is to establish rapport with the child, and to gain his or her confidence, rather than ascertaining facts. Children being interviewed should feel that they, and their points of view, are respected and valued (Barker 1988). It is probably also best to start talking about topics which do not relate directly to the problem area. As rapport is established, more difficult aspects of the child's life can be gently explored. Being seen alone in this way gives the child an opportunity to talk about any potential difficulties away from his or her parents, especially if any abuse is suspected or if young people wish to talk in confidence. Topics which may be broached include worries, anxiety, thoughts of self-harm, obsessions and other experiences about which the child is sensitive or embarrassed.

MENTAL STATE EXAMINATION

There can be no set routine for the psychiatric examination of children as much depends on the child's age, language skills, willingness to talk and personality (Barker 1988). However, it would be important to explore the following areas before reaching a diagnosis and making treatment recommendations:

- reasons for referral
- previous medical problems
- previous mental health problems
- any history of physical, emotional or sexual abuse
- suicidal ideation and past episodes of self-harm
- sleep and appetite
- current or past medication, and any possible allergies
- habits and mannerisms
- temperament and personality
- past separations and attachment-linked behaviour
- peer relationships
- relationships with adults
- ability to cope with new situations
- contact with the law
- appearance and behaviour
- parent–child interactions
- speech
- any unusual thoughts or ideas
- inappropriate visual or auditory experiences
- intellectual function
- mood and affect
- attention, concentration, distractibility and fidgeting
- fantasies and wishes.

PHYSICAL EXAMINATION

As child psychiatrists are qualified doctors, physical examination may be warranted, especially if the clinician is concerned about possible medical problems as a result of the comprehensive assessment. The aim would be to exclude any of the conditions described in Chapter 8 (Behavioural phenotypes), Chapter 12 (Epilepsy) or Chapter 15 (Obstetric complications and neuro-developmental problems), as well as any other medical problem that may be contributing to the presenting symptoms. General examination may include measurement of height and weight, measurement of head circumference, assessment of cardiovascular and respiratory function, examination of the abdomen, examination of the musculo-skeletal system and review of the central nervous system.

A basic neuro-developmental examination is especially important if the child's history suggests possible neurological problems. This would include any concerns about fits or seizures, developmental regression, loss of acquired skills, dysmorphic features, deviation of weight or height from normal parameters and abnormal gait. In addition to the general examination, central nervous system review should include examination of the cranial nerves, examination of the motor system and testing of reflexes. It is also essential to observe for any skin lesions, such as café-au-lait spots.

If the child or adolescent may be started on any medication, it is important to establish baseline measurements. For example, height and weight must be recorded before prescribing stimulant medication, and blood pressure must be recorded before starting children on clonidine.

INVESTIGATIONS

Unlike some areas of medicine, such as a fractured bone showing up on X-ray or a blood test identifying an infection, there are no specific diagnostic tests for mild neuro-developmental difficulties. Investigations are therefore rarely needed, unless specific clinical indications are found in the history or on examination. For example, if there is a history of fits, abnormal movements or fluctuating behaviour, then an EEG should be performed (see Chapter 12). Equally, a history of severe learning disability, unusual behaviour, loss of skills, unremitting headaches, recurrent vomiting or variable levels of consciousness may require urgent review by a paediatrician. As brain scans cannot help to identify diffuse neuro-developmental problems or mental health difficulties, this approach should only be instigated if the paediatricians or other medical practitioners have concerns about a focal brain lesion, if there has been a head injury or if the EEG indicates overt abnormalities. However, chromosomal investigations may be needed if the clinician suspects underlying problems such as Fragile X or other dysmorphic syndromes (Chapter 8).

TREATMENT

Child psychiatrists may have competencies in a wide range of different psychological therapies such as behavioural work, cognitive behavioural therapy, family therapy, individual psychotherapy and group therapy. However, these approaches are discussed in more detail within their specific chapters in Part 4. Instead, as child psychiatrists are usually the only qualified doctors within the multi-disciplinary setting, and therefore uniquely able to prescribe drug treatments, this section will focus on the use of medication in children with mild neuro-developmental processing problems.

Medication

When prescribing medication, or even when considering the use of drug treatments, several basic principles should be applied:

- Only prescribe medication if other non-pharmacological interventions have first been tried but proved unsuccessful.

- Medication should be used to treat a specific problem, such as aggression or hyperactivity, rather than being used in the hope of some general benefit.

- The use of medication should focus on individual signs and symptoms, rather than being used routinely to treat specific diagnoses or syndromes.

- Establish a base-line measurement of the presenting problem before starting any medication to provide a guide against which improvement or deterioration can be measured.

- Follow national guidelines on the use of medication and appropriate dosages.

- Warn parents and children of common side-effects.

- Always start medication with the lowest dose possible, and maintain the drug treatment at the lowest effective dose.

- Avoid using more than one medication (poly-pharmacy) if possible.

- Arrange regular review appointments.

- Consider reducing or stopping medication at each review appointment as children should not remain on medication indefinitely.

Specific groups of drugs

Table 20.1 summarizes the various medications which are most likely to be prescribed by child psychiatrists for the treatment of emotional and behavioural problems in children and adolescents. This is accompanied by a brief explanation of these drug treatments for general reading. However, since recommended dosages change, child psychiatrists are advised to consult specialist prescribing guidelines before issuing medication to children with mild neuro-developmental difficulties.

Table 20.1 Summary of symptoms and useful drugs

Symptom	Medication
Hyperactivity	Methylphenidate
	Dexamphetamine
	Clonidine
	Imipramine
Agression	Risperidone
Tics	Clonidine
	Risperidone
	Halopridol
	Sulpiride
Depression	Fluoxetine
	Sertraline
Obsessions and	Sertraline
compulsions	Fluoxetine
	Clompiramine

Stimulants

Methylphenidate and dexamphetamine are used in the treatment of hyperactivity disorders. They work by activating inhibitory neuronal pathways, which often results in a general reduction in hyperactive behaviour. However, it is important to note that, while stimulants will reduce hyperactive behaviour, they will not 'cure' it. Hence the need to consider any medication alongside appropriate psychological management approaches. Side-effects of these drugs include a reduced appetite, insomnia and the exacerbation of tics.

Neuroleptics

These medications are traditionally used for children and adolescents who present with clear evidence of psychotic behaviour, such as auditory hallucinations or delusions. However, they are also helpful in managing aggression and for reducing tics. Neuroleptics include risperidone, sulpiride and halopridol. Risperidone works by blocking dopamine receptors, adrenoceptors, serotonin (5HT) receptors and histamine receptors. Side-effects of risperidone include weight gain, headache and dizziness. Sulpiride is a specific dopamine receptor antagonist, and side-effects include unusual movements, tremors, muscle rigidity and motor restlessness.

Alpha 2 adrenergic agonists

Clonidine is usually prescribed for the treatment of high blood pressure in adults, but it has also been found to be useful in reducing tics and hyperactive behaviour in children and adolescents. However, clonidine does not effectively improve concentration or inattention. Side-effects of the medication include low blood pressure, depression and sedation.

Tricyclic anti-depressants (TCAs)

These drugs are generally used to treat depression in adults. However a number of TCAs are useful in children, including the management of bed-wetting. Imipramine may be used for hyperactivity if stimulant medication and clonidine have failed. Clomipramine acts primarily on serotonin receptors and prevents reuptake of serotonin (5HT). Because of this, it is used in children with obsessive compulsive disorder. General side-effects may include a dry mouth, blurred vision, constipation and cardiac difficulties in high doses.

Selective serotonin reuptake inhibitors (SSRIs)

These drugs work by inhibiting the removal of the monoamine neurotransmitter serotonin (5HT) from synapses in the brain, thus prolonging their effect on the receptors. SSRIs, such as fluoxetine and sertraline, are useful in depression and in obsessive compulsive disorders. Side-effects of these medications include nausea, anxiety, a dry mouth and diarrhoea.

Multi-agency liaison

The child and adolescent psychiatrist should be able to hold in mind a holistic overview of the child's difficulties. They should therefore have some knowledge of the child's cognitive and physical abilities, an awareness of the child's emotional state and an understanding of both family and peer relationship difficulties. Because of this comprehensive overview, the child psychiatrist is often well placed to liaise closely with other relevant agencies and professionals, such as schools or social services. In these situations, they may even act as an advocate for the family.

Liaison may simply involve keeping other agencies informed of medication changes or the results of investigations. However, as disorganized children often struggles in school, teachers are likely to hold numerous review meetings during the school year and other involved professionals are often invited. This provides a useful opportunity for the psychiatrist to emphasize the child's neuro-developmental difficulties, and the way in which these problems may impact on emotional, social and educational progress. Helping teachers and other professionals to understand that the disorganized child has subtle but significant processing problems, and that he or she may need help with self-esteem and self-confidence, may bring about considerable changes in the child's functioning at school.

REFERENCES

American Academy of Child and Adolescent Psychiatry (1997) 'Comprehensive Psychiatric Evaluation.' *Facts for Families* (No. 52). Washington: American Academy of Child and Adolescent Psychiatry.

Barker, P. (1988) *Basic Child Psychiatry*. Oxford: Blackwell Scientific Publications.

Goodman, R. and Scott, S. (1997) 'Medication and diet.' In R. Goodman and S. Scott (eds) *Child Psychiatry*. Oxford: Blackwell.

Graham, P., Turk, J. and Verhulst, F. (1999) 'Treatment.' In *Child Psychiatry: A Developmental Approach*, 3rd edn. Oxford: Oxford University Press.

Royal College of Psychiatrists. (1999) 'Child and adolescent psychiatrists – how they can help.' *Factsheets for Young People* (No. 36). London: Royal College of Psychiatrists.

Chapter 21

A clinical psychology approach

Helen Rodwell and Estelle Macdonald

INTRODUCTION

Psychology is a scientific study of the mind, with an emphasis on trying to understand how people think and behave. Clinical psychologists work alongside other mental health colleagues to determine how best to promote the psychological well-being of children, adolescents and families. They are trained to work with both children and adults, across a wide range of mental health problems, bringing to bear a systematic approach to assessment and therapy informed by current psychological knowledge and theory. Clinical psychologists are also trained in a variety of therapeutic approaches, and are particularly able to offer psychometric assessments where appropriate. They can play a key part in providing teaching, training, liaison and consultation for other professions and agencies such as teachers or social services.

As described in previous chapters, the disorganized child experiences a wide but variable range of difficulties that are not always easy to identify. A clinical psychologist who specializes in working with children is therefore in a unique position to offer comprehensive assessments and to devise intervention programmes specific to each individual child. In this chapter, some of the most commonly used assessment approaches will be outlined, including assessment of cognitive ability and behavioural assessments. The usefulness of these assessments will be discussed, and an overview of the most common interventions will then be presented, including some ideas about techniques that parents can try at home.

CLINICAL PSYCHOLOGY ASSESSMENT

The assessment phase of any intervention is extremely important, and clinical psychologists often require significant time to focus on and gather in the most useful information. They may achieve this through observation, measurement, testing and statistical analysis. However, their thoroughness can sometimes prove frustrating for parents who want to move quickly on to clinical intervention that will potentially lead to an improved quality of life for both their child and their family. Unfortunately, it takes time to fully understand a child's individual difficulties, their strengths and weaknesses, and how they function in the wider worlds of family and school.

During assessment appointments, the clinical psychologist may therefore ask a wide range of questions about the child, about his or her family and about life at school. This can sometimes feel intrusive to both parents and young people, but the questions being asked invariably have a purpose and logic. If children, adolescents or parent are ever unsure as to why certain information is being sought, they should simply ask the clinical psychologist for clarification. The importance of any questions and information can then be explained, including whether or not the answers will be kept confidential.

The insight gained into the thinking and behaviour of the child or adolescent, based on this comprehensive assessment, is essential for determining the most appropriate, and ultimately the most effective, treatment package for the distressed young person. While parents may compare their child's treatment with that of another child, which can prove useful, it is also important to remember that each child is unique and that their circumstances are often different. All young people therefore deserve their own individually tailored approach, focused on their specific problems and environment.

Finally, it is important to note that, while clinical psychologists have all been trained in comprehensive assessment and intervention skills with children and adolescents, in practice not all clinical psychologists working with young people will be able to offer the full range of skills outlined below.

Cognitive assessment

Clinical psychology addresses a wide range of problems related to thinking and learning, such as intelligence, memory, attention and executive function. A cognitive assessment will therefore focus on how the brain, or how the different areas of the brain, function. For example, how do we learn, why do we remember, what makes us perceive things in a certain way and how do we make sense of the information which we receive? These complex and complicated abilities are usually investigated and assessed by the administering of different psychometric tests. Some of the investigations are more general, relating to overall levels of functioning, while others are very specific, dealing only with comprehension or reading.

Most children enjoy doing these tests, and rise to the challenge in an age-appropriate manner. The child is usually seen alone for the duration of the testing, with a typical testing session lasting between one and two hours. The number and length of sessions may alter depending on the tests used and on the problems being investigated. It is often best to test children in the morning after breakfast when their concentration is at a peak. However, testing can be done at any time during the day or evening. After the tests have been completed, they need to be scored and analysed, which again takes time. The clinical psychologist should then give feedback, either face-to-face or in a report. It is important that the child's parents understand what the assessment has highlighted, what the analysis of any results show and what this will mean for the child or adolescent.

Most of the investigations recommended for cognitive testing in young people are designed to give 'scaled scores'. As these scaled scores take active account of the child's age, they therefore give a good indication of how well that child is functioning compared to other children of the same age. While some psychologists will provide a detailed breakdown of the different test scores, many will instead focus their feedback and report on whether the child is performing at an average, above average or below average level. This should be accompanied by conclusions and recommendations aimed at improving the child or adolescent's life, both at home and at school. However, should parents or young people find that the feedback or report is too complicated or technical, they should ask the clinical psychologist concerned to explain it again until they fully understand what it means, both theoretically and practically.

Intelligence

The measuring of intelligence by empirical testing has long been a source of controversy. While some professionals find the results helpful in terms of guiding clinical practice, others are concerned about constraining children's natural ability and restricting their inherent potential. However, when working with disorganized children, such assessment can provide valuable insights into a wide range of different cognitive abilities. It may also help to identify subtle deficits in cognitive functioning, and explain why the child is not performing well in school in spite of being seen as intelligent.

While cognitive testing may provide an intelligence quotient (IQ) score, it can also provide information about a child's intellectual strengths and weakness. Assessment is therefore useful in identifying specific problems and in providing an overview of the child's general abilities. However, it is important to remember that scoring on these tests depends on other factors such as attention, language and organization.

Broadly speaking, intelligence testing measures both verbal and performance ability. Verbal sub-tests include measures of comprehension, vocabulary, information storage and retrieval, concept formation, abstract thinking, short-term memory and arithmetic. Performance sub-tests include picture completion, block design, picture arrangement, object assembly, mazes and visual–perceptual abilities. These assessments will also give some indication of a child's memory and concentration skills, and can provide a 'freedom from distractibility' score that is potentially useful when assessing for possible attention problems.

The most common assessment tools in use are the Wechsler Pre-School and Primary Scale of Intelligence – Revised (WPPSI-R) for children aged 3 to 6 years (Wechsler 1990) and the Wechsler Intelligence Scale for Children – Third Edition (WISC-III[UK]) for children aged 6 to 16 years (Wechsler 1991). The WISC-III[UK] is being updated into a fourth edition called the WISC-IV[UK]. There is also a short screening version, the Wechsler Abbreviated Scale of Intelligence (WASI) (Wechsler 1999), which is very quick and which can be used to determine whether a full assessment is needed. However, it should not be used instead of a comprehensive assessment.

Clinical psychologists use these assessment tools both to understand the child's general level of ability and to highlight their strengths or weaknesses. An overtly bright child may therefore present with excellent arithmetic skills, average vocabulary and weak visual perception skills. The clinical psychologist can then introduce more specialized tests to clarify emerging problems. For example, if a child's score on the WISC-IIIU[UK] indicates poor memory function, then further memory testing may be offered. Similarly, the Leiter International Performance Scale – Revised can be used with children who have motor impairment or for whom English is a second language (Roid and Miller 1997).

Memory

Memory is an extremely complex brain function which is made up of many different but inter-locking cognitive processes. For example, memory is closely linked to attention and concentration as, to remember something, we first have to focus our attention on it. Memory also requires the ability to retain information over time, such as learning multiplication tables by repeating them over and over to ourselves. Memory is further organized into short-term and long-term memory, as well as being classified as visual, auditory and spatial depending on the source of information.

Due to these very different components of memory functioning, it can prove a difficult and complicated area of assessment. A commonly used assessment tool is the Children's Memory Scale which measures all aspects of memory including immediate visual memory, delayed visual memory, immediate verbal memory, delayed verbal memory, attention, concentration, learning capacity and delayed recognition (Cohen 1997). This scale provides a good indication of memory functioning in children and adolescents from 6 to 16 years.

Other memory assessment tools include the Wide Range Assessment of Memory and Learning (WRAML) which measures verbal and visual memory (Sheslow and Adams 1990), the Rivermead Behavioural Memory Test which measures memory associated with everyday tasks (Aldrich and Wilson 1991) and the Rey–Osterith Complex Figure which measures visual, immediate, delayed and recognition components of memory (Kolb and Wishaw 1990).

Attention

Attention is an important skill that children increasingly develop over time. Like memory, attention can be sub-divided into different aspects of functioning. For example, sustained attention is when we concentrate on something over a long period of time. In contrast, selective attention is where we focus on one object while ignoring other stimuli, like playing the popular card game 'Snap'. A well-used assessment is the Test of Everyday Attention for Children (TEACh) which measures the different aspects of attention (Manly, Robertson and Anderson 1999).

Children with ADHD, as described in Chapter 6, present with a core diagnostic feature of inattention. This can be measured using validated rating scales such as the Connors' Questionnaires (Connors 1973) and the Strengths and Difficulties Questionnaire (Goodman 2001). However, this feature is an overt clinical symptom rather than an indication of potentially impaired cognitive function. The clinical psychologist, in measuring attention, is seeking to identify subtle deficits in multi-facetted brain function rather than trying to quantify gross behavioural changes at home or in the classroom.

Executive function

Executive functioning is made up of a complex array of abilities including self-monitoring, planning, organization and problem-solving. These skills develop throughout childhood and adolescence, and even into early adult life. Executive function can therefore be seen as the 'control centre' of cognitive processing. It makes possible tasks involving the integration of information, the ability to act on sensory stimuli, forward planning and the implementation of behaviour. These abilities are therefore needed both to use and to respond to information in a thoughtful and organized manner. The daily task of getting up in the morning, and organizing oneself for the day ahead, is an example of executive functioning.

Children with neuro-developmental difficulties, such as ADHD and autistic spectrum disorders, invariably have executive function deficits. It is therefore an important area for assessment with regard to disorganized children as they equally often present with decreased executive abilities. A clinical psychologist may use a range of different tests to assess these areas of cognitive function including the executive subsets from the NEPSY (Psychological Corporation 1997), the Stroop Word and Colour Test (Golden 1978), the Wisconsin Card Sorting Test (Heaton 1993) and Behavioural Assessment of the Dysexecutive Syndrome for Children (Emslie *et al.* 2003).

Mood, behaviour and family functioning

The clinical psychologist will often explore the child's mood within the comprehensive assessment as this may influence how the child performs during the cognitive testing. For example, an anxious children may find it difficult to concentrate. The child's mood is also a useful barometer for understanding how he or she is getting on in day-to-day life.

Children often reflect their mood through the activities in which they do or do not take part. In particular, children who are struggling or depressed may give up previously enjoyed activities. Assessment of the child's mood can be achieved by asking both the parents and the child mood-related questions such as 'how do you feel at school?' and 'what activities make you feel happy?'

Children who are having difficulties with learning often find school very challenging, not least because of the criticism and negative feedback which they may experience from their peers, their teachers and their parents. Disorganized children, with their neuro-developmental processing problems, can therefore find the world to be a baffling, confusing and adversarial place. Unfortunately, as they invariably lack the organizational and verbal skills to express how they feel to parents or teachers, these problems may instead present with anxiety and low mood.

There are numerous scales available for assessing depression and anxiety, such as the Birleson Depression Scale and the Spence Children's Anxiety Scale, which can be found in the *Child Psychology Portfolio* (Sclare 1997). A parent's observation of his or her child's mood is also invaluable as parents are in the best position to know their child's general level of functioning and how he or she behaves. It is also important for the psychologist to assess basic family functioning (Chapter 24) as this too can impact on how the child presents, and the degree to which he or she will engage in psychological testing.

PSYCHOLOGICAL INTERVENTIONS
How to use information from the cognitive assessment

The cognitive assessment, and the resulting report, should give a clear indication of both the child's strengths and weaknesses. It is therefore valuable to discuss these finding with other professionals involved in the child's care, especially the school. Most parents choose to share their child's report with schoolteachers and specialist educational staff, and this is always a good idea. The report should therefore include specific recommendations for both parents and teachers as to how the child's strengths can be capitalized on, and how any weaknesses can be remedied.

For example, if a child has difficulties with visual memory (not being able to remember what he or she sees) then this can be aided by encouraging the child to practise 'using his or her memory. The popular game of finding card pairs can be helpful. Hiding different items under a tea towel and asking the child to remember as many as possible after one minute of exposure is another enjoyable and beneficial exercise. Some children can improve their visual memory by silently talking to themselves, which works by making the visual information which needs to be remembered into something verbal.

While cognitive testing can provide extremely helpful information, it is essential to keep in mind that these assessments are administered under strict conditions, which are almost always very quiet and one-to-one with the psychologist. The results of these assessments are therefore primarily a good indication of how well a child will function under ideal learning conditions. It is crucial that the clinical psychologist then considers, based on the testing, how well the child might perform within other settings, especially within the classroom. While a child might show average cognitive abilities within the assessment, this may not be reflected in his or her academic work due to the distractions and stimuli inherent in classroom learning. The clinical psychologist, in the report, will therefore provide some practical ideas about how the child might best use his or her cognitive abilities, and avoid processing weaknesses, within the classroom.

However, it is also important to remember that cognitive abilities develop over the course of childhood and adolescence. This means that any weaknesses identified at a young age may not prove to be a weakness at a later age. For this reason, many clinical psychologists will recommend that a child is re-tested periodically, at one- or two-year intervals, to see how they are progressing.

Behavioural management

Clinical psychologists often approach problems, such as anxiety attacks or temper tantrums, from the perspective of psychological behaviour theory. They implement this model by using what is called an ABC analysis. This is dependent on a detailed chronology of what happens prior to the incident (**A**ntecedent), the response of those around the child (**B**ehaviour) and the impact of their responses on the child (**C**onsequence). For example, a child who wants to buy sweets at a supermarket may start screaming loudly if thwarted (A). His or her mother, through embarrassment and fatigue, may quickly give in (B). This will encourage the child to resort to screaming whenever his or her demands are not met (C).

These patterns of behaviour are assessed in terms of both the individual child and the wider family. Once an ABC assessment has been completed, the psychologist will discuss key issues with the parents and agree potentially desirable outcomes. The same child may then find that his or her screaming does not lead to sweets but that, in contrast, improved behaviour is most likely to lead to the desired effect. This will soon make the temper outbursts redundant. The core issue in behavioural management is therefore not the elimination of unwanted behaviour but rather the promotion of desired behaviour in its place. This approach can be applied to a wide range of situations, such as children being dressed for school on time or adolescent boys putting their dirty football kit in the washing basket after use.

The behavioural approach to increasing desired behaviour is through positive reinforcement. Once a desirable behaviour has been agreed by the parents with the clinical psychologist, it is then introduced into the child's life and rewarded when it starts to appear. This can be achieved by simple praise or by using inexpensive rewards that are important to the child. Possible options may include staying up later at the weekend or watching a favourite television show. It is always essential to set up an interesting variety of rewards so the child does not get bored and become demotivated. At first, the child will need to be rewarded as soon as possible after the desired behaviour has occurred in order to maintain momentum. However, the rewards can gradually be extended over time or even be phased out completely.

In contrast, negative reinforcement involves the removal of an aversive stimulus or unwanted response after the desired behaviour has occurred. For example, a parent will only stop complaining after the child has finished all of their vegetables. Extinction, as an alternative approach, involves the removal of a previously identified reward, such as parental attention or a flexible bedtime. Whether using positive or negative reinforcement, it is important to work with fairly simple behaviours at first as, if faced with something difficult and unattainable, the child might just give up. He or she may then prove reluctant to engage in any future attempts to change his or her behaviour. Also, for some children, these tasks may need to be broken down into several smaller steps, indicating exactly what needs to be done in concrete terms, and detailing the positive or negative consequences equally clearly.

Another behavioural approach to reducing undesired behaviour is the use of 'time-out'. This involves taking, or sending, the child away from the area in which the undesired behaviour has occurred to a quiet place. It is best to agree with the child when this approach may be used, and to agree an appropriate place for time-out. This should be a quiet place where the child can slowly settle. It is important to emphasize that the approach is not a punishment, but instead represents a chance for the child to calm down and regain his or her composure. The general rule for time-out is one minute for every year of age, so that a 6-year-old child will remain in the time-out area for six minutes.

Anger management

If anger is a major issue, and it is dominating family life, then it may prove easier for a neutral person, such as a clinical psychologist, to help in resolving the problem. The psychologist could approach these difficulties by talking to the parents about different and more effective ways of dealing with the child. He or she may also talk directly, and separately, with the child. This could include cognitive behaviour therapy sessions in which the child is taught how to monitor his or her emotions, and how to actively change any thoughts which lead to angry feelings and acting out behaviours. Relaxation strategies can also be shown to the child. However, especially if his or her anger is a serious problem, then the child must have a reasonable degree of motivation and engagement if there is to be any chance of success with these approaches.

At the same time, parents need to explain to their children that it is normal to become angry at times, and that this might be the appropriate response to a difficult situation. As anger is not, by definition, wrong, it is therefore more important to help children to manage their anger more effectively rather than trying to eradicate it entirely. Children need to learn when it is acceptable to be angry, and keeping an anger diary may help to identify situations and thoughts that lead to unwanted and unacceptable angry outbursts. Using this approach, the child can then start to think of ways in which to avoid or manage those situations and thoughts better. As the ancient philosopher Aristotle once said: 'one needs to use the right amount of anger, with the right person, at the right time'.

Box 21.1 Tips for dealing with anger

- Relax
- Use helpful self-talk ('I am calm and relaxed')
- Drink a glass of water
- Move away from the problematic situation
- Listen to music
- Count to 50

Planning ahead and organization

Structure and routine are essential in keeping children organized, with the degree of routine and structure closely matching the child's level of disorganization. For some disorganized children, it may even prove helpful to have timetables and instructions for basic home-related activities such as meal-times, bathtimes and bed time. These timetables and instruction flowcharts can be pinned up on a wall in the child's bedroom, stuck to the bathroom mirror if linked to personal hygiene or attached to the fridge. It may also prove useful to colour code and label drawers and shelves, which will allow the child to store and retrieve items easily. These visual cues and concrete instructional pathways will help the child more than complex verbal communications.

There are also a range of essential daily living activities which may quickly spark off adverse behaviour and reactions in disorganized children. These could include shopping in crowded centres or long waits at the post office. Parents know their children better than anyone else, and can usually predict the situations in which they may start to play up. These activities can then be planned for in ways which will reduce both parental and child stress, for example, only doing shopping with the child if it is absolutely necessary. If unavoidable, make sure that there is a reward available for good behaviour. Also plan for food and toilet breaks to reduce boredom and over-stimulation, and make sure you know where the public conveniences are. If going out for a meal, fast food restaurants or buffets may help to avoid long and potentially frustrating waits. Going to the cinema or theatre may prove more difficult, but these problems can be overcome by attending at times when there are fewer people in the audience and by arranging to sit in aisle seats should a quick escape be needed.

Some disorganized children can be extremely fussy when it comes to deciding what to wear, and this may cause major disruption in the mornings before school. It may then prove helpful for the child to decide on what to wear for the next day at school, and to set out these clothes the night before. Children with neuro-developmental problems may also have an increased sensitivity to certain fabrics, particularly non-cotton clothes which are constraining, ticklish or prickly. Many of these children complain about sleeves, seams or labels causing irritation. It may again help to cut off all labels, and to consider pre-washing all new clothes several times to render the material softer.

The very nature of the clinical psychology assessment is to help in identifying these potential triggers, and then finding ways in which the child and his or her family can overcome these problems.

Box 21.2 Tips for parents

- Don't place your child in situations which he or she cannot manage
- Avoid surprises
- Visual and concrete messages help
- Written messages are usually better than verbal messages
- Use humour to diffuse situations
- Be specific with praise
- Expect ups and downs
- Role play difficult situations with your child and model flexible responses to frustration
- Identify feelings which your child cannot verbalize, and talk these through once the crisis has settled
- Look after yourself and treat yourself occasionally – it's hard looking after a disorganized child!

REFERENCES

Aldrich, F.K. and Wilson, B. (1991) 'Rivermead Behavioural Memory Test for Children: A preliminary evaluation.' *British Journal of Clinical Psychology 30*, 161–168.

Cohen, M. (1997) *Children's Memory Scale.* Georgia: University of Georgia.

Connors, C.K. (1973) 'Rating scales for use in drug studies with children.' *Psychopharmacology Bulletin: Special Issue on Pharmacotherapy with Children 9*, 24–84.

Emslie, H., Wilson, C., Burden, V., Nimmo-Smith, I. *et al.* (2003) *Behavioural Assessment of the Dysexecutive Syndrome for Children.* Bury St Edmunds: Thames Valley Test Company.

Golden, J.C. (1978) *Stroop Word and Colour Test.* Chicago, IL: Stoelting Co.

Goodman, R. (2001) 'Psychometric properties of the strengths and difficulties questionnaire.' *Journal of the American Academy of Child and Adolescent Psychiatry 40*, 1337–1345.

Heaton, R. (1993) *Wisconsin Card Sorting Test Manual – Revised and Expanded.* USA: Psychological Assessment Resources.

Kolb, B. and Wishaw, I. (1990) *Fundamentals of Human Neuropsychology*, 3rd edn. New York: Freeman.

Manly, T., Robertson, I.H. and Anderson, V. (1999) *Test of Everyday Attention for Children (TEACh).* Bury St Edmunds: Thames Valley Test Company.

Psychological Corporation (1997) *NEPSY.* San Antonio, TX: Psychological Corporation.

Roid, G.H. and Miller, L.J. (1997) *Leiter International Performance Scale – Revised.* Wood Dale, IL: Stoelting Co.

Sclare, I. (1997) *The Child Psychology Portfolio.* Windsor: NFER-NELSON.

Sheslow, D. and Adams, A. (1990) *Wide Range Assessment of Memory and Learning (WRAML)*. Wilmington, DE: Wide Range.

Wechsler, D. (1990) *Wechsler Pre-school and Primary Scale of Intelligence (WPPSI): Revised UK Edition.* Sidcup: The Psychological Corporation.

Wechsler, D. (1991) *Wechsler Intelligence Scale for Children*, 3rd edn. (WISC-III). London: The Psychological Corporation.

Wechsler, D. (1999) *Wechsler Abbreviated Scale of Intelligence (WASI)*. San Antonio, TX: The Psychological Corporation.

Chapter 22

A child psychotherapy approach

Samuel M. Stein and Uttom Chowdhury

INTRODUCTION

Sigmund Freud, in trying to relieve adult patients of their neurotic symptoms, realized that many of their problems had roots in infancy and childhood. This ongoing and adverse influence indicated a potential interference in and restriction of the developmental process. Child psychotherapy is therefore the application of psychoanalytic understanding to the treatment of children with emotional and behavioural problems. Melanie Klein, who applied many of these theories to children, was enthusiastic about the potential widespread provision of child analysis to enhance healthy emotional development in young people. Many child psychotherapists today would still hold that the primary aim of child psychotherapy is the promotion of emotional growth and the relief of mental suffering. If this is carried out judiciously and appropriately, later problems, such as disturbance in adulthood, can potentially be avoided. Almost invariably, it will be accompanied by symptom relief and behaviour change (Byrne 1999).

THEORY AND PRACTICE

Child psychotherapists of all orientations are trained in theories of child development and developmental psychopathology. They take into consideration the changes which individuals, families and communities undergo over time. Child psychotherapy also recognizes that the child's development is determined at several levels: from the genetic and constitutional, through physical and psychological influences, to influences emanating from the family, neighbourhood and cultural spheres of life. Childhood symptomatology and disorders are therefore more likely to be perceived as developmental deviations than as childhood illnesses. However, it is not the external experience by itself which determines the impact upon the child, but the internal response to it and how it is interpreted by the child. According to Reeves (1977), psychological illness is both the product of, and an indicator of, significant failure by the individual psyche to deal adequately with internal conflict.

Child psychotherapy is not strictly concerned with the external functioning of the child, such as practical, familial and social behaviours. Instead, because it gives priority to the presence and influence of the unconscious in the child's conflicts, child psychotherapy places the internal world of the child at the heart of treatment. As described by Byrne (1999), there are several core principles common to all schools and approaches of child psychotherapy:

- the importance of play as a means of communication
- the concept of containment of anxieties
- the transference relationship between the patient and the therapist
- the use of interpretation to promote insight into the patient's inner world
- the constancy of the setting of the therapy.

The importance of play as a means of communication

Sigmund Freud observed a small child at play with a cotton reel, throwing it out and reeling it back in again. He understood this to be symbolic of the repeated but temporary loss of the mother, which the small child was attempting to master through play. In this observation, he affirmed play as a very serious business indeed. Melanie Klein developed her play technique, and provided toys for the child in therapy, but not to reassure the child or to provide a creative outlet. These items are primarily there to provide the child with a means of facilitating the expression of thoughts and feelings. Klein considered that the child's play could be understood and interpreted in very much the same way as the psychoanalyst interprets adult dreams.

Containment of anxieties

The child psychotherapist provides a reliable and regular presence in a familiar and safe setting. His or her deep attentiveness to the child, in all aspects of the inner world, is reminiscent of the mother–infant relationship. The infant projects intolerable feelings into the mother who acts as a container for these feelings; a container strong enough not only to bear these feelings but also to digest them and then feed them back to the infant in a more tolerable form. By understanding and introjecting the concept of a containing and understanding mother, the infant begins to builds up a capacity for thought and a growing sense of self. The child psychotherapist is similarly available to the child as a container. This is communicated through the attitude of attentiveness, interest in the child's feelings and state of mind, and a willingness to tolerate and understand painful communications from the child. The child's experiences of the therapist as able to contain his or her feelings and anxieties, and later to interpret them, strengthens his or her sense of self and changes occur in the child's internal world. Improved relationships to people in the external world will follow improvements in the internal relationships within the child's mind. A common aim to all approaches is also to increase self-esteem in the child.

The transference relationship

Through the child psychotherapist's availability as a container for the child's projections, the transference relationship develops. Transference describes the ways in which the child interacts with the therapist, and the therapeutic setting, as an expression of the child's relationship with internal representations within his or her own inner world. Thus, in exploring the transference and counter-transference relationship, the child psychotherapist aims to explore the internal world of the child including his or her fantasies, wishes and understanding of the external world.

The use of interpretation to promote insight

It is a central idea of psychotherapy that interpreting and naming what is going on in a child's internal world brings relief, facilitates insight and creates room for change. The process is one of 'reflecting the patient's view of the world back to them, but with more light let in' (Wallace 1997). Interpretations are offered in simple words, appropriate to the child's capacity to understand. The child can then increase his or her capacity to think something through, and to see the choices that might be available, having had the opportunity to negotiate difficulties thoughtfully rather than impulsively act them out. This can further protect the child from the adverse impact of later life events.

ASSESSMENT

Broadly speaking, psychotherapy is appropriate for children in whom confusion and conflict in their internal world affects their adaptation to the external world. The list in Box 22.2 includes many of the difficulties manifested by children which are amenable to psychotherapeutic treatment. Some child psychotherapists also work successfully with patients who have significant learning disabilities (Sinason 1992; Simpson and Miller 2004).

Child psychotherapists work both within health care services and privately, and referrals may come via a number of different routes. In the private sector, parents concerned for their child and acting on advice from other health care professionals are the most frequent referrers. Otherwise, referral for psychotherapy

Box 22.2 Problems amenable to child psychotherapy treatment

- Enuresis (bed-wetting)
- Encopresis (soiling)
- Eating disorders
- Withdrawal and depression
- Attachment difficulties
- School refusal
- Conduct disorder
- Suffering sequelae to sexual, physical or emotional abuse
- Struggling to cope with major life events such as bereavement, divorce or chronic illness in self or family member
- Physical or mental handicap
- Neuro-developmental and processing problems

may be made by professionals who, following their own assessment of the child and family, may wish for a psychodynamic assessment of the child in their own right. In the public sector, referrals are most often received from primary health care including general practitioners, paediatricians, community nurses and health visitors. For those children who manifest difficulties in coping at school, concerns by teachers and educational psychologists may prompt a referral for assessment. In all referrals, permission and cooperation from the parents or main carers is essential.

The psychotherapist meets with the parents and the referred child, invites them to describe current difficulties and gathers information about the child's early development. This may include information about pregnancy, birth, the nature and quality of early attachment relationships, how the child slept as a baby, how the feeding relationship and early separations were negotiated, and so on. In some cases, it may be necessary to have a separate meeting with parents, who may need to express some of their concerns and give sensitive historical details, which they feel might be harmful for the child to hear. It is also important to explore the parents' understanding of the referral, and to think with them about which aspects of the child's functioning might be best helped by a child psychotherapy intervention.

If the parents, the therapist and the child are all in agreement that an individual assessment should follow, the therapist will arrange to see the child on his or her own for a few sessions in order to explore further the usefulness of psychotherapy. During these sessions, the therapist attends very carefully to the child's play and, where possible, explores the child's views on his or her difficulties and the child's understanding of what is happening to him or her. In these exploratory sessions, it is important for the therapist to pose 'trial interpretations' to obtain some idea of the child's receptivity and responsiveness to the insights offered. These interpretations are kept at a general level, for instance talking about the patterns of the child's relationships with family members and others external to the therapy. In parallel with these meetings, another worker may offer the parents a separate meeting to address parental anxieties, and to gather more information about life at home in the interest of informing the assessment as a whole.

While the confidentiality of patients' material has always been considered of central importance to the building of the therapeutic relationship, it is also important, especially in the case of children with complex disorders, that the psychotherapist is able to communicate with parents in an open way about the child's response to the assessment and treatment process. However, because psychotherapists stress the importance of the child's experience of the process, they will always discuss with the child what they plan to share with parents, so that it becomes part of the therapeutic relationship and is not experienced as a betrayal of it. This allows the child to be part of the thinking about what the difficulties are and how best to address them. In the case of adolescent patients, the process described above may, naturally, take a somewhat different course as their need for a space more separate from, but still supported by, parents is developmentally appropriate and therapeutically more effective.

The psychotherapist will always have in mind the degree of commitment needed to bring a child once weekly, or more, for therapeutic sessions. The recommendation of psychotherapy for a child can also be emotionally testing for parents in a way untypical of other treatment approaches. Parents sometimes feel that their relationship with the child has been judged lacking, or that the offer of treatment implies that the child is 'mad'. Some parents find it difficult to countenance a close relationship developing between therapist and child, and fear that the therapist will be a rival for their child's affections. Others have to weigh up the practicalities of travel, transport, the needs of siblings, ordinary after-school activities and the educational timetable of the referred child against a commitment to regular psychotherapy. These worries and concerns can and should be addressed before treatment begins. In some cases, individual psychotherapy is not appropriate and the psychotherapist may then make recommendations for a different type of help.

Case example: Dylan

Dylan was referred for child psychotherapy by the community paediatrician at the age of 8. His difficulties included a speech impediment, and involuntary tics which had no identifiable cause. Dylan was also presenting with bed-wetting, nightmares and excessive fearfulness of animals. His parents felt supported by the initial meeting with the child psychotherapist, and requested further help and advice on how to deal with Dylan's difficulties. After several weeks, Dylan's individual assessment took place. The psychotherapist who assessed him found him to be an articulate little boy who played and talked freely, and who responded well to her interest in his unconscious thoughts and feelings. However, despite some diminishing of his fears during this period, his parents felt that practical help from occupational therapy and speech and language therapy should take priority over psychological therapy for Dylan. They expressed their worry that the psychotherapy might make him feel more unhappy, rather than just lessening his symptoms. He had apparently become more outspoken, and even somewhat aggressive towards them, in the course of the assessment. They instead asked if they could come alone, as parents, to discuss their concerns about Dylan and the ways in which they managed him. The child psychotherapist was able to offer this, and Dylan's difficulties improved through the work with his parents which took place in parallel with his directly accessing other therapeutic interventions.

Case example: Lara

Lara, aged 10, was adopted from an institution in China at the age of 4 months. Nothing was known about her birth history but, when found by her adoptive parents, she was very underweight. She was also being bottle-fed on cow's milk in spite of an intolerance to lactose. Lara had a history of slow motor and language development, as well as sensory difficulties, especially hypersensitivity to noise. She had developed fears and phobias about normal household appliances, such as the washing machine and lawn mower. Lara's concentration and attention were poor. Her learning at school was also slow, and she was functioning nearly three years behind her chronological age in most subjects. During her assessment for psychotherapy, her play revealed a preoccupation with her own identity and her profound confusion about it. Her adoptive parents elected for psychotherapy, although the idea of Lara forming an important attachment with her therapist was quite painful for them. However, they brought her consistently to sessions throughout the three years spent in treatment.

TREATMENT

If all agree to proceed, the therapy commences. The child's life is full of transference processes, and internal object relationships are regularly externalized and acted out upon other people, pets and toys. Transference processes may find particular expression within psychotherapy, helping to reduce high levels of arousal and anxiety through the provision of repeated, reliable and attentive contact and understanding by the child psychotherapist. Thus, over the first weeks of therapy, transference processes tend to gather in on the therapeutic situation. This is facilitated by the therapist's interpretation of any anxieties which seem to manifest in the session material.

The function of the therapeutic setting is to provide the child with some personal space in which there is a minimum of interference from external and internal distractions. The total setting includes the external realities of the room, the toys, the timing of the therapy and the mental receptivity of the therapist. Consistency and reliability are essential, and help to create an atmosphere of physical and emotional containment. It also helps the therapist to detect subtle changes in the child's play and communications, which arise more from his or her internal world rather than as a response to external factors. For example, the therapist's lateness may accenuate the child's anxiety about abandonment.

As described by Byrne (1999), the room should be simply furnished and ideally have access to water. Drawings or work by other children are not displayed as this may provoke envy. The session should occur at the same times and on the same days and any breaks, such as holidays, should be prepared for well in advance. Toys and drawing materials are necessary, and many therapists prefer to provide a box or drawer of toys exclusively for each child. These include small human figures, wild and domestic animals, fences, building blocks, small cars and other transport vehicles, a ball, string, paper, Plasticine, Sellotape, glue, scissors and crayons or colour pencils. Other therapists prefer to provide a communal box of toys which is available to all patients who come into the room, although difficulties can arise with this arrangement. It may prove impossible to know if changes in a child's behaviour are in response to his or her encountering evidence of another child's use of the toys or if they are due to internal processes. Communal toys cannot be safely left from one session to the next in a particular arrangement or construction as subsequent children may rearrange them. This can, at times, be an inhibition to the degree to which the child feels free to play.

Traditionally, therapists found it best if their contact with parents was kept to an absolute mimimum. It was also felt that any meetings should preferably be conducted in front of the child. This can be enormously helpful in allowing the therapist and child to do the necessary therapeutic work while unhindered by outside information and anxieties. However, this practice is changing. A therapeutic approach which includes regular meetings of another worker with the family or parents is strongly recommended, even in the case of some adolescent patients. This allows cross-fertilization between the parent meetings and the child's psychotherapy, which can be particularly helpful in complex cases. In addition to this input, the child's therapist will review progress with parents or carers, along with the worker who has been meeting with them, at regular intervals. It is not helpful if the difficulties with organization and communication with which these children and their families often struggle are re-enacted by a professional network which fails to synchronize, coordinate or communicate effectively. The child's therapist may also attend network meetings and planning meetings, for example, at school.

Case example: Graham

Graham was referred to the local Child and Adolescent Mental Health Service at the age of 5 due to persistent soiling. Although toilet trained by the age of three and a half, and consistently dry for over a year, at nursery he started having a few accidents. On starting school, his soiling became more frequent and soon occurred on a daily basis. The school was concerned that the soiling was a manifestation of anxiety whenever Graham was asked to do anything beyond his capabilities.

Background

Graham was born prematurely by caesarian section after his twin sister died in utero shortly before the birth. As an infant, he fed well but struggled to establish sleep patterns. His milestones were mild to moderately delayed, and he did not speak until he was 3. His problems with expressive and receptive language had already been assessed by educational psychologists, speech therapists and occupational therapists, and various different diagnoses had been made.

Graham lived at home with his mother, two older brothers and a younger sister. His mother had suffered a miscarriage before he was conceived, and his father left home shortly after Graham's birth and the death of his twin sister. Although he maintained regular contact, Graham's father had difficulties in managing Graham. Graham's older brothers also teased him, and his younger sister was rapidly catching up with him in terms of educational and emotional development.

At times, Graham's frustrations became overwhelming. This led to uncontrollable outbursts of aggression, particularly towards his sister. His mother was understandably protective of Graham, and was particularly concerned about his lack of educational progress. Graham was becoming increasingly aware of the gap developing between himself and his peers, particularly in the acquisition of literacy skills. He also had poor impulse control and was clumsy. Graham was unable to dress himself, and had very poor organizational and spatial skills too. His fear of failure was acute, and he would avoid tasks that he found difficult to manage.

Assessment

Graham's low self-esteem, combined with his confused state of mind, suggested that assessment for individual psychotherapy was appropriate. This provided a deeper understanding of Graham's complex emotional difficulties, and his internal sense of chaos and disorganization. As the surviving twin, the impact of this loss and his mother's postnatal depression created a confusing early infantile experience. He presented as an isolated and sad child, who could also be anxious and aggressive. Graham was clearly unable to process simple communications, and often appeared to be in a dream world.

The psychotherapist felt that Graham was struggling to control a world of which he could not make sense, a world in which he felt hopeless and helpless. As some aspects of his development were still at a toddler stage, he was regressing to this earlier developmental level in the face of ongoing stress at school, peer pressure and the demands of socialization. This was preventing him from moving forward, and he was offered weekly psychotherapy to address the discrepancy between his emotional development and his chronological age.

Treatment

Graham was of average height with an open face, gentle eyes and a shy manner. His clothes were always messy and muddy. At the beginning of his treatment, which lasted two years, Graham was very worried about 'what he would do'. To manage this anxiety, he would bring along objects from home. His therapist understood this as an attempt to overcome separation concerns by creating a concrete link with his mother. The 'doing' – drawing, painting and clay modelling that he chose to do in his sessions – was a chaotic, confused and messy process. Graham would smear, drop and spill, jumping from idea to idea. There was no sequencing to his thoughts, and the room would end up with mess and fragments of objects everywhere. This seemed to represent accurately Graham's internal world.

At this stage in his therapy, Graham was not very interested in playing with the therapist, but preferred to become completely immersed in his own activities. He found it difficult to think about and respond to the therapist's thoughts, leaving her feeling very shut out. It was as if he became lost in his own separate but chaotic world and found it difficult to differentiate between thoughts, ideas, actions and feelings. At times he seemed bewildered and disorientated. By becoming immersed in his disorganization, he did not have to think.

Graham gradually felt more contained and was able to enter into dialogue with his therapist. He began to 'understand' the beginning and endings of the sessions. While unable to tell the time, he began to experience internally the rhythm of the regular weekly sessions. Although Graham lacked a capacity for symbolic functioning in his play, and his thinking was concrete, he became increasingly able to think for himself and to reflect on his own thoughts and feelings. He was also discovering an experience of being held in mind by someone who was emotionally available, and his relationship with the therapist was starting to have meaning.

During a subsequent session, Graham completed his model, a grumpy tortoise. His therapist wondered just how much he identified with the tortoise – was he like an animal that hibernates for long periods with a tough shell and a vulnerable soft inside that only comes out when he is feeling brave enough? She thought with Graham about this, and about what the tortoise might be feeling. It soon emerged that he was alluding to his own feelings about being grumpy. However, for Graham, it was safer for the tortoise to be grumpy than for him to think about his own grumpy feelings. Interpretation of his cross feelings about himself, and towards his therapist, began a process of understanding and acknowledging the problems which he had with his own aggression.

Initially, Graham found it difficult to convey feelings or experiences in words. However, it became increasingly possible to think together with his therapist. He began to make less mess in the room, and to think about what he was making. By his therapist being along with him in the process, trust developed and a therapeutic alliance was built up. It became possible to begin deeper interpretative work which helped to bring unconscious fears, fantasies, conflicts and wishes to the surface. Graham's internal conflicts became more manifest as the transference shifted from his therapist being someone who criticized, told him he was failing and judged him like a teacher, to being a more benign helpful person.

This gradual process of working through helped Graham's capacity for thinking. He was becoming internally more organized and therefore more able to understand. He could think about his therapist's interpretations in a meaningful way, taking them in and thinking about them for himself. Some insight was developing, and Graham was beginning to understand his own aggression. He was able to express these feelings in words, instead of feeling helpless and hopeless, and this impacted on his self-esteem. Talking about his feelings and thoughts was also helpful in bringing more clarity to his world, particularly his capacity to think and listen. He began to ask questions and be curious rather than just accepting that he did not understand and remaining in a disorganized and confused state of mind.

Parent work

Graham's mother attended regular sessions with another clinician. Her grief about his difficulties, the complexity of mourning for one child while caring for another, her struggles with assessments and diagnoses, her battles for suitable educational placement and the painful end of her marriage were all addressed in this therapy. Working through her feelings about these external realities, and understanding her responses to them, helped to free a space within her mind within which Graham could be seen as a separate and viable son. This in turn contributed to his psychological development.

Summary

Graham's soiling, his presenting problem, improved considerably. By the end of his therapy, he had very few accidents. His improved self-esteem made him more motivated to try at school, and his language problems improved to such an extent that he moved out of the special unit which he had been attending and into mainstream class. He also made considerable progress in developing a capacity to listen, to understand and to acknowledge his frustration, while learning to communicate his thoughts and feelings more effectively.

ACKNOWLEDGEMENTS

We would like to thank Pamela Bartram and Tessa Dalley, both child and adolescent psychotherapists, for their contribution to this chapter.

REFERENCES AND FURTHER READING

Alvarez, A. (1992) *Live Company: Psycho-Analytic Psychotherapy with Autistic, Borderline, Deprived and Abused Children*. London: Routledge.

Byrne, G. (1999) 'Child Psychotherapy.' In S.M. Stein, R. Haigh and J. Stein (eds) *Essentials of Psychotherapy*. Oxford: Butterworth-Heinemann, pp.232–252.

Kazdin, A.E. (1991) 'Effectiveness of psychotherapy with children and adolescents.' *Journal of Consulting and Clinical Psychology 59*, 785–798.

Reeves, A.C. (1977) *Freud and Child Psychotherapy*. London: Wildwood House.

Simpson, D. and Miller, L. (eds) (2004) *Unexpected Gains Psychotherapy with People with Learning Disabilities*. London: Karnac.

Sinason, V. (1992) *Mental Handicap and the Human Condition*. London: Free Association.

Wallace, W. (1997) 'Children on the couch: Is three the perfect age to meet your shrink?' *The Independent Newspaper*, London.

Chapter 23

A classroom approach

Val Burgess and Uttom Chowdhury

INTRODUCTION

School days are meant to be 'the best days of our lives'. They are a time for making friends, having fun, learning new things and generally acquiring skills that will, one hopes, help in adult life. However, for disorganized children, school can quickly become a very unhappy place where the child struggles to learn, has difficulty keeping up with peers, has few friends and may be subjected to severe bullying. This chapter aims to highlight some of the key educational difficulties facing disorganized children in the classroom, and attempts to offer some basic strategies for making things more manageable for the disorganized child.

CLASSROOM OBSERVATIONS

Teachers and other educational support staff are in a unique position in that they work with children outside and away from the home environment. They can carefully monitor individuals to assess how they approach tasks, and ascertain whether they are accessing lessons. They can also observe children's general behaviour, their social interaction with peers and their self-esteem. Educational colleagues therefore have an essential role in providing input to any medical or psychological assessments that may be carried out by other professionals such as doctors, psychologists, family therapists and occupational therapists.

Some basic principles underpinning classroom observations

The aim is to build up an understanding of how individual children learn most effectively. This is especially important with regard to disorganized children as they often present as a diagnostic conundrum. The teacher can therefore provide valuable information on the child's specific strengths and difficulties, which may help determine the diagnosis or, at the very least, provide a better understanding of the child's presenting problems. Gathering information from parents and professionals, and careful observations of the child in the school context, can help to clarify individual difficulties and then to identify appropriate strategies to support the child. Children should be observed across a range of different situations and in different contexts, such as in the classroom, in the dining hall and in the playground.

Parents can share their observations and experiences from home and within the wider community. Observations of the child at work and play, in both individual and group settings, may further help to identify some of the child's difficulties. In particular, the child's social and communication skills, and ability to cope in different situations, can impact on both academic learning and the acquisition of life skills. A problem-solving approach to these difficulties will therefore enable development of effective strategies for supporting the disorganized child, with the aim of promoting his or her independence as a thinker and learner in both classroom and social contexts. However, any strategies which are introduced must be refined in the light of further observations, with ongoing and close communication with other child care professionals involved with the child.

CLASSROOM PROBLEMS AND SUPPORTIVE STRATEGIES
Internal organizational difficulties
Problems

- 'Filing' information and organizing thinking
- Making connections with previous learning
- Processing of information
- Long-term and short-term memory
- Retrieval of information and word-finding.

Supportive strategies

- Make connections with previous learning explicit
- Allow the child time to process questions and information
- Encourage active listening
- Cue a child that you are going to ask him or her a question next
- Use visual cues, pre-recorded questions or prompt sheets
- Encourage use of diaries and note-books as reminders
- Use check-lists.

Sensory integration

Problems

Modulation of sensory information may prove difficult for the disorganized child. Emotional states can influence a child's response, such as heightened anxiety resulting in an over-reaction to being pushed in the corridor. The sensory demands of a dining hall can be overwhelming, including trying to balance the tray and body awareness in the queue. Tactile, visual, auditory, olfactory and gustatory systems can all be assaulted!

Supportive strategies

Pre-planning and anticipation of possible problems, together with problem-solving solutions, are applicable to any situation. Use of the dining room provides an example of this process:

- Ensure that the child knows what to expect in the dining hall.

- A description of the situation, and possible management strategies, can be provided through a social story.

- Practise a 'walk through' in quieter moments or before the queue develops.

- Cater to the child's organizational and coordination difficulties, such as using a non-slip mat on the tray or a special receptacle for cutlery.

- Making choices can be challenging for some children, and a preview of the menu prior to lunchtime can be helpful.

- Other opportunities to practise making choices can be deliberately built into the school day.

- Some children are very particular about the texture of food, or may not like different foods touching on their plate, and this knowledge needs to be shared with those serving the food.

- Seating position in the dining room needs as much careful consideration as in the classroom.

- Some children prefer sitting with their back to a wall as they find movement behind them disconcerting, while others can become easily over-stimulated by activity in front of them.

- Knowledge of the individual child should actively influence any decisions.

Motor difficulties

Problems and supportive strategies

- Some children may have difficulty in integrating the two sides of their body.

- Problems with the vestibular system can lead to difficulties with balance, especially on smaller and precarious furniture such as stools.

- A lack of awareness of their body in space can result in children finding it difficult to make motor judgments or to manoeuvre around the classroom.

- Difficulties with tactile processing may render the child hypersensitive to touch, and create difficulties in judging pressure when playing with peers or when writing.

Handwriting

Problems

Letter formation, spacing and layout of work can prove challenging and tiring.

Supportive strategies

- It is important to improve posture.

- Chairs should be the correct height, and arms may offer additional support.

- Encourage children to plant their feet firmly on the floor when in a seated position, and a footstool can help children to stabilize their body.

- Grip may need to be improved and the occupational therapist can offer suggestions for exercises to develop upper muscle strength.

- It is worth experimenting with pens which have comfortable grips, and it is often easier to maintain flow with roller ball pens.

- Graph paper can be useful to encourage spacing between words.

- Allow use of word processors or dictaphones.

- It may prove helpful to give separate marks for content and presentation.

Attention and impulse control

Problems

Attention difficulties can take many forms:

- Children may be side-tracked by visual and auditory distractions.

- The child may attend to absolutely everything, and find it difficult to focus on the task at hand.

- There may be an inability to persevere.

- As the child cannot maintain attention, he or she may miss important information or essential parts of multi-task instructions.

- Some children find it difficult to identify the relevant details of a task, and to then focus on the key elements.

Lack of impulse control refers to children who have an inability to think before they speak or act. They are therefore impulsive, without consideration of any consequences. They may also say or do things without apparent regard for others. This has implications for relationships, for understanding of safety and for working within classroom settings.

Supportive strategies

- Minimize auditory and visual distractions.

- Avoid sitting the child near heaters or overhead projectors, which may emit background noise.

- Avoid notice boards or classroom displays which may act as visual distractors.

- Consider creating an office space by using a portable screen on the desk.

- Sitting at the front of the classroom or on teacher walkways can be effective.

- Consider seating arrangements, and which pupils should sit nearby.

- Structured lessons with clearly defined tasks and expectations are easier to access.

- Keep things simple.

- Tasks should be broken down into chunks, although too many steps may result in the disorganized child losing track.

- Some children may find it helpful to manipulate a small object while listening.

- Visual timers can be useful to cue a child into changes of activity.

- Highlight key words in questions and the relevant details of text.

- Provide clear boundaries for behaviour, and set clear rules and consequences.

- Reward and acknowledge appropriate actions or steps in a positive direction.

- Fatigue management is important as remaining focused may drain the child's energy resources.

- Social behaviour may need to be consciously regulated, and social rules can prove helpful.

Mathematics

Problems and supportive strategies

- Allow use of calculator.

- If writing numbers is a problem, allow use of graph paper to keep numbers within small cells.

- Break work down and only present very few questions at any one time.

Aggression

Problems

Children with neuro-developmental problems may become quickly and easily frustrated, which then often leads to outbursts of aggression. Sometimes they are unable to articulate their needs, or they may misunderstand innocent comments made by peers. They may even just feel overwhelmed by noises within the classroom. Teachers need to be aware of these potential problems when dealing with outbursts in the classroom, and disorganized children need to be taught strategies for releasing frustration appropriately.

Supportive strategies

Interventions should focus on helping the child to understand that aggression is unacceptable, and that there are other ways of dealing with frustration and conflict. Strategies may include distraction, talking to someone else, having a drink of water and breathing deeply. Teaching the child to walk away or 'make a graceful exit' can also be effective in preventing incidents. However, the disorganized child is not always able to articulate the need to leave, and a private agreement with the teacher that he or she can leave the classroom whenever he or she is feeling overwhelmed may serve to diffuse any potential aggressive outbursts.

Motivation

Problems

Motivation is often a problem for the disorganized child. This may, in regard to academic work, be due to poor concentration and problems in understanding the topic. It may also stem from poor self-confidence and low self-esteem.

Supportive strategies

- Focus on strengths.

- Negotiate manageable targets with the pupil.

- Make it safe for the child to risk failure.

- Welcome mistakes as a way of learning.

- Reduce the fear of criticism and any fears of looking stupid.

Homework

Problems and supportive strategies

Homework demands traditionally increase as children progress through school. However, encouraging the disorganized child to do homework after school can prove very difficult and create conflict within families. As he or she is enjoying school or mastering learning skills, the last thing that a disorganized child wants to do on returning home is more academic work. Some schools therefore allow children to complete their homework in the library at lunchtime, or run study clubs which teach children how to approach homework tasks. This not only ensures that homework gets done, but also keeps the disorganized child out of trouble during unstructured activities.

Other strategies include:

- ensuring that homework is presented to the child in a written format

- providing a clear structure for homework, with clear expectations

- giving clear and succinct instructions

- allocating classroom time for children to record their homework tasks

- using a self-contained homework folder, with an internal wallet for a homework diary, to improve organization

- clearly labeling and/or colour coding different subject materials

- providing a written reminder on the front of the folder to remember to hand in homework.

Exams

Problems

Many examination boards are sympathetic and understanding if a child has difficulties at school. With a little planning, and letters of support from doctors and psychologists, simple changes can be introduced to make exams less stressful and more manageable.

Supportive strategies

- Give support and extra time for academic work.
- Allow extra time to do the exam.
- Allow tests to be read to the child.
- Allow the child to respond verbally if this proves helpful.
- Allow use of word processors.
- Provide breaks during the exam.

STRUCTURE AND ORGANIZATION DURING THE SCHOOL DAY

Disorganized children require significant levels of support from teachers and other school staff throughout the day. This can be provided in many different ways including visual timetables, established routines, structured lessons, differentiated learning materials and help with coping strategies.

Establishing routines

Effective routines for when school begins, and again for when it ends, can help to ensure a positive start and successful finish to the school day. Following a sequence of pictures, or similar flowcharts, can help young children to establish good routines at school. These can instruct the disorganized child about what to do on entering school, where to hang up his or her coat, where to keep his or her bag and what to do during class registration. Without such structure and visual supports, ineffective and undesirable routines may become quickly established and these can prove very difficult to change later on. Using similar sequences of pictures, or written lists, is equally applicable within the home setting to facilitate bathroom routines or getting dressed for school in the morning. They can also prove effective in helping disorganized children to conceptualize family holidays or to understand better what can be expected on a school trip.

Visual timetables

Visual timetables are an invaluable tool for the disorganized child in all school settings from nursery through to college. These timetables can be presented in a wide variety of different formats, taking into account the child's age and his or her level of understanding. Pictorial representation of large part-day segments of time may prove suitable for one child, whereas another may benefit from a more detailed written full-day timetable which clearly identifies all subjects, rooms, teachers and support staff. While the possible variations are extensive, the essential component is that the visual timetable is accessible to the disorganized child and easily understood even when the child is having one of his or her worst days.

The disorganized child needs to be encouraged to check the timetable regularly as a matter of routine. However, mechanisms for subtle but persistent change also need to be built into the schedule and arrangements. This potential to introduce changes needs to increase as the child moves through the school system and encounters more complex educational arrangements. These organizational strategies will help the child to become more independent, although even children of the same age may find themselves at different points along this journey. Within the timetable, forewarning of any changes can help to reduce anxiety and help to ensure the child has an opportunity to arrive at the right place, at the right time, with the right equipment – a real challenge for the disorganized child!

Pictorial and written lists

Some children will respond well to pictorial or written lists. These can again be provided in a wide array of different and personalized formats including equipment lists, reminders of classroom rules and lists of tasks to be completed in a lesson.

ACCESSING LESSONS
Classroom layout and seating position

The optimum position for each individual child within the classroom needs to be established. For disorganized children, a position near the front of the class, or on a teacher walkway, may prove most helpful. In contrast, highly distractible children may be better seated in a corner position where nearby movement is at a minimum. Wall displays can also be a distraction, as can objects on the desk. Similarly attention should be given to which other children are seated near the disorganized child, and it can even be helpful to leave a vacant seat next to him or her in some circumstances. Unfortunately, the physical layout of the classroom may unavoidably influence the selection of seating positions.

Giving instructions

Instructions that are simple, and which are tailored to the child's level of comprehension, are likely to be most successful. Lessons should also be supported by visual information, and by explicit links which help the child to connect current topics with previous learning. It is often helpful to back up verbal instructions with visual instructions, and significant levels of repetition may be needed. However, care must be taken only to repeat, and not to rephrase, the instruction as this may otherwise confuse the disorganized child. For children with primarily attentional difficulties, it may help to maintain eye contact while giving oral instructions, whereas this may be better avoided in children with problems which approach the autistic spectrum.

Learning materials and learning strategies

- Clear visual instructions need to be given for all tasks.
- A breakdown of the task may be provided in the form of a diagram or list.
- Planning aids or writing frames can help the child to organize his or her homework.
- Relevant details and the key words in question may be highlighted to help the child focus on important details.

SOCIAL SKILLS AND GROUP WORK

Many children with neuro-developmental problems have difficulties with social skills. Similarly, disorganized children may present with autistic spectrum traits and symptoms, even though lacking the full condition. Their restricted social skills can be actively addressed through social stories, comic strip conversations and group work. Pair and group work can also be introduced into almost any area of the curriculum while serving as a useful vehicle for improving social skills. Subjects such as drama and literature can explore how different people respond within various situations, using the child as either a participant or an observer.

Social stories

A social story is a short description of a realistic situation written according to a special style and format (Gray 1997; Gray and White 2002). There are four basic sentence types, which follow a specific written formula. The result is a story, which could otherwise prove incomprehensible or anxiety provoking, but which now has a patient and reassuring quality. It is important when drafting a social story to reflect the child's perspective of the given situation. The language and format used also need to reflect the child's level of understanding and developmental maturity. Social stories aim to teach social understanding through such visually presented material in which expected behaviours are described and different people's perspectives are presented.

Comic strip conversations

Comic strip conversations (Gray 1997) incorporate the use of simple line drawings to illustrate what people say, see and think. Symbols and colour are used to clarify communication and to improve comprehension. Joint attention is focused on a marker board, and each person has a marker pen to illustrate what will or has happened. Participants draw and discuss possible ways to handle given situations. This provides the disorganized child with an opportunity to try out a wide range of different social strategies in a non-threatening environment.

Strategies to promote participation in group work

Teachers may find it helpful to provide a group schedule which lists all of the activities to be covered in the planned group work. These group schedules can be presented in picture, symbol or word format. In particular, the schedule could include a turn-taking board which clearly identifies and lists who will talk next.

Table 23.1 Examples of group schedules

For younger children	For older children
Look at the big book	Look at the script
Read pages 1–6 with the teacher	Decide who will read which part
Find the verbs on each page	Read through the script together
Remember to put your hand up	Read your part at correct place
Return to your seat	Stop after the group has read the script through twice
Fill in your work	

Social demands of working with a partner or groups

Group work places high levels of demand on children with limited social skills, including:

- remaining seated in an allocated place
- turn-taking and negotiation skills

- actively listening to, and reporting back on, the comments of others
- adopting different roles within a group
- reaching consensus and accepting group decisions.

THE 'HIDDEN CURRICULUM'

The school is a social environment which makes social demands on the children within it. However, some children need help to develop the necessary social skills. Just as academic learning skills need to be specifically taught, it is equally important to teach skills which relate to this 'hidden curriculum'. It includes attitudes, the climate of relationships, styles of behaviour and the general quality of life available through the school community. Without acquiring these skills, the disorganized child will find it very difficult to cope and anxiety, frustration, aggression, demotivation and other associated behaviours are likely to increase.

In *Skillstreaming* (1997), Goldstein and McGinnis make some useful suggestions about the development of social skills in adolescence. Tony Attwood, in *Asperger's Syndrome – A Guide for Parents and Professionals* (1998), puts forward similar ideas for establishing and maintaining friendships, understanding the thoughts and feelings of others, enhancing conversational skills and developing useful life skills. Other novel approaches include the use of 'conversational colours' to help children understand emotions (Gray and White 2002), whilst traffic lights and temperature gauges may prove equally helpful. Interactive computer software such as *Mind Reading*, developed by the Autism Research Centre in Cambridge, has also been implemented to help individuals improve their ability to recognize emotions in others.

It is therefore essential that social skills are taught in context wherever possible since many children do not easily transfer these skills. If anything, disorganized children need the hidden curriculum to be made explicit, and they need to be given significant opportunity to develop their social understanding. Awareness of their subtle but specific difficulties needs to be raised so that social skills can be planned into the wider school curriculum.

Break and lunch times

Unstructured periods, such as breaks and lunchtimes, can be particularly stressful for children who do not understand social rules, such as the unwritten rules of the playground and how people relate to one another. Supportive strategies which can be implemented include the following:

- Introduce and teach social rules.

- Teach structured games.

- Teach games where they will be played as some children find it difficult to transfer skills into other contexts.

- Social stories can be used to present social information and strategies.

- Consider forming a circle of friends for the individual.

- Encourage attendance at clubs which provide structure and mutual interests.

- Respect the individual's views as children sometimes want time alone.

- Introduce strategies to manage anxiety, especially when the child is calm.

Bullying

Although many children are bullied for no apparent reason, children who are prone to being bullied often present as anxious and have low self-esteem. They may be loners, with a tendency towards being passive and easily dominated. The disorganized child has many of these characteristics, and it is especially important that teachers and parents are alert to any possible signs of bullying. This may includes signs of withdrawal, escalating school phobia, deterioration in academic work, uncharacteristic aggressive outbursts, poor sleep, depression, bed-wetting and even soiling. If a child is being bullied, whether disorganized or not, then it is essential for this to be addressed as soon as possible so as to ensure that the child feels safe both inside of school and out.

COMMUNICATION BETWEEN TEACHERS AND PARENTS

If a child is experiencing difficulties in the classroom, it is always a good idea for parents and teachers to remain in close communication. This is especially important for children with mild neuro-developmental and processing problems as parents may be unaware of any particular difficulties until the child starts school and is confronted by the demands of everyday learning. Teachers are usually first to recognize these problems, and they are also in a good position to make comparisons with a peer group. Parents equally have a responsibility to inform teachers about any home-based issues which they suspect may be adversely affecting the child in the classroom. While primarily left to parental discretion, if a child has a medical diagnosis or is on medication, then it is usually in their best interests for the teacher to be aware of it.

REFERENCES AND FURTHER READING

Attwood, T. (1998) *Asperger's Syndrome: A Guide for Parents and Professionals.* London: Jessica Kingsley Publishers.

Cambridge University/Baron-Cohen, S. (2004) *Mind Reading: The Interactive Guide to Emotions.* London: Jessica Kingsley Publishers.

Goldstein, A.P. and McGinnis, E. (1997) *Skillstreaming the Adolescent – Student Manual.* Illinois: Research Press.

Gray, C. (1997) *Social Stories and Comic Strip Conversations.* Michigan: Jenison Public Schools.

Gray, C. and White, A.L. (2002) *My Social Stories Book.* London: Jessica Kingsley Publishers.

Howlin, P. (1998) *Children with Autism and Asperger Syndrome – A Guide for Practitioners and Carers.* Chichester: John Wiley.

Smith Myles, B. and Adreon, D. (2001) *Asperger Syndrome and Adolescence – Practical Solutions for School Success.* Kansas: Autism Asperger Publishing Company.

Chapter 24

A family therapy approach

Danièle Wichené and Samuel M. Stein

INTRODUCTION

Contemporary family therapy is not a single model, but a number of different paradigms which have evolved from other psychotherapeutic approaches, both recent and more established. As a consequence, many therapists work with concepts and techniques from a number of different schools of family therapy (Thwaites 1999). It is also a common misunderstanding that family therapy has to involve the family, the whole family and nothing but the family. In reality, family therapy may involve couples, individuals, part of a family or even wider networks.

HUMAN SYSTEMS

The principle that govern human systems suggest that personal beliefs, actions and relationships are all inter-related. They will also influence the beliefs, behaviours and relationships of others, and will similarly be affected by others. This is not simply a case of cause and effect (linear action), but of multiple impacts and feedback (systemic effect). Suppose a mother believes that a father is pushing their child too hard over school work. She then attempts to moderate the father's effect by protecting the child. If the father interprets her behaviour as holding the child back, he may push the child still harder. This may be seen by the mother as further evidence that the father's over-zealous approach needs moderating (Thwaites 1999). When two behaviours act to intensify each other in this way, the pattern is said to be symmetrical. When an increase in one behaviour leads to a decrease in another, the pattern is instead complementary.

STRUCTURAL FAMILY THERAPY

Structural family therapy is inseparable from the charismatic approach of its prime originator, Salvador Minuchin. It is perhaps the most easily understood model, and its strengths lie in its clarity, relative simplicity and usefulness with a wide range of family problems. Change is achieved by the therapist using a directive approach to alter family patterns to a 'healthier functioning form'. The family need not gain insight because appropriate change in their interactional patterns should result in a reduction of symptoms. The therapist uses a normative model of healthy family functioning that considers the family in terms of its boundaries, hierarchies and its life cycle stage. Relationships that are regarded as too close or over-involved are described as enmeshed, and those that are too distant as disengaged.

STRATEGIC FAMILY THERAPY

Strategic therapy works by using interventions that reduce the power which the symptom has over the family. Strategic therapy does not use a normative model of functioning, but instead aims to provide a brief intervention that moves the family to a healthier way of relating. Symptoms are seen as an indication that a family is at a life cycle transitional stage but is having problems re-structuring around it. For example, a parent may develop agoraphobia at a point where his or her last child is preparing to become more independent, thus necessitating the delay of that independence. Unhelpful repetitive sequences, such as occasional relapses, then occur whenever change is threatened. These will be in place of more complex adaptive changes, such as adjusting to life without children. Therapy, which can change deeply entrenched behaviours in a potentially short time, involves getting the family to interrupt these repetitive sequences and move to a new (and more adaptive) range of responses.

MILAN AND POST-MILAN APPROACHES

These methods work through the exploration and clarification of how family ideas, beliefs, relationships and actions relate to the presenting problems. As well as personal beliefs, therapy will explore the influence of family myths and family scripts, such as 'we are a family who always look after each other'. The therapist will use a stance of 'curiosity' to explore and challenge existing links, and to introduce possible new connections. Post-Milan therapy focuses more on explanations which have been co-constructed by the therapist and the family together, rather than by therapist alone (Jones 1993; Palazzoli *et al.* 1980).

OTHER MODELS OF FAMILY THERAPY
Brief therapy and solution focused therapy

These methods seek to achieve expedient resolution of presenting problems or symptoms. The therapist works with clients or 'customers' who are motivated to change by using a range of strategies and techniques that work toward desired change rather than past problems. Solution focused therapy is particularly noted for emphasizing clients' coping strategies by concentrating on occasions when they have overcome other difficulties (De Shazer 1984).

Medical family therapy

This approach is used to help families and individuals affected with chronic physical conditions that have, or are seen as having, a biological foundation. The family therapist uses a bio-psycho-social systems model to address the role which the illness plays in family dynamics and for the individual. The aim of therapy is to help the patient, and his or her family, to cope with the effects of chronic illness or disability, and to reduce conflict around the illness (Doherty, McDaniel and Hepworth 1994).

Behavioural family therapy

Following a thorough assessment that may involve individual interviews, interventions are designed to produce specific behavioural change. This model places great emphasis upon using proven techniques such as parent training and problem-solving. It claims to be particularly useful with conduct disorders and adult mental illness (Falloon 1991).

AIMS OF THERAPY

The aims of therapy will relate directly to the clinical context, and to the style of therapy being used. Structural therapy aims to improve family functioning and to reduce symptomatic behaviour through the introduction of appropriate boundaries and structures. Strategic therapy aims to help individuals and families to become 'unstuck' from patterns of behaviour that are problematic, and which prevent them from moving on in their life cycle. The aim is not to provide insight but to change behaviour in an expedient and effective fashion. Milan systemic therapies aim to develop a systemic understanding within the family that allows individual members to have greater choice in their actions (Thwaites 1999).

Box 24.1 Common applications of family therapy

- Family-based problems (sibling conflict, marital disharmony)
- Psychiatric illness (family support, education or therapy)
- Unresolved intergenerational issues (parental authority problems)
- Adjustment issues for foster, adoptive and step-families
- Life cycle issues (death of parent, children leaving home)
- Adjustment difficulties for immigrant families
- The impact of chronic or life-threatening illness on a family
- Child protection work (disclosure of child abuse)

REFERRAL

As many families find themselves referred for family therapy without sufficient explanation or discussion, it is important to establish the appropriateness of the referral and how well the family have been prepared for such an approach. A good referral will include a comprehensive description of family composition, ideas of how the problems relate to family dynamics and a summary of how these issues have been addressed to date. It is also helpful to know what expectations the referrer and the family have for outcome.

Family therapy can be counterproductive where its use inappropriately delays important processes such as child protection investigations or divorce proceedings. There are also instances where individual therapy needs to precede any family intervention so that an individual is sufficiently prepared to work in a family context. Working with the survivors of sexual abuse commonly falls into this category. Another important contra-indication is when therapy contributes to maintaining the problem (Thwaites 1999).

ASSESSMENT

Family therapists seldom view families simply as systems to be observed and analysed from the outside. Also, they often see families as 'experts on themselves'. Assessment for family therapy should therefore be regarded as a two-way process. Both the family and the therapist will need to assure themselves that the timing, the setting and the nature of their problems makes family therapy the right choice.

Assessment appointments focus on who in the family will attend, how the family interact, how this relates to their difficulties, how motivated they are to change and what style of therapy is most likely to be helpful. Even after an initial meeting, the family may be given feedback, and possibly a therapeutic task, both as an intervention and to assess their degree of motivation. This will also allow the family to judge how they feel about a family approach.

If further therapy is agreed, it may be either a fixed number of sessions or a more open contract. The family therapist will then work with the thoughts and feelings which family members bring to these sessions, with an emphasis on how they make sense of their current difficulties. Both individually and as a family, therapy will explore how presenting problems are worsened or alleviated, and how feelings are shared. Active work is also undertaken on the relationships that are created within the room between parents, children and the therapist.

THERAPEUTIC SETTING

Purpose-designed settings for family therapy usually include a one-way screen, an observation room, a connecting telephone and video equipment. Such settings are seldom found outside of mental health clinics and training agencies. A quiet and private room, comfortable chairs and pleasant surroundings are all obvious contributors to a positive working environment. The therapy room must be big enough so as not to become oppressive during the 60–90 minutes that sessions normally last, particularly when some of the family may be restless or angry. Where young children are included, toys and drawing materials can prolong their involvement, and therefore that of the adults. Sometimes the whole family will be seen together. At other times, the therapist may meet only with the child, or only with one parent, or only with the couple or only with the siblings. These decisions are made during the course of therapy, in conversation with the family, as themes and ideas develop. Family therapy in the home is only indicated when a family has genuine difficulties attending a clinic or when it is used to engage a family who would otherwise be unlikely to come to therapy (Reimers 1994).

TREATMENT
Stories

As all families have stories to tell, about both the past and the present, family therapists often use this approach to reflect on ideas that are meaningful to the family, beliefs that run within the family, values that inform their actions and views expressed by and within the family. Family therapists may also encourage the use of stories as a way of exploring such issues as experiences of being the youngest child in a family, the meaning of authority in a family of origin, views on relationships or who used to misbehave as a child. Frequently, within the course of family therapy, a story about the past may find new meaning in the present, and a new story may only start to make sense when it has been connected to an older story or an ancient family secret.

Family therapy can, using this approach, help people who have become stuck with both living and telling their story. The challenge for families and family therapists is therefore to slowly demolish the old story, while moving toward a new story that opens up novel possibilities and opportunities. These 're-authored' life stories can edit out unwarranted attributions of weakness or helplessness, and instead substitute in stories of strength and responsibility. By moderating problem-saturated family stories in this way, individuals and families can take on greater ownership of their own lives.

By being mindful of the different voices making themselves heard in the therapy sessions, the family therapist helps new and more useful stories to emerge. These therapeutic conversations provide an understanding of how each person involved in the problem views its origin, its maintenance and its possible solutions. For families, this may allow new meanings to be attributed, and for stories to be rearranged along different lines with greater prominence on positive aspects that had previously been missed or ignored.

Externalizing the problem

This is a useful method of working with children who appear to be defined and identified solely by their presenting problem or condition. Devised by Michael White (1988/9), it consists of a collaborative exploration by the therapist and the family, actively involving the child, of the influence of the problem on their collective lives. By identifying the problem, and by describing it in a way that portrays it as having a character and will of its own, it becomes possible to generate and organize a more problem-free way of talking. Therapy may then help the family or individual to resist, and even overcome, the now named and externalized problem that wishes to dominate their lives.

Naming the problem is therefore, in itself, a very important first step. By talking about the problem as something which is external to the child, with its own unhelpful and negative characteristics and aims, its influence on the child and family can slowly but surely be mapped. This is achieved by recalling moments when the problem was, for whatever reason, overcome and kept at bay. It marks the beginning of a joint effort on the part of the child, the family and the therapist to create together a new, happier story. It also gives meaning to what has been happening, which can help people make positive changes without losing face. It also enables their improved relationship to become instrumental in making things better. The child and his or her family are thus provided with a set of tools that can give them back a sense of power over the problem, which they can all fight together. It has indeed been known for the problem to decide to disappear!

Using a genogram

Genograms are used within all family therapy approaches to lay out family information in a concrete and graphical form. They can also be used to 'map' family processes. Drawing the genogram as part of the therapeutic approach can facilitate engagement and inform subsequent work by the family. It should ideally include three generations of family, to give information about intergenerational patterns. It may also include other significant people, and even illustrate significant events and relationships.

Genograms aid the family therapist in considering the family structure in terms of sub-systems. These can be core structures within a family such as an individual, a dyad of husband and wife or a generational grouping of children and grandparents. Sub-systems can also represent a common connection, such as family members with the same illness. The family itself can equally be considered as a sub-system of a larger system, such as a cultural group or a social group.

Reframing

Reframing seeks to explore the positive intention behind a particular behaviour. It explicitly aims to alter the meaning of behaviours or beliefs by considering them in a more positive light. A reframe is therefore the process whereby the therapist challenges the existing description of a problem and offers an alternative that may fit equally well. The intention is to change interactional patterns within the family by the 're-description' of behaviours. For example, an anorexic teenager's refusal to eat might be reframed from 'illness' to 'challenging behaviour', thereby moving it from the domain of medical treatment to that of different parenting approaches. Reframing could be used equally well in helping a couple who have become stuck in a pattern of mutual blaming. With a knowledge that each had been raised in a depressed household, the blaming could be seen as a genuine wish to avoid replicating problems from their own family of origin, and as a way of energizing the other partner so that they did not lapse into depression. The therapy, by reframing these behaviours, could then focus on the couple's shared concerns and fears rather than simply looking at who was to blame.

Neutrality

Neutrality refers to a specific stance originally adopted by the Milan team which has become a core concept of systemic therapy. In its original form, the therapist's aim was to avoid making moral judgements and to be seen as a non-allied figure working at a more removed level (Palazzoli *et al.* 1980). The concern about this approach is that therapy could endorse a 'moral neutrality' (Jones 1993), for example where both an abuser and the abused would be afforded equal validation. This is clearly unacceptable, and the concept of neutrality – while still of central importance – must be used judiciously and with great care. The post-Milan approach views neutrality more as a recognition and measured use of the therapist's beliefs rather than a suspension of them. The therapist has an idea of what desirable outcomes might be, but, within this, has to work with the family's capacity to change (Thwaites 1999).

Working with a team

The Milan approach often makes use of a peer team who observe the therapy specifically to provide the therapist with consultation on the therapy process. The team will also assist in the formulation of hypotheses, and introduce ideas and comments about the therapist–family system. This team structure is always explained to and agreed with the family before therapy commences. The therapist remains in the interview room with the family, while colleagues follow the session via video-link or one-way screen. From time to time, they will offer comments or be invited to share their ideas and questions with the family. In a reflecting team (Anderson 1987), the observers discuss their thoughts openly in front of the therapist and family. This enables the family to become observers to a discussion on their own family processes. While it may seem an unusual practice, when done with therapeutic intent and genuine respect, it is often appreciated by families who feel listened to, valued and supported in their efforts.

DISORGANIZED CHILDREN AND THEIR FAMILIES

A large number of children and young people are referred to Child and Adolescent Mental Health Services each year with behaviour that is difficult or unmanageable. While some of these children may have a formal diagnoses of attention deficit hyperactivity disorder (ADHD), Tourette syndrome, Asperger syndrome or obsessive compulsive disorder, far more frequently there is no accompanying diagnosis. Instead, the referral has been precipitated by the sheer relentlessness of incomprehensible behaviour, both within the family and outside in the wider community. In all cases, even though a single individual may be seen as the primary problem, the whole family has been disrupted to some extent by the adverse behaviours and endeavours to accommodate these behaviours safely and effectively.

Family therapy, in keeping with its theoretical approaches, considers illness and behaviour from a relational perspective. Emphasis is placed not only on the possible meaning of the presenting symptoms to the directly affected patient, but also on the potential meaning of these symptoms to close relatives, friends and peers. Health and illness are therefore seen in terms of socially constructed patterns and interactions. There is less focus than before on illness as residing entirely within the sick person, in favour of more emphasis on the multiple levels of meanings which influence our approach to health and illness. Disorganized children, instead of being perceived within either a culture of blame or a culture of illness, may instead need to be seen within a culture of relationships and interactions.

Family therapy would therefore consider not just the disorganized child, but a whole family and social system with a disorganized child in its midst. Parents are often left feeling utterly overwhelmed, placing strain on their own relationship. Frictions may also creep in over how best to respond to the child's challenging behaviour, with views becoming more and more polarized. The extended family, the school environment, the child's peer groups, the parents' professional life and even their own health may all be affected by the situation. Whether the child presents with diagnosable symptoms or not, the family therapist would work with the way in which the family perceive and interpret the presenting problems. A diagnosis, or the absence thereof, may also hold very different meanings for each family, or for different members of the same family. It is essential to keep in mind that a child's behaviour may sometimes serve not to cause but to highlight other difficulties within the family. If these problems escalate, then the disorganized child may become more and more disorganized.

When managing disorganized children, parents often ask 'what belongs to the condition?' and 'what is deliberately naughty?' Family therapy would not consider these aspects of behaviour as mutually exclusive. After all, children who are disorganized are still only children. They will therefore behave in ways expected of their peers, and often in ways expected of slightly younger children, which may include some elements of disobedience and rebelliousness. What matters is how family relationships are affected by the behaviour, and how these relationships can be used to influence adverse behaviours for the better. Even with the use of medication, patterns of behaviour may not change until the meaning of the child's condition for the family has been addressed. Ian Law, a Canadian family therapist, actively questions the medical construction of ADHD, and instead tries to create a context in which there is greater opportunity for the discovery of strengths, competence and success (Law 1997).

Along similar lines, Everett and Volgy Everett (1999) have developed a programme for treating young people and families with ADHD focusing on five life cycle stages of family experience. At each stage, the child's experience, parental responses, sibling attitudes and marital issues are seriously considered.

These are viewed from multiple perspectives including scapegoating, resentment and diminished communication. Identified themes are addressed through a range of different sessions: with the individual child, with the child and parents, with the siblings, with the parents on their own and with the intergenerational system. As therapy progresses, they use anecdotes from the family's history as a way of dealing with problems, to provide a chance to 'live stories', to improve the 'quality of intimacy' and to assess resources for joint problem-solving.

David Pentecost (2000) has reflected on the implications of ADHD for systemic practice. He observed that these families appear physically depleted, show high levels of stress, experience feelings of stigma and guilt, feel isolated with their difficulties and have poor estimation of their parenting abilities. These families also appear to focus heavily on constraint, coercion and commands. His approach has been to redefine ADHD as a relational issue, shifting the focus onto turning vicious circles into virtuous circles, hearing the child's voice, re-editing fixed narratives, exploring family scripts and highlighting strengths. His method involves talking to children and families about ADHD, and how it has been influencing all of their lives. By building on the positives, parents help their children to regain self-esteem and begin to feel better about themselves, making it easier to see and praise what is going well. Discipline and authority are replaced by a more caring and supportive approach for the whole family.

Case example: Paul

Paul, a 12-year-old boy, was referred to the Child and Adolescent Mental Health Service because of increasingly difficult and unmanageable behaviour. He had previously seen a wide range of health care specialists, and diagnoses such as ADHD, Asperger syndrome and Tourette syndrome had been considered. However, Paul did not seem to fit into any particular category or condition, and he had only responded to medication in a limited way. When he was identified as a 'disorganized child', this brought immense relief to his mother as it explained both his behaviour and her inability to manage it more effectively over the years. However, it also brought great sadness as possible long-term implications needed to be acknowledged. While Paul's mother was concerned about labelling her son, and possibly limiting his potential, she also recognized that specialist help at school might not prove forthcoming without some form of diagnosis.

Paul lived with his mother, Lynn, who had been single for many years following an abusive marriage. His father, Mick, had serious problems with alcohol, and had endangered their lives on several occasions.

Although divorced, Lynn still felt guilty about having protected Mick by keeping his alcoholism secret, and about having chosen the wrong man to marry. These feelings influenced how she responded to Paul's challenging behaviour, and any attempts to show autonomy and authority. Recently, Lynn had met Peter, and they had decided to live together as a family. He liked Paul very much, and they had many interests in common.

The family were seen in various combinations: Lynn on her own, Lynn and Peter, Paul with his mother and Paul on his own. In a family session, Peter talked of having been adopted and about his child from a previous marriage. He enjoyed a good relationship with his son, in spite of being separated from his wife, something which Paul had been unable to achieve since his parents split up. In the days that followed, Paul became more disturbed, being abusive towards his mother and telling Peter 'you're not my dad'. Lynn was concerned that Peter wouldn't want to remain in the family given these problems, while Peter felt unwanted and useless.

During the therapy, Peter explained how he had come along in order to protect Lynn. However, subsequent sessions brought to light Lynn's concerns about the way in which Peter felt a need to rescue her. She had built up an identity as a brave woman who had managed to bring up her son, in spite of his major difficulties, while protecting herself from a dangerous man. While Peter's concerns were clearly well intentioned, they were adversely affecting Lynn's sense of identity and ways of functioning. Discussion therefore took place about the meaning that vulnerability might have for her within relationships, and how she and Peter could manage this problem more effectively.

For Paul, being seen on his own provided an opportunity to talk about wanting more freedom. As he was almost 13, he wanted his mother to allow him to go into town with his two friends. Sessions focused on how he could reassure his mother that it would be safe to let him go out, and how this capacity to be trusted could be concretely demonstrated. Paul came up with some very sensible answers, which were then fed back to his mother in a joint session. However, Peter raised concerns that Paul only wanted to go to town because he hoped to see his father.

Paul became very upset, and started crying. This seemed to verify that something important needing doing in relation to his father. His mother and Peter were able to recognize this, and offered to set a search in motion. Peter, in particular, was supportive of Paul trying to build a new story about mutual trust with his father. At the same time, Peter's own issues relating to his adoption kept being awakened, and he felt utterly confused. It emerged that he was terrified of getting close to Paul in case the new relationship with his father led Paul to reject him and even push him out of his life.

At the last session, Lynn, who could barely stop smiling, described how the search had been done, letters written and responses received. Although these were not everything that Paul might have hoped for, they seemed to satisfy him and he soon calmed down. There had been no further episodes of nastiness or silliness, and 'a lot of normal life'. The whole family had played a part in naming and externalizing the problem, while recognizing its influence on them all. They had engaged in a process of change, as a family, as well as exploring what this meant for each of them individually. While Lynn and Peter had been forced to explore painful and frightening issues from their own pasts, by letting go and supporting Paul's quest, they had shown just how much they cared.

REFERENCES AND FURTHER READING

Anderson, T. (1987) 'The reflecting team: Dialogue and meta-dialogue in clinical work.' *Family Process 26*, 415–428.

Barker, P. (1981) *Basic Family Therapy*. London: Granada.

Burnham, J. (1988) *Family Therapy*. London: Routledge.

De Shazer, S. (1984) 'The death of resistance.' *Family Process 23*, 11–17.

Doherty, W., McDaniel, S. and Hepworth, J. (1994) 'Medical family therapy: An emerging arena for family therapy.' *Journal of Family Therapy 16*, 31–46.

Everett, C. and Volgy Everett, S. (1999) *Family Therapy for ADHD: Treating Children, Adolescents and Adults*. Guilford: Guilford Press.

Falloon, I. (1991) 'Behavioural family therapy.' In A. Gurman and D. Kniskern (eds) *Handbook of Family Therapy Volume II*. New York: Brunner/Mazel, pp.65–95.

Jones, E. (1993) *Family Systems Therapy*. Chichester: John Wiley.

Law, I. (1997) 'Attention deficit disorder: Therapy with a shoddily built construct.' In C. Smith and D. Nyland (eds) *Narrative Therapies with Children and Adolescents*. Guilford: Guilford Press.

Palazzoli, M., Boscolo, L., Cecchin, G. and Prata, G. (1980) 'Hypothesising-circularity-neutrality: Three guidelines for the conductor of the session.' *Family Process 19*, 3–12.

Pentecost, D. (2000) *Parenting the ADD Child: Can't Do, Won't Do*. London: Jessica Kingsley Publishers.

Reimers, S. (1994) 'Bringing it back home: Putting a user-friendly perspective into practice.' In S. Reimers and A. Treacher (eds) *Introducing User Friendly Family Therapy*. London: Routledge, pp.220–240.

Thwaites, S. (1999) 'Family therapy.' In S.M. Stein, R. Haigh and J. Stein (eds) *Essentials of Psychotherapy*. Oxford: Butterworth-Heinemann, pp.274–291.

White, M. (1988/9) 'The externalising of the problem and the re-authoring of lives and relationships.' *Dulwich Centre Newsletter*.

Chapter 25

An occupational therapy approach

Sharon Drew

INTRODUCTION

Acquiring the ability to both sequence and organize is an essential component of child development (Part 1). These skills enable us to orientate ourselves within a framework of time and space. They are attained as part of a developmental progression from sequencing of movement, to sequencing of events throughout the day, to sequencing of symbols, letters and numbers and finally to sequencing of time. Disorganized children generally present with difficulties in many of these sequencing and organizing tasks. This has serious implications with regard to how they function at home, in school and within the wider community. Therefore, if these problems are not proactively addressed in childhood, they may have significant ramifications in adulthood, especially in the work place.

As individuals, we are not born organized, and need to learn ways and means of bringing order to our day. However, disorganized children will require a more formalized and pragmatic approach. Occupational therapists who specialize in working with such children will understand the nature of their difficulties and how this affects their everyday living and learning. They will therefore be able to help the child to develop the essential skills necessary for coping with day-to-day life. This may be achieved through direct therapy with a disorganized child. However, the occupational therapist may work not only with the child, but also with the family and the school, asking parents and teachers to facilitate very practical solutions. This holistic approach aims to ensure that the child has every opportunity to reach his or her optimum potential.

MAKING A START

Before attempting to implement any occupational therapy strategies, it is important to consider the following guidelines:

- If there are several areas of difficulty, consider which problem is the main priority.

- The child's priorities may not be the same as those of his or her parents and teachers, and compromises often need to be made.

- If the child does not see any relevance to the task, he or she may prove less motivated to master it.

- A 'contract' may need to be established to ensure cooperation.

- In order to remain motivated, not only the child but also the adults need to feel that progress is being made.

- Tackle the areas of difficulty in 'bite-size chunks'.

- Keep in mind that, when learning anything new, children with organizational difficulties may continually feel that they are getting it wrong.

- New skills should be taught from the bottom up, starting with the first component of the skill and then adding steps until the end result is achieved.

- Many children may fail to get beyond the first step, which can prove very frustrating for children, parents and teachers.

- It is important to maintain motivation and self-esteem through the initial use of instant reward.

- Teaching a task from the end to the beginning, instead of the other way around, may help the child to feel that he or she has achieved something.

- Remember that different children learn in different ways; some through listening, some through seeing and some through doing.

- It is important to use a multi-sensory approach when teaching new skills.

- Learning needs to be active and fun, or it soon becomes a chore.

- When teaching or introducing new skills, keep things simple.

- Monitor the time being spent closely as it is better to succeed with a 5-minute target than to fight over completing a 20-minute piece of work.

Table 25.1 Aiming for success

Strategies and plans are not successful if there is:	Success happens with:
A lack of consistency	Clear instructions and a small number of rules
A lack of time	
A lack of understanding	Potential rewards that are achievable
A poor response to reinforcement	Prioritizing the important
Unrealistic expectation	Understanding the child
A lack of rules	Rewarding improvement, however small

HELPING THE CHILD WITHIN THE HOME SETTING

Being a parent is difficult at the best of times. However, being the parent of a disorganized child is even harder and can be extremely frustrating. As the child grows and develops, the once-manageable toddler becomes more difficult to handle. Not only is the parent having to deal with the complexities of poor processing and disorganization, but also with normal developmental stages such as temper tantrums and puberty. As adolescence approaches, young people increasingly want to exercise their own views and to become empowered as their own person. Entrenched responses to problematic situations and events, which once worked effectively, can then lead to discord within the family as the child gets older. The remainder of this chapter will therefore focus on some of the practical difficulties which may be encountered across the age groups, with some ideas and suggestions that may prove helpful.

THE YOUNGER CHILD
Difficulties with daily routine

Children of this age seldom have a well-developed sense of space and time, and continually ask questions such as 'how far is it?' or 'are we there yet?' However, most children can already cope with the fact that they may have to wait. In contrast, for the disorganized child, these delays can feel quite scary as they do not know 'what is coming next'. They may therefore 'keep on' asking the same or very similar questions, even when these issues have only just been. answered. Their inability to sequence and organize information means that they need to seek reassurance and responses persistently, which can easily prove frustrating to parents and teachers, and may even be misinterpreted as negative behaviour. This problem can be better managed by listening to what the child has to say, accompanied by reassurance and a cuddle, rather than trying to eradicate the behaviour through punishment.

As adults, we often look forward to days in which jobs can be done at leisure or when friends stop by unexpectedly for coffee. However, children with organizational difficulties cope very badly with unstructured days. Holidays and weekends, which lack the rigidity of school timetables, can therefore prove particularly trying for parents. Disorganized children cope better when there is a structure and a routine to their daily lives. This can be catered for by creating schedules and timetables for most of their waking hours, or just for those periods of time which prove problematic. However, the information cannot only be given to them verbally. It needs to be reinforced with visual references, such as picture diaries pinned onto the wall. The child should be encouraged to contribute to these visual reminders, or even to make his or her own, using photographs of people and places or cutting pictures out of magazines. White boards, notice boards or magnetic boards can also prove very useful when implementing these strategies. It is often helpful to have some 'blank' spaces built into the child's day which can be used to represent 'quiet time' or 'free play'. They can also provide scope for the 'unexpected', and be used to help the child understand that sometimes things don't quite go according to plan.

While children can be taught to tell the time, this is very different from knowing what 'time feels like'. For the disorganized child, this can provedifficult as it is something which comes with normal growth and development rather than lending itself to being taught. However, parents can help the child with processing problems to understand something about how time passes by using sand timers, kitchen buzzers or a stop watch. It is important to be consistent in the approach used, and to ensure that all family members are bound by the same rules and boundaries. Be especially mindful of the language used with disorganized children as saying 'in a minute' but meaning 'I'll deal with it when I am ready' may prove confusing and impede any attempts to learn about the passage of time.

Sleep

Disorganized children often present with sleep problems. Getting the child intobed may present a challenge, and he or she may then struggle to fall asleep. It is always helpful to establish a 'bedtime routine', which needs to be consistent and implemented at the same time each evening. This could include using a timer to bring evening activities to a planned rather than a sudden and unexpected end, ollowed by a period of quiet before bed. As the aim is to ensure that the child feels secure at bedtime, leaving a night-light on or a door open may help him or her to settle. Similar effects may be achieved using a story tape, calming music or even tapes of natural sounds to relax the child and encourage sleep.

A warm bath may help to settle the child. However, when drying him or her, avoid light and tickly movements as these may prove too excitatory and stimulating. Instead, use firm movements and swaddle the child in a large warm towel, encouraging him or her to feel calm and settled before getting into bed and going to sleep. Similarly, children who do not sleep well can sometimes be helped if they are 'tucked in' tightly. This can be achieved by using a sheet over the top of thequilt which is then tucked in firmly under the mattress, or by using heavier blankets on the bed. Some children may even sleep better in a sleeping bag. Alternatively, pillows or soft toys can be packed down the sides of the bed to create this 'swaddling' or 'cocooning' effect, which has been anecdotallyreported to provide reassurance and thus aid sleep.

Box 25.1 Improving sleep patterns

Try to ensure that:

- the bedroom environment is not too noisy
- the bedroom is not too light, especially in summer
- the bedroom is not too dark, especially if the child has fears
- the temperature is just right for the child
- doors are positioned according to what is comfortable for the child
- scary television programmes and books are avoided before bedtime
- activities that are too stimulating are avoided before bedtime
- the bed is comfortable the child is not allergic to the pillows or the duvet

---

Play

The disorganized child often does not know how to play games or how to use toys imaginatively. They frequently misunderstand the rules, are ungracious winners or poor losers, and struggle to maintain attention throughout the activity. This can be frustrating, not only for them but also for those playing with them, and can affect how the child makes and maintains friendships. They therefore need someone to guide them through the play process, learning from experience about how to play but under the direction of an adult.

Play is a two-way process, and disorganized children may be unable to play purposefully or constructively on their own. Adults should therefore not be afraid of getting down on the floor and joining in with these activities. If anything, the more whole-hearted the effort, the more fun will be had. The more fun an activity, the more likely that children will want to continue with or repeat it, and learning then takes place. Rewards should also be inherent in the game or task, and it may prove helpful to use toys which have an instant benefit. This can take the form of pressing a switch and seeing something happen, experiencing the joy of discovery or the satisfaction of completion. It is important that the tasks are developmentally appropriate for the children and, to ensure that they experience some success, initial activities must fall well within their abilities.

Children who cannot sit still and attend, struggle to learn. They then have little reason to participate, setting up a cycle which is difficult to break. It is therefore important to keep any games short, simple and achievable. Working for even small periods of time, five or ten minutes a day, will ensure that interest is maintained. As the child's skills improve, the time spent working on a task can be gradually increased. Disorganized children also find it difficult to end tasks or games, and using a timer to provide external reinforcement may prove helpful. Play can be used to encourage the child to use problem-solving skills. For example, as the game commences, the child can be asked 'what are you going to do in the game?', 'why are you going to use that...?' or 'can you do it another way?' Materials must also be interesting to the child, providing something that is unusual or colourful to provoke exploration. Multi-sensory toys and games which involve touch, sight and noise are particularly beneficial. Even turning everyday activities into games and fun may help children to develop their organizational skills. A simple cooking activity can encourage them to plan what ingredients are needed, and allow them to think through the sequence in which they will need to be used.

Box 25.2 Successful play

- This will occur if it focuses on success rather than failure
- the children are interested in the game
- only just enough help and encouragement are provided
- it is fun and enjoyable rather than drab and boring
- it makes sense, rather than feeling that it is something devised to fill time.

Dressing

This can be an area of significant contention, especially when time is at a premium. Problems usually arise first thing in the morning, when parents not only need to get their children ready for school but are also trying to get themselves to work on time. Despite repeated instructions, which invariably increase in volume and stress level, the disorganized child remains sat on his or her bed or watching television. Alternatively, he or she may appear fully dressed but wearing completely the wrong outfit.

Some children will therefore need help to organize their clothes, and these can be set out the night before, layered in the order in which they need to be put on. This will help with both sequencing and with keeping the child on task when dressing. While it is important to increasingly promote independence in these skills, this can be worked on when time pressures are less intense, such as on weekends or during holidays. It may also prove helpful to break the tasks down into smaller chunks, and to encourage the child only to complete one aspect independently, rather than trying to manage the whole lot. Success is then more likely, and motivation for both the parent and the child will be sustained.

If there are physical problems with dressing, because of poor coordination or clumsiness, parents should review both the clothes in the child's wardrobe and those which they are buying. Garments which have elasticized waistbands avoid the need to manage buttons and other fasteners, while items with labels or logos can help with orientation. If putting on socks is proving difficult, then a little talcum powder can be used together with socks which have a coloured heel toshow which way they should go. Trainers with velcro fasteners, or shoes with springy laces, may overcome the need to tie knots, and the child should be encouraged to sit on the floor, or a little stool, with his or her feet placed firmly on the floor when dressing.

Some disorganized children are able to manage buttons, albeit very slowly. As it is particularly important to ensure that each button is fastened through the correct hole, beginning to button at the lower edge of the shirt or blouse will make it possible to see if the corresponding button and button hole have been chosen. This will save the frustration of having to repeat the task because the buttons have been mismatched with their holes. Also, if the child is finding it difficult to get the buttons through the holes because of poor manipulative skills, these can be sewn on with shearing elastic to provide some 'give' when pushing the button through the holes. If other fasteners or zips are not being managed easily, this can be approached by attaching a novelty key ring or some other interesting item which is big enough for the child's hands to grasp more effectively.

Organization of personal belongings

Disorganized children constantly lose their personal belongings, much to the frustration of parents and teachers. This can be combated by designating a specific place or container for each item, both at home and at school. Colour-coded storage bins and drawers are helpful, especially if labelled with pictures that make it easy to see what goes where when putting things away. Net hangers can be used for keeping soft toys and small objects accessible but out of the way. It may prove sensible to purchase multiple sets of stationary for school, even if these are personalized with their name, as losing these items during the first few weeks of term is almost guaranteed. Finally, it is always helpful to put labels inside school uniforms and sports kit and, whenever feasible, choose brightly coloured garments, such as coats, so that the child can easily see which belongs to him or her in the cloakroom.

Meal-times

Meal-times are an important time for families. It is where information is shared about the day, and it is also a time for developing social skills within a 'safe' environment. However, meal-times require the child to sit in one place, to listen to others around the table, to take turns and to wait for the meal to end. These activities, in turn, establish the requisite skills for young children to be able to sit still, to listen and to learn in school. The early use of cutlery also prepares the child for holding and using pencils, scissors and other tools with control.

To help children get the most out of meal-times, ensure that they are sitting in a balanced position on their chair at the table. Their feet ideally need to be placed upon a firm surface, such as flat on the floor. This will maximize the amount of control that they have over their arms, which is essential for the control and use of cutlery. If the child's feet do not reach the floor, an upturned box may help, as may pushing his or her bottom nearer to the front of the seat by placing a firm cushion behind his or her back. Also check that children can reach the table easily, and that they do not have to reach up, as this will make them tire very quickly. A firm block of foam may prove better for sitting on than a cushion, and chairs with arms on the sides can prove useful. Alternatively, a child's table and chair set can be used.

Disorganized children may struggle with the practicalities of eating. A plate with higher sides can help to load food onto a fork or spoon, and fatter barrelled cutlery is often easier to hold and control. If the child has difficulty with accurately getting the spoon or fork to his or her mouth without spillage, this can be addressed by twisting the bowl-end of the spoon/fork by about 20 to 25 degrees. This modification should prevent the hand from tipping food over sideways as the child transfers the contents from plate to mouth. If necessary, consider using smaller child-size knives, forks and spoons. Plastic crockery is also less likely to break

If spillage occurs when drinking from a cup, it may help to pour less fluid into the cup in the first place. This not only makes it easier to handle, but there is less mess if it is mismanaged. Also consider using other containers, such as 'round bottom' beakers which only 'rock' when knocked over, or drinks cartons with integral straws. If plates and cups are tending to slip on the table, this can be rectified by placing a small damp piece of cloth under the crockery or drinking utensil.

To help develop the child's independent skills at meal-times, he or she should be encouraged to pour his or her own drinks and cereals. Unfortunately, this can end up being a very messy process. Parents should try not to reprimand the child, as it is unlikely that it was done on purpose. Instead, they can help the disorganized child by storing food or drinks in plastic see-through containers with easy-pour spouts, preferably with handles. Children should be taught not to over-fill their bowls or beakers, which can be achieved by using a marker to indicate how far up the container or bowl they need to fill. Remember, plastic containers are lighter to lift and hold.

Using the toilet

Many children who are disorganized can find bottom-wiping difficult. This isexacerbated by the fact that toilets are generally adult-size, except perhaps innursery or infant school. The child will therefore struggle to place his or her feet firmly on the floor, which is essential for balance while sitting on the toilet. Furthermore, in order to wipe their bottom, children need to shift their weight forward over their feet to allow a big enough gap behind for their hand to use the toilet paper. Keep in mind that the aperture of an adult toilet seat is large, and the child may fear 'falling down the hole'. These problems can be overcome by using a toilet inset, and by providing a small step or block so that the child's feet are placed on a firm surface. Disorganized children can also be encouraged to support themselves by holding on to a basin or towel rail, and a small 'grab' bar can even be fixed to the side of the toilet.

When wiping their bottoms, children need to know where their hands are when they go behind their backs. However, children with organizational difficulties often need to monitor what they are doing with their eyes, making the task of bottom-wiping even harder for them. They may then either avoid using the toilet or get into a mess. It may prove helpful to use wet wipes as well as toilet tessue, and to place picture cue cards beside the toilet to give children a visual reminder of what they need to do next. It is important to prevent the use of the toilet from becoming problematic as children may start to avoid using it altogether, resulting in constipation and overflow.

THE OLDER CHILD
Organization of self and belongings

Structure and routine are as important to the older child as they are for the younger child. However, the older child needs to gradually consolidate these skills as they are important for independent living, for further study at university or college and for the world of work. This can be facilitated by encouraging disorganized children to always start by identifying the different steps needed to begin and to accomplish a task. They can then repeat these directions to them-selves, or to a listener, for clarity and recollection. It may also prove helpful to write down the various steps, either in long-hand or in shorter notations and flowchart form.

Young people with processing problems often benefit from improved note-taking skills. They can then use a specific note-book to record essential tasks and deadlines, or pin these up on a highly visible and accessible notice board. Detailed diary-keeping can prove helpful, as can developing the habit of writing up a 'things to do list'. This sheet can be placed somewhere that is frequently passed and easily seen. The list should include the dates by which tasks need to be done, and finished items should be crossed out when they have been completed. A laminated timetable placed strategically in their bedroom may help to remind them to prepare appropriate clothes for the next day, or to pack the correct sports kit for school on the following day. Another copy can be placed on the inside of their school bag, and a third copy can even be stuck up in their locker at school, to act as a reminder at all key points of contact.

Other strategies can include the use of a dictaphone or talking pen to record important reminders. The use of see-through containers or clear files to store documents may help, as may colour-coded labels and the use of clearly labelled coloured files for different subjects, events and projects. A key on a chain, attached to their clothing, could be used if locker keys and front door keys are frequently lost.

Homework and study skills

The disorganized child often finds it a struggle simply to get through the school day, without the added stress and burden of homework or preparation for exams. These issues can quickly become an area of family contention. The problem can be addressed by parents and children establishing a strategic approach to homework and studying. The young person should be encouraged to plan his or her academic activities, and to organize all required tasks according to an agreed schedule and routine. However, it is essential to allow plenty of learning breaks in between tasks, and to avoid letting homework go on for too long. Ensure that homework assignments are reviewed nightly, checking for thoroughness, neatness and accuracy. If the child is receiving more homework than can be realistically managed in one night, parents should approach the school, who may be willing to make adjustments if they understand that a problem exists.

Consider the child's learning style carefully. Some individuals find it easier to work when there is music playing, or prefer reading while walking around. Not all tasks need to be done sitting at a desk or table, and it may prove helpful to allow the young person to complete their homework while lying on the floor. Other children may find it helpful to use alternative methods of recording written information such as using a computer or dictating the answers for their parent to write out. However, good communication with the school is essential to ensure that these methods are acceptable to teachers and other educational staff. When revising, the disorganized child can read his or her revision notes out loud into a tape recorder, which can then be played back again and again in the build-up to exams. The use of fluorescent markers to highlight key information may prove useful, as may the writing of salient points onto 'post-it notes' which can then be fixed to prominent places around the house, allowing the child to read them each time he or she passes by.

It is essential for parents and teachers to help disorganized children to avoid boredom and frustration in relation to their academic work, with the focus instead being on maintaining interest and learning through novelty and creative approaches.

Personal care

Increasingly complex personal care issues come to the fore in older children with organizational difficulties. While remaining aware of their problems and potential limitations, it will still be important to encourage the young person to develop a sense of pride in his or her personal appearance. After all, the way in which people present will influence how others perceive them, including social relationships and employment. As before, it is important to encourage the disorganized child to establish a routine so that his or her personal care becomes automatic. Disorganized children should also actively prepare for events in advance, and allow themselves plenty of time to get ready. This can be aided by setting alarms and using timers to ensure that each step is completed on time. Disorganized children should be encouraged always to check their appearance in a mirror before leaving the house.

Dressing

Managing buttons may still be an issue for the older child, particularly collars and cuffs. Those with small hands may be able to slide the cuff over their hand without undoing the button. Otherwise, it may help to sew on the cuff buttons with shearing elastic to allow the hand through without needing to undo or fasten the button. Collar buttons may prove particularly difficult to fasten as the task cannot be monitored visually, there is often very little material on which to hold and collars can be quite stiff. This problem may be overcome by sewing the button onto the buttonhole, so that it looks like a conventionally fastened button, while the neck of the shirt is fastened more easily with velcro sewn into the neckband under the buttonhole. Another approach would be to choose 'easy to wear' garments that can be quickly and efficiently coordinated with matching items in the wardrobe, and parents can also look for 'easy care' fabrics so that clothes always look neat.

Most children start to tie bow-knots at approximately 6 years of age. However, many disorganized children may still find it problematic to manage shoelaces even in their teens. When teaching shoelace tying, ensure that the child is sitting comfortably and is well supported. Parents can then sit next to the child, or directly behind him or her, when demonstrating the task. It may help to stabilize the toe of the shoe against an immovable object to prevent the shoe from slipping when the foot is inserted. Directions need to be clear, and language should be kept to a minimum, with few distractions. It is important to give the child sufficient time to complete the activity, generating a feeling of success, although slip-on shoes can be purchased if laces remain a problem.

Hair and make-up

Make-up is very important for young girls, and wearing it helps them to be accepted as part of their peer group. However, for the disorganized child, reversing images in the mirror can prove very difficult. It may help to have make-up lessons on a one-to-one basis, or to ask a beautician for advice on easy-to-apply options, such as tinted moisturiser. Applying make-up is easier in a well-lit room, using a large mirror, and it should be removed using moist facial wipes. It may also help to apply make-up according to a set routine, such as tinted moisturiser, followed by eye-shadow and then lipstick.

Managing their hair can prove difficult for disorganized girls, especially if they wear it very long. It is therefore important to consider the most manageable style, and advice can be obtained from the hairdresser about products which lend themselves to ease of styling. For disorganized boys, shaving may prove problematic. Electric razors are easiest to use, making small circular actions, and working from one side of the face to the other.

Bathing and washing

A regular bathing routine should be encouraged, with showers often proving easier to manage than baths. The use of 'all in one' shower gels that can also be used on the hair may help, as may adopting a routine of working down from the head to the toes. It may also prove helpful to include a non-slip shower or bath mat within the shower or bath to reduce the risk of slipping.

Domestic skills

It is important for the young person to develop domestic skills for independent living in adulthood, but domestic activities also help to reinforce organization. For example, cooking may require the disorganized child to follow a recipe, and specific chores around the house may have to be done on certain days, such as putting out the garbage. Young people with processing problems should be actively encouraged to learn about using household equipment, such as washing machines, and the need to keep colours and whites separated. If necessary, some individuals may need to use modified apparatus to help them with food preparation, such as electric can openers. The microwave oven is also a very useful piece of kitchen equipment, and there are now a wide selection of easy-to-prepare foods on the market.

Out and about

Going out and about can be nerve-racking for disorganized young people. They can easily get lost, and seldom think to use landmarks for orientation. When going out with others, they should always establish a meeting point and time, and even a back-up plan. They may find it helpful to practise the arrangements or routes beforehand, as well as knowing whom to ask or where to go for help if necessary. The disorganized child may benefit from carrying a mobile phone, or even a phone card, in case of emergencies. Getting his or her name and address printed on a 'business card' may also prove helpful. It is essential to ensure that the young person understands, and can demonstrate, road safety before he or she is allowed out and about independently.

Hobbies and leisure activities which may help the disorganized child

- *Aerobics* may help to improve motor control and coordination.

- *Astronomy.*

- *Badminton* may prove a useful introduction to racquet sports as the racquet is light and the shuttle moves relatively slowly.

- *Biking activities* using tricycles, quad bikes or tandems may prove easier than riding a two-wheeler, allowing improvement of motor coordination and concentration, and allowing the disorganized child to join in safely with the family on cycling trips.

- *Canoeing.*

- *Chess* can prove a positive and successful experience for some children with specific learning difficulties, as well as prompting them to join clubs and to meet others with similar interests.

- *Computers*, as an interest or as a later occupation, can enable disorganized individuals to produce high-quality written work that could not be achieved using pen and paper.

- *Cookery* can help with fine and gross motor skills through activities such as rolling, cutting, shaping, spooning and pouring. It may also promote organization and conversation, producing a concrete end-product of which the child can be proud.

- *Drama classes.*

- *Horse riding* can promote balance and rhythm.

- *Line dancing,* which is often something new for all of the participants, can prove a good form of exercise while also helping with social skills, coordination and self-esteem.

- *Martial arts* such as Tai Chi, Judo and Karate all require and promote self-control, motor control and self-discipline.

- *Non-competitive hobbies* such as bird watching, singing and sailing canprove to be fun while also serving as excellent opportunities for improving motor coordination and self-esteem in a non-threatening environment.

- *Photography* can be an enjoyable and creative hobby, easier than drawing or painting, especially if using a Polaroid or digital camera for almost instant results.

- *Pottery* is good for coordination and for improving muscle tone, starting with 'coil pots' built up from 'snakes' rolled out by the child.

- *Rambling and orienteering* are excellent forms of exercise that are non-threatening and sociable, while also promoting planning and organization.

- *Swimming* allows the child to strengthen both upper and lower body.

- *Trampolining* helps with sequencing of movement but the child needs to develop an awareness of safety and the potential impact of his or her actions on others.

- *Yoga* is non-competitive and allows individuals to progress at their own pace, while helping with relaxation and improving body awareness.

Chapter 26

Group therapy approaches

Estelle Macdonald and Uttom Chowdhury

INTRODUCTION

In 1907, Joseph Pratt, a physician from Boston, wrote about the benefit of treating tuberculosis patients in a holistic way. As well as attending to their physical illness, he brought 25 of them together each week in a 'tuberculosis class' to discuss their symptoms and progress. He observed an improvement in morale, and a reduction in emotional symptoms. This was probably the first description of a therapeutic group (Haigh 1999).

Today, group therapy, in its widest sense, takes place in numerous different settings. Examples include nurses organizing anxiety management groups in community mental health centres, probation officers running anger control courses for convicted offenders, psychologists taking cognitive-behavioural groups for eating disorders, occupational therapists conducting skills groups, management trainers running personal development courses, psychiatrists running doctor–patient relationship seminars, staff from voluntary agencies setting up self-help groups and many others.

Group therapy is unusual among the analytically based psychotherapies in believing that change can come before insight. The more psychoanalytical task of understanding the meaning and dynamics of symptoms in a rational way is deemed to be less important than the actual experience of being part of a group in which developmental processes take place. These begin with attachment and containment, then move through communication and involvement to a more mature and autonomous position of agency. These stages can be construed as the 'culture' required for therapy to be effective: attachment corresponds to a culture of belonging; containment to a sense of safety; communication to a culture of openness or enquiry; involvement to inclusion or a living–learning experience; and agency and autonomy to a culture of empowerment (Haigh 1999).

These developmental stages all correspond to various aspects of Yalom's (1986) therapeutic factors, which are described in Box 26.1. A therapeutic factor is a component of group therapy which contributes to an improvement in the patient's condition. They result from the actions of the group therapist, the actions of other group members and from the actions of the patient him- or herself. There are also 'non-specific therapeutic factors' which are frequently described in the literature, and which refer to the many general benefits accrued by participants who take part in groups.

Group therapy therefore aims to make patients more aware of themselves in relationship to others, to be better equipped to behave adaptively with others and to gain more fulfilment in all human relationships. Groups achieve this by providing an environment in which emotional development takes place, which can in turn make a considerable difference to behaviour, symptoms and someone's concept of their core self (Haigh 1996).

Box 26.1 Yalom's 12 therapeutic factors

1. Interpersonal input (learning from one's constructive relationship with others)

2. Catharsis (feeling and expressing powerful emotions)

3. Cohesiveness (belonging, acceptance and loss of isolation)

4. Self-understanding (insight into previously unacknowledged parts of oneself)

5. Interpersonal output (experience of successful relationships with others)

6. Existential factors (meaninglessness, isolation and responsibility)

7. Universality (the recognition that one's problems are not unique)

8. Installation of hope (seeing improvement in others)

9. Altruism (being able to help, and therefore being a value, to others)

10. Family re-enactment (understanding how childhood patterns are repeated)

11. Guidance (accepting help and advice from others)

12. Identification (modelling behaviour on others)

TYPES OF THERAPEUTIC GROUP

The use of therapeutic groups can often benefit children and parents who are attending various different clinical services. Groups are also a useful therapeutic forum for seeing several people in one session, and they may thus prove valuable when resources are limited. Participants may benefit in terms of self-esteem and self-confidence simply from being in the group. Many hospital departments therefore recognize the importance of such groups for parents and children with medical conditions (Leonard 1991).

There are three main types of group:

- *Support groups:* these are often run by voluntary organizations, and they provide a place for parents and children to express themselves in a supportive environment. Group members are also able to help others by giving advice, as well as learning from those who have undergone similar experiences.

- *Educative groups:* these groups often use a cognitive-behavioural approach, and they are a useful way of teaching children and families coping strategies collectively. Examples include social skills groups, and groups focusing on a specific problem such as self-esteem.

- *Experiential groups:* these groups utilize psychoanalytic methods to explore unconscious group dynamics. Often what takes place in the group is a reflection of the individual's inner world, and also represents how members may behave outside of the group when in their own environment.

In the past, patients with 'biological' or neurological conditions were often not considered as suitable for group work, and group psychotherapy was primarily geared towards patients who presented with 'neurotic' conditions such as post-traumatic stress, bereavement or anxiety disorders. However, in recent years, more and more therapeutic groups have been set up for children with neuro-developmental disorders by various clinical services. These have included groups for children and adolescents with Asperger syndrome (Marriage, Gordon and Brand 1995), obsessive compulsive disorders (Chowdhury *et al.* 2003a) and Tourette syndrome (Lambert and Christie 1998).

While this represents a significant step forward, many of the children who do not fit neatly into the exact criteria for a specific diagnosis or disorder may still be excluded from these potentially helpful groups. These disorganized children, who present with a mixture of neuro-developmental problems, are often aware that they are slightly different from their peers. They may have been the victim of bullying because of their behaviour, or may have been teased about their educational abilities at school. Many disorganized children are therefore extremely sensitive and have low self-esteem. They would undoubtedly benefit greatly from therapeutic groups involving similar children of a similar age, bringing welcome support and improved self-confidence.

Clinical services planning to set up such groups should therefore give considerable thought to patient selection. This may require some flexibility regarding diagnostic criteria. Entry into the group can still prove beneficial to individuals who fit the picture of a disorganized child, even if they lack diagnostic specificity. They should, as a result, be actively considered for inclusion in social skills groups for children with Asperger syndrome or self-esteem groups for children with attention deficit hyperactivity disorder (ADHD). Educative groups with a specific focus on anger management or social skills are particularly helpful to disorganized children, while more analytical and experiential groups would not be suitable for younger children with neuro-developmental processing problems. However, older adolescents who are disorganized may respond well to this type of group therapy if orchestrated by an experienced group therapist with a sound knowledge of their difficulties.

PARTICIPATING IN THERAPEUTIC GROUPS

The most common format for therapeutic groups is a weekly session lasting for approximately 90 minutes, which starts and finishes punctually. Some therapists may run more intensive treatments, with groups meeting twice weekly, but this is seldom practicable outside of specialist settings such as in-patient units and thera-peutic communities. Wherever possible, out-patient groups are timed to accom-modate participants' school, work and domestic obligations.

Therapeutic groups normally have one or two therapists, and between six and ten participants. In selecting group members, the mixture of patients must always be seriously considered. While some groups may benefit from all participants being very similar, in general groups work best when the members are heterogeneous or different. Issues such as age and gender may need to be more evenly balanced, whereas a wide range of social, educational and occupational backgrounds could be an advantage. However, in trying to achieve such a mix, care must be taken to avoid isolating single members.

The room which is to be used for group therapy needs to be large enough to hold an evenly spaced circle of chairs, provide space for structured activities, be free from interruption, as quiet as possible and not too hot or cold. The chairs need to be comfortable enough to sit on for an hour and a half, but not so large and soft that group members are likely to fall asleep in them. They should all be of a similar height, and there may be a small table in the middle of the circle. The room, especially if being used with disorganized children, needs to appear constant from one session to the next, without major changes of decoration, furnishing or other features. Most therapists will set up the circle of chairs before participants arrive, and may choose either to include or exclude chairs for members who have sent apologies.

Therapeutic groups may be *slow-open* or *closed*. A slow-open group runs continuously, often over many years, and has new members join as old ones leave. The length of stay can thus vary considerably according to the individual members' needs. In a closed group, all of the members start together, and the group is set up to run for a specific time. If there are early drop-outs, new members can be recruited after it has started. However, late starters will receive a shorter period of therapy, and this needs to be seriously considered when recruiting them. Newer and less common formats of groups include *block* and *termly*. Block groups meet for intensive periods of group work which are widely spaced, while termly groups have specific dates – for example, four ten-week terms per year with gaps between.

Group therapists differ in their views on the minimum acceptable number for conducting a group. Some therapists will cancel a group if less than three members attend, while others will consider the group is existing 'in mind' even with a single member present. Groups and therapists differ, and some closed groups run satisfactorily to a planned ending with three members while others struggle considerably with five or six. Attendance of groups is often cyclical: there can be spells of weeks or months of full attendance, alternating with times during which there are many absences, often with good practical reasons given. Attendance may serve as a particularly robust measure of how successfully a group is functioning.

Fears which patients may have about participating in groups include forced exposure, unwelcome intimacy, their 'turn' coming round and not being taken seriously. In a well-conducted group, none of these should happen. It may help to explain to potential group members that the group 'becoming a safe place' is an important part of therapy itself. Taking turns, being in 'the hot seat' or 'under the spotlight' is not how group psychotherapy works. Worries about not being taken seriously, or embarrassment about the reasons for being there, can also be helped by an accepting and empathic therapeutic demeanour, and a number of preparatory sessions.

SOCIAL SKILLS GROUPS

Effective and competent social skills, including empathy and social problem-solving, have been identified as an important factor in protecting children from difficulties such as poor relationships with peers and behaviour problems (Walker *et al.* 1996). It is therefore essential, in order to help prevent future mental health problems, to offer social skills training to disorganized children, who invariably present with difficulties in this area of functioning. Carr (2000), in his book on the most effective therapies for children and adolescents, notes that social skills training over 12 sessions, together with behaviour management programmes and parent education, can help to reduce home and school-based behaviour problems in the short term.

Social skills groups are generally well received by participants and parents alike, and have been perceived as clinically successful by professionals (Dogra and Parking 1997; Lambert and Christie 1998; Schaefer, Jacobsen and Chahramanlou 2000). However, although disorganized children seem able to learn social skills within a therapeutic group setting, many have difficulty in generalizing the skills which they have learnt to the environment outside of the group. Marriage *et al.* (1995) noted that participants had all made significant gains while in the group environment, including improved self-confidence and the acquisition of some concrete social skills. Unfortunately, feedback from parents and teachers suggested that the skills which had been effectively learnt by the participants within the group had not generalized well to the home, school or community setting.

Having said this, it is becoming increasingly apparent that, with the intensive and active involvement of both parents and teachers, social skills can be transferred outside of the group setting. Clark *et al.* (1992) provide evidence which highlights that involving parents in group work can positively influence the outcome for children. Similarly, Macdonald *et al.* (2003) orchestrated a social skills group for children with social skills deficits based on cognitive-behavioural techniques. Parents were invited to a parallel parents group, and extensive liaison with parents and teachers took place before and after each group session. Homework tasks were also specifically designed to include parents and teachers. Pre-group and post-group questionnaires were sent to parents and teachers for evaluation purposes, and analysis of these results indicated an improvement in social functioning, both within and outside of the group, for most of the children.

The running of social skills groups

Thorough planning and preparation are necessary if these groups are to be successful. Success also depends on the careful selection of participants for the group, based on its aims and targets. Adequate planning needs to take place before the group begins, as well as before and after each session. Opportunities for extensive liaison with parents and teacher, to enhance the transferring of social skills, should also be actively built into the programme. Finally, appropriately qualified facilitators need to be selected and, if necessary, trained in the specific approaches inherent in successful social skills training groups.

Selection of participants

As described earlier, careful attention needs to be given to the selection of participants within any therapeutic group. This may prove especially important when running social skills groups. While children with ADHD, and also those with Asperger syndrome, may present with social skills deficits, placing them in the same group can be problematic. The group should preferably include children with roughly similar difficulties, with some children who are higher functioning available to serve as role models. Children with severe problems may benefit from involvement in a group, but no more than two of these participants should be included within any one programme.

Facilitators

To implement a successful social skills training programme, quite a number of different facilitators are needed. Several professionals are required for the children's group alone, as the participants invariably need a great deal of individual attention. It is also helpful to have at least one facilitator who is skilled in the running of groups and in the interpretation of unconscious group processes. Given the number of staff needed to run these programmes, they can prove instrumental in training up other facilitators who have more general mental health skills. It can serve as a powerful learning experience, within the group context, for children to obtain immediate interpretation of and feedback about their social skills.

Planning

Adequate time needs to be set aside for planning of the social skills group. Not only is time needed beforehand, with all the facilitators involved, but time also needs to be set aside for planning before and after each session. This can prove very time-consuming but it is essential for the smooth and successful running of the therapeutic groups. It is particularly important to make time available for all facilitators to meet after each group as this enables the exchange of information between those running the children's group and those running the parallel parents' group. Together, the facilitators can think about what worked well in the sessions, what worked less well, and also generate new and creative ideas in response to unexpected directions or processes within the group. These therapeutic groups can prove emotionally taxing for facilitators, who may benefit from the chance to talk about and process their own experiences of the group. This is very important for their well-being as therapists, and as the containers of unconscious group dynamics.

The structure of the children's group

Cognitive-behavioural techniques are used in the children's group, as well as interpretation of unconscious group processes. Three main themes are usually addressed within the children's social skills training group. These are *feelings, developing friendships* and *communication skills*. There is also significant focus on the handling of frustration, anger and aggression. Small group discussions, role-play exercises, art activities and group feedback are used to explore these different themes. It is also important to build in 'free' time, during which the children can engage in unstructured play with one another. This is a useful exercise for determining if they are able to use, and extend, the social skills which they have learnt within the therapeutic group. A different child can also be asked to lead the group each week in a game which they have chosen. This gives all of the children an opportunity to practise their newly acquired leadership, cooperation and negotiation skills.

The parallel parents' group

This group acts primarily as a support group for parents of disorganized children, and is not as structured as the children's group. The first part of each session would involve informing parents about what the children would be dealing with in their group. It also provides an opportunity for addressing any concerns which have arisen as a result of, or since, the last meeting. Thereafter, the parents set their own agenda for the group. However, at the end of each session, a facilitator from the children's group will join them to inform the parents of how the other group went. They also use this opportunity to give parents a copy of the homework tasks for the week, and address any other specific issues raised by the parents. It is essential to remind parents about the importance of remaining actively involved in the homework tasks, as these are joint activities and not tasks for the children to complete by themselves.

Liaison work

A vital component of social skills training is comprehensive liaison work with both parents and teachers. While this may prove very labour-intensive, it is essential for ensuring the transfer of skills from the therapeutic group to the outside environment. Liaison work involves sending detailed weekly letters to parents and teachers, after each session, outlining what has taken place within the group. These letters should also explain the weekly homework tasks for home and school. Parents need to play an active role in the homework tasks throughout the training. Teachers can also help by reinforcing activities from the social skills group within the classroom. As these tasks are designed to promote social interaction, it is essential that the child is not left to complete them alone.

The children are also given contact books in which parents and teachers can provide written feedback to the facilitators of the group. The facilitators can similarly pass information and instructions back to the parents and teachers in the same way. At the halfway stage, direct telephone contact is made with both parents and teachers to review the anticipated external application of the social skills which the children have learned within the group environment. Again, any concerns which are emerging can be discussed early on in the treatment process. Once the group has come to an end, feedback interviews are held with parents, teachers, referrers and facilitators to discuss the progress of each of the children who participated in the group, and to think about any further work that needs to take place.

SUPPORT GROUPS FOR PARENTS

Parents of disorganized children may be left feeling 'blamed' by professionals, or they may feel that 'busy' clinicians do not really understand what it is like living with a child who has neuro-developmental processing problems 24/7. Parents often find that they receive more empathy and reassurance from other parent who are in, or who have been in, a similar position or who have been through similar problems. For this reason, support groups for parents of disorganized children can prove extremely valuable. They are easy to set up and require few basic resources, such as a large room which is available regularly. Quite often, the members of the group will take over its organization and running for themselves.

However, even if run autonomously by parents for parents, the group will still need to actively decide on its own structure and function. The participants and organizers must reach a decision on whether to have an open-ended drop-in group which is on-going, or a closed group which only operates for a set number of sessions before ending. In the authors' experience, an open-ended drop-in group may prove most effective, although the number of participants may increase steadily. Such a group has been in place through the Child and Adolescent Mental Health Service in Bedfordshire for several years, providing on-going support to parents of disorganized children. The majority of parents have found these groups helpful, either attending regularly or just tending to 'drop-in' when crises occur.

If there are adequate resources, combining elements of a support group with elements of an educational group can prove very beneficial. Chowdhury *et al.* (2003a) set up a semi-structured group for parents of children with ADHD along these lines. In the first session, group members were asked about the problem areas with which they would like help. Psychological techniques which related directly to potential resolution of the problems initially raised were then taught and implemented. This would take place during the first half of each group session. The second half of the therapeutic group consisted of unstructured and general discussion among group members. All of the parents who participated said that they had found the group helpful and supportive. A similar semi-structured group for parents of disorganized children could almost certainly provide a similar level of much needed practical advice and support. Since parents set the agenda, by identifying the problems with which they want help, they will gain a greater sense of ownership of the therapeutic process. This may encourage them, in turn, to set up other support groups from which parents of disorganized children can benefit.

REFERENCES AND FURTHER READING

Bloch, S. (1982) *What is Psychotherapy?* Oxford: Oxford University Press.

Carr, A. (ed) (2000) *What Works with Children and Adolescents? A Critical Review of Psychological Interventions with Children, Adolescents and their Families.* London: Routledge.

Chowdhury, U., Caulfield, C. and Heyman, I. (2003a) 'A group for children and adolescents with obsessive compulsive disorder.' *Psychiatric Bulletin 27,* 187–189.

Chowdhury, U., Elsworth, J., Viljoen, D. and Stein, M. (2003b) 'Implementing NICE guidelines: A group for parents of children with attention deficit hyperactivity disorder (ADHD).' *Quality in Primary Care 11,* 241–244.

Clarke, G., Hops, H., Lewinsohn, P.M., Andrews, J. *et al.* (1992) 'Cognitive-behavioural group treatment of adolescent depression: Predictions of outcome.' *Behaviour Therapy 23,* 341–354.

Dogra, N. and Parkin, A. (1997) 'Young person's social interaction group.' *Journal of Clinical Child Psychology and Psychiatry 2,* 297–306.

Haigh, R. (1996) 'The ghost in the machine: The matrix in the milieu.' In J. Georgas, M. Manthouli, E. Besevegis and A. Kokkevi (eds) *Contemporary Psychology in Europe: Theory, Research and Application.* Göttingen: Hogrefe and Huber.

Haigh, R. (1999) 'Group psychotherapy.' In S.M. Stein, R. Haigh and J. Stein (eds) *Essentials of Psychotherapy.* Oxford: Butterworth-Heinemann, pp.253–273.

Lambert, S. and Christie, D. (1998) 'A social skills group for boys with Tourette's syndrome.' *Clinical Child Psychology and Psychiatry 3,* 267–277.

Leonard, J. (1991) 'Parent support groups.' *British Medical Journal* (Editorial) *303,* 1152.

Macdonald, E., Chowdhury, U., Dabney, J., Wolpert, M. *et al.* (2003) 'A social skills group for children: The importance of liaison work with parents and teachers.' *Emotional and Behavioural Difficulties 8,* 43–52.

Marriage, K.J., Gordon, V. and Brand, L. (1995) 'A social skills group for boys with Asperger's syndrome.' *Australian and New Zealand Journal of Psychiatry, 29,* 58–62.

Schaefer, C.E., Jacobsen, H.E. and Ghahramanlou, M. (2000) 'Play group therapy for social skills deficits in children.' In H.G. Kaudsen and C.E. Schaefer (eds) *Short-Term Play Therapy for Children.* New York: Guildford Press.

Walker, H.M., Horner, R.H., Sugai, G., Bullis, M. *et al.* (1996) 'Integrated approaches to preventing antisocial behaviour patterns among school-age children and youth.' *Journal of Emotional and Behavioural Disorders 4,* 194–209.

Yalom, I.D. (1986) *The Theory and Practice of Group Psychotherapy,* 3rd edn. New York: Basic Books.

Useful information

ADHD

NICE have produced *Guidance on the Use of Methylphenidate for ADHD* which supports the use of stimulants in treatment. It highlights the need for further research into treatment (NICE 2001). This is a helpful document for clinicians and can be accessed via the website www.nice.org.uk.

The ADD Information and Support Service (ADDISS) website contains a great deal of information about conferences, support groups, and other resources in the UK: www.addiss.co.uk

Adult mental health

Royal College of Psychiatrists
17 Belgrave Square
London SW1X 8PG
Website: www.rcpsych.ac.uk

Autistic spectrum disorders

The National Autistic Society
393 City Road
London EC1V 1NG
Tel: 020 7833 2299
Website: www.nas.org.uk

Child psychiatry

The *Mental Health and Growing Up* series contains 36 fact sheets on a range of common mental health problems. Available on the Royal College of Psychiatrists' website at www.rcpsych.ac.uk.

The Strengths and Difficulties Questionnaire (SDQ) is available for download free on the internet, from www.sdqinfo.com. This is available in young person, parent and teacher versions.

Child psychotherapy

British Association for Counselling and Psychotherapy
Website: www.bacp.co.uk

Clinical psychology

British Psychological Society
St Andews House
48 Princes Road East
Leicester LE1 7DR
Website: www.bps.org.uk

Developmental dyspraxia

Dyspraxia Foundation
8 West Alley
Hitchen
Hertfordshire SG5 1EG
Website: www.dyspraxiafoundation.org.uk

Dyslexia

The Dyslexia Institute
Park House
Wick Road
Egham
Surrey TW20 0HH
Tel: 01784 222300
Website: www.dyslexia-inst.org.uk

Epilepsy

National Society for Epilepsy
Chesham Lane
Chalfont St Peter
Bucks SL9 0RJ
Tel: 01494 601300
Website: www.epilepsynse.org.uk

National Centre for Young People with Epilepsy: www.ncype.org.uk

Family therapy

Institute of Family Therapy
24–32 Stephenson Way
London NW1 2HX
Tel: 020 7391 9150
Website: www.instituteoffamilytherapy.org.uk

Obsessive compulsive disorder

OCD Action
22/24 Highbury Grove, Suite 107
London N5 2EA
Tel: 0845 390 6232
Email: info@ocdaction.org.uk
Website: www.ocdaction.org.uk

Occupational therapy

British Association of Occupational Therapy and College of Occupational Therapy
Website: www.cot.co.uk

Schizophrenia

www.schizophrenia.com

Semantic pragmatic deficit syndrome

www.mugsy.org/spd.htm

www.hyperlexia.org/sp1.html

Special educational needs

National Association for Special Educational Needs
Website: www.nasen.org.uk

Department for Education
Website: www.dfes-gov.uk/sen

Independent Panel for Special Education Advice (IPSEA)
Website: www.ipsea.org.uk

Speech therapy

Royal College of Speech and Language Therapy
2 White Hart Yard
London SE1 1NX
Website: www.rcslt.org

Tourette syndrome

Tourette Syndrome Association (United Kingdom)
P.O. Box 26149
Dunfermline KY12 7YU
Website: www.tsa.org.uk

List of Contributors

M. Tanveer Alam is a specialist registrar on the South London and Maudsley rotation.

Kerry Bennett was born in Plymouth, and has lived in Iraq, Bahrani, Dubai and Egypt. She graduated from King's College London in 1999 with a BSc Honours Degree in Human Biology. Kerry Bennett has dyslexia which was recognized at the age of 14. Her career involves generating awareness about dyslexia.

Frank M. C. Besag studied at Birmingham University, obtaining the Queen's Scholarship (top student). He subsequently trained at the John Radcliffe, Great Ormond Street, Hammersmith and Maudsley Hospitals, before becoming Medical Director at the National Centre for Young People with Epilepsy. He is currently a consultant neuro-psychiatrist in Bedfordshire and visiting Professor of Neuro-psychiatry at the University of Luton. He has published a number of papers on epilepsy and is particularly interested in brain-behaviour relationships.

Val Burgess is a specialist teacher/adviser for children with autistic spectrum disorders. She works at the Service for Sensory Impairment and Communication Difficulties, The Child Development Centre, Bedfordshire, UK.

Iris Carcani-Rathwell is a specialist registrar on the South London and Maudsley rotation.

Rebecca Chilvers is a research psychologist and PhD student at the Institute of Child Health and Great Ormond Street Hospital. Her interests include autism, neuro-developmental disorders in females and the development of lexical memory. She is also interested in the role of DVD-based technology in the diagnosis and treatment of childhood and adult disorders.

Deborah Christie is Head of Service for Paediatric and Adolescent Psychology and Honorary Senior Lecturer at University College London and Middlesex Hospitals, London. She trained in neurobiology, neuro-psychology and clinical psychology in London and Oxford. Her research interests include psychological and neuro-psychological aspects of chronic illness in children and adolescents.

Deba Choudhury graduated in Behavioural Sciences from University College Northampton. She has an MSc in Applied Developmental Research from the University of Hertfordshire. She worked as a research assistant for Bedfordshire and Luton Mental Health and Social Care Partnership NHS Trust and has completed a Diploma in Practitioner Skills for Eating Disorders with the National Centre for Eating Disorders. She is currently working as a Graduate Primary Care Mental Health Worker in Southall, Ealing, London.

Uttom Chowdhury is a Consultant in Child and Adolescent Psychiatry for Bedfordshire and Luton Mental Health and Social Care Partnership NHS Trust and an Honorary Consultant in the Social Communication Disorders Clinic at Great Ormond Street Hospital, London.

Sidney Chu is a Paediatric Occupational Therapy Service Manager for Ealing Primary Care Trust. He has special interest in the assessment and treatment of children with attention deficit hyperactivity disorder (ADHD), developmental coordination disorder (DCD), dyslexia, autistic spectrum disorder, Asperger syndrome, cerebral palsy and tics disorders. He has published research and clinical articles in different professional journals, and also chapters in books. He presents regular clinical workshops to different health, educational and psychological professionals within the UK and also overseas.

Ashlee Clifford has worked as a research assistant at the Child and Adolescent Mental Health Service, Dunstable. She has a Masters in Health Psychology and has carried out research looking at stress in parents of children with autistic spectrum disorders.

Sharon Davies works as a consultant child and adolescent psychiatrist at the Huntercombe Maidenhead Hospital and is also an honorary consultant for the Tourette's Clinic, Great Ormond Street Hospital, London. She runs an adolescent in-patient unit, specializing in long-term treatment and rehabilitation of adolescents with severe enduring mental illness. Other interests include early onset psychosis, neuro-developmental disorders and the psychiatric aspects of epilepsy in children.

Sharon Drew is an independent consultant occupational therapist by profession with a special interest in providing integrated working practice between health and education for children with special education needs. Sharon has written several professional text books as well as a fictional book for children, entitled *Jack and the Disorganised Dragon*. She has presented academic papers and regularly lectures to professionals and the general public at international and national level. Sharon has written and teaches accredited courses at Masters, Bachelors and Foundation degree level.

Christopher Gillberg is a professor of Child and Adolescent Psychiatry at Gothenburg University, Sweden and at St George's Medical School, London. He is Editor in Chief of *European Child and Adolescent Psychiatry*, and author of several scientific and educational books on autistic spectrum disorders and child neuro-psychiatry. He has published widely on all aspects of child neuro-psychiatric disorders.

Alex Horne is a consultant child and adolescent psychiatrist and medical director for North East London Mental Health Trust. He has worked for the past 12 years in East London. He has a special interest in social communication disorders working with paediatricians and teachers, as well as with parents and siblings of children with these disorders and with the young persons themselves.

Sue Jennings is a consultant in child and adolescent psychiatry for North East London Mental Health Trust. She trained as a specialist registrar on the Great Ormond Street Hospital and Royal London Hospital rotation.

Estelle Macdonald qualified as a counselling and educational psychologist in South Africa. She moved to the UK and qualified as a chartered clinical psychologist. She worked for several years in the UK in the NHS in the areas of child and adolescent mental health and neuro-psychology. She is currently working at the Meyrick Bennett Children's Assessment and Therapy Centre and in private practice in South Africa.

Alison Mantell is a consultant in child and adolescent psychiatry for Bedfordshire and Luton Mental Health and Social Care Partnership NHS Trust. She has a special interest in liaison child psychiatry and child protection issues.

Sarah O'Reilly has worked as a research assistant at the Child and Adolescent Mental Health Service, Dunstable.

Christopher Roberts is a consultant child and adolescent psychiatrist at the Wolverton Gardens Child and Family Consultation Centre, Hammersmith, West London Mental Health Trust.

Helen Rodwell is a clinical psychologist for Bedfordshire and Luton Mental Health and Social Care Partnership NHS Trust. She has a special interest in neuro-psychology.

Paramala Santos is a consultant in child and adolescent psychiatry at the Department of Psychological Medicine, Great Ormond Street Hospital, London. He has a special interest in paediatric psycho-pharmacology, and dual diagnosis of pervasive developmental disorders with mental health difficulties. He has published numerous papers on clinical neuro-psychiatry and neuro-developmental disorders.

Samuel M. Stein is a consultant in child, adolescent and family psychiatry in Bedfordshire. He is an honorary senior lecturer at University College London, and has edited three books: *Essentials of Psychotherapy, Psychotherapy in Practice: A Life in the Mind* and *Beyond Belief: Psychotherapy and Religion*.

Danièle Wichené is a family therapist at the Dunstable Clinic, Bedfordshire. She trained in systemic and family psychotherapy at the Kensington Consultation Centre and has worked as a therapist in Child and Adolescent Mental Health Services and in school. She is particularly interested in sibling relationships, and constantly fascinated by how revisiting the past can bring out differences in meaning which have a liberating effect on all persons concerned.

Subject index

Author index

Aarts, J.H. 130
Abwender, D.A. 184
Adams, A. 257
Achenbach, T.M. 114
Ainsworth, M.D.S. 57, 58
Airaksinen, E.M. 108, 131
Albright, F. 92
Aldrich, F.K. 257
Allen, D. 161
American Academy of Child and Adolescent Psychiatry 73, 243
American Psychiatric Association 19, 66, 68, 76, 98, 109, 140, 168
Anderson, G. 79
Anderson, T. 295
Anderson, V. 257
Arnold, L.E. 139
Artner, J. 139
Asarnow, R.F. 170, 171
Asperger, H. 76
Attwood, T. 101
Austin, J.K. 133
Ayres, A.J. 97

Bailey, A.J. 79
Baker, D. 137
Barker 244, 247, 248
Barkley, R.A. 101, 108
Baron, D.A. 174
Baron-Cohen, S. 51, 79, 164
Barratt-Boyes, B.G. 93
Barrett, P.M. 145
Bartsch, K. 54
Beard, A.W. 129
Bell, J. 90
Bell, S.M. 57
Berg, C.J. 144
Besag, F.M.C. 125, 130, 132
Bishop, D.V.M. 161, 164
Bornstein, R.A. 101

Bourneville, D.M. 91
Bowlby, J. 57
Bradley, C. 66
Brand, L. 318
Byrne, G. 265, 266, 271

Campbell, T. 43
Carey, W.B. 137
Carr, A. 320
Cermak, S.A. 96, 97
Chakrabarti, S. 78
Chambless, D.L. 145
Chen, Z. 43
Chowdhury, U. 318, 324
Christie, D. 318, 321
Clarke, G. 321
Clements, S.D. 134
Cohen, D.J. 182
Cohen, M. 256
Connors, C.K. 71, 139, 257
Cooper, R.G. 50, 58
Corbett, J. 173
Crawford, S.G. 124

De Shazer, S. 290
de Silva, M. 130
DeHart, G. 50, 58
Denhoff, E. 135
Dennett, D. 50
Dennism, J. 88
Dogra, N. 321
Doherty, W. 290
DuPaul, G.J. 101
Durkin, K. 57

Eapen, V. 180
Edelbrock, C. 114
Eden, G.F. 120
Egeland, B. 58
Einfeld, S.L. 87
Emslie, H. 258
Erenberg, G. 184
Erikson, M.F. 58
Everett, C. 296

Falloon, I. 290
Fawcett, A.J. 120
Fianu, S. 136
Fisher, S.E. 121
Flament, M.F. 144

Flint, J. 87
Fombonne, E. 78
Fonagy, P. 55, 60, 61
Fowler, M.S. 120
Fox, A.M. 97
Fox, N.E. 58
Frank-Pazzaglia, L. 131
Frith, U. 79, 117, 164
Froster, U. 121

Geller, D. 142, 144
Ghahramanlou, M. 321
Giedd, J.N. 182
Gillberg, C. 101, 108, 109, 110, 111
Gillberg, I. 110
Gilmour, J. 37
Giuliano, J.D. 182
Goei, V.L. 121
Golden, J.C. 258
Goodman, R. 72, 129, 257
Gordon, V. 318
Gray, J.M. 88, 286, 287
Grigorenko, E.L. 119, 121
Gross-Tsur, V. 132
Gubbay, S.S. 96, 100

Hadwin, J. 51
Hagberg, B. 108
Haigh, R. 316, 317
Hall, W. 87
Handford, H.A. 135
Hanna, G.L. 149
Hansen, B.H. 182
Hardie, T.L. 174
Heaton, R. 258
Hepworth, J. 290
Hersov, L. 134, 135, 136, 140, 159
Heyman, I. 142
Hobbes, T. 44
Hollander, E. 147
Hollis, C. 170
Hornsey, H. 180
Howlin, P. 51, 54, 84

Ingram, T.T.S. 135
Inoff-Germain, G. 143, 171, 174, 181

340